FROZEN FOOTSTEPS:

Memoir of a Mountaineer

TIMOTHY C. LEWIS

1st Edit by Maraya Loza Koxahn
2nd Edit by Nona Allison
Final Edit by Julia M Wallace

We were drenched, shivering, and exhausted. With no food left between us, we knew we had to find the route back before we ran out of daylight. The snow was deep, and hard to negotiate with heavy packs on. Everything looks the same when you're lost: the trees, the rocks, the snow. We trudged on as if in a trance. It wasn't until we felt broken and defeated, bereft of hope, that we came upon a set of frozen footsteps. Our hearts were gladdened; our spirits began to soar—for we recognized them as the same footsteps we had created on the way up. They would lead us back home safely.

Sunday, June 4, 1989—Glacier Peak Wilderness Area

I am a cat and have lived my nine lives.

ACKNOWLEDGEMENT

The completion of the book could not have been possible without the encouragement and help of so many people whose names may not all be enumerated. Their contributions are sincerely appreciated and gratefully acknowledged.

However, the people I would like to express deep appreciation and indebtedness to are the following:

My Mother, Madge Lewis, for giving me the insight to write down all the events that I witnessed and experienced throughout my climbing history.

My Daughters, Melissa Shipley, Amanda O'Brien, and Michaela Scattaregia, for being so patient with me, loving me, and accepting my obsession to climb mountains. I love you all so much.

My ex-wife, Debra Lewis. Thank you for teaching me the value of living in the moment and being so understanding.

My Brother, John Lewis, for being the best brother I could ever wish for, always having my back, being patient, and teaching me the proper way to pack a pack.

My late friend, Alan Coxon, for saving my life more than once, teaching me the fundamentals of mountaineering, and showing me how to be confident.

My late friend, Garry Past, for showing me how to find my inner strength.

My friend, Rob Sesko, for pulling me up to the summit when I was too tired to go on. You will always be my dearest friend and climbing partner.

And to Jacqueline Annette Morris for helping me to learn how to take things to fruition and completion. Without her pushing me to my full potential I would have never finished this project.

All quotes that were used with author notations were derived off the internet. All quotes that have no author notations were written by Timothy Lewis.

This book is dedicated to Fred Beckey. An extraordinary mountaineer that every climber that set foot on a summit knew of, loved, and respected.

Cover: Inside the ice cave. Photo by John Lewis. Creative design by Diane Mueller

Back cover: Mt Rainier from Alta Visa. About the Author written by John Lewis

CONTENTS

FROZEN FOOTSTEPS:

Memoir of a Mountaineer

INTRODUCTION

IN THE WINTER OF 1974, AT THE AGE OF EIGHTEEN, I survived a near-death experience in the mountains near my home. It wouldn't be my last. Never tell your mother that she almost lost her son—mine forbade me to ever go climbing again. *What?!* I had just started and I loved it! There was no way I could do what she asked. But once she recovered from the shock of my admission and realized that I had grown into a young man whom she could no longer control, we struck an agreement.

My mother asked me not to tell her I was going climbing before I left, but only after I had returned home safely. I agreed. She suggested that I keep a journal about my experiences. I thought it was a good idea. After more than thirty years of recording my stories I decided to compile them into this book, to share with those who may have experienced similar expeditions and others who have never found themselves facing a life-threatening situation on the top of a mountain.

Mountains are mysterious. Not only is the air thinner up there, so is the veil between worlds. Things happen that I don't completely understand and can't adequately explain.

"But, isn't it dangerous?" is a question I've heard so many times that I've grown tired of trying to answer it. Yet, here I am, trying to explain in such a way that we might both understand. Together we might discover what it is that makes us seek something bigger than ourselves.

Learning to climb at a young age helped me to build not only physical strength but mental endurance as well. The Pacific Northwest has produced some of the most renowned climbers in the world and I have been fortunate to have met some of them. You will find their names laced throughout my story.

There are no road maps to life, no definitive books on how to live perfectly; it's up to you to figure it out as you go along. All mountains are climbable if you choose the correct route and carry the right equipment. You have to be prepared and persistent to get to the top. Never give up. If you take a wrong turn or a make a bad choice, you can always go back down and try climbing again another time. If it doesn't kill you.

There are two types of mountaineering: Rock climbing, which is exactly what it sounds like, normally involves two or more climbers, but you can do what's called "bouldering" or "free climb" by yourself. The usual two-person rock climbing method is when one climber is anchored to the bottom of a climbing wall using an assortment of anchors, sometimes even tied to a tree. The two are roped together. The lead climber begins up the wall using protection devices that are placed into cracks. Or, in many cases, there are bolts screwed into the rock face. The climber uses a device called a carabiner. It's a metal loop about the 2 1/2 to 3 inches long and 2 inches wide. It has a spring loaded gate that you can push open with one finger. The carabiner is clipped into the bolt or protection device and the rope runs through it. Once it is clipped in place it keeps a climber safe. The climber below, using what is called a belay device, slowly lets out rope as the lead climber ascends. If the lead climber should fall, it would only be as far as the protection device or bolt he or she last placed.

Alpine climbing encompasses glacier climbing, snowfield climbing, and rock scrambling. The climbers rope themselves together and carry ice axes—an anchor tool that can save you from a deadly fall. The head acts like a handle and, used like a cane, it helps your ascent. If you should slip, the pick side of the axe is plunged into the ice or snow and it will stop you. This action is called a "self-arrest." If two or more climbers are roped together, and one should slip, the other climbers work together as a team, plunging their ice axes into the snow and putting their weight on them to brake a falling climber from going too far—possibly into a crevasse. This is called a "team arrest." Belaying is probably the most important thing in climbing. It's the foundation of what makes climbing safe.

The word "belay" is similar to "ballet." Rock climbing is sometimes referred to as ballet on rock. But that was not where the word belay comes from. It's actually an Old English nautical word from the sixteenth century. The American Alpine Institute adopted it in the twentieth century. One member of a climbing party becomes the stationary member by tying himself to a firm rock projection or anchored device. This safeguards a moving climber and allows him to proceed. When I climb up a large rock wall with a rope tied to me and the other end to my belayer, my life is in my belayer's hands. If I fall, I'm confident he or she will save me from death. If I'm on belay traversing around a crevasse, I know my belayer will do everything he can—short of dying—to rescue me if I fall in. We trust our lives to our climbing partners; we have to. You share a love of climbing, and of each other, that goes beyond friendship.

If the desire to climb can be something you're born with, then I was. Maybe it was just a desire to push myself to the extreme, to live on the edge—and, later, some kind of spiritual quest—that caused me to go forth and climb. Growing up surrounded by mountains, being introduced to climbing at an early age, and having the influence of great mentors all led me to ask, (ask what?)

Whether it be rock climbing or an obsession to climb Mount Everest, something drives us to be near rock or kicking steps in ice. The sound of an ice ax being plunged into the frozen snow. The tinkling of ice particles as they blow by you in a gust of freezing wind. The sound of your heavy breathing as you reach up and grab onto a handhold as metal carabineers and anchors bang against the rock and echo off into the distance. There is an unparalleled power that engulfs you and a fire in your soul that pushes you to your limits and beyond. A climber never tires of this. Once you have reached a summit, you dream of climbing another one. Or the same one by a different route.

Chapter 1

My 'Wearabouts'

"At the height of what you believe you can do,
is where you will stand."

I WOKE UP IN THE MIDDLE of the night after having fallen asleep on the couch.

In an evening in early October 2012, after eating a cheap TV dinner and getting my pack ready, I opened a bottle of 3 Blind Moose, poured a glass, sat down on the couch and put on my favorite movie, *Castaway*. I fell asleep shortly after Chuck ended up on the tiny island, but awoke to see him standing at the crossroads of his life wondering what to do next. I love that part. After all he went through—getting stuck on that island, fighting to stay alive, failing to commit suicide—he found his way back and started his life over. I watched the rest of it, then got up and grabbed my water bottle out of the fridge. I gulped down about half of it and looked around my apartment. I felt out of touch with reality, everything looked sort of surreal, like I wasn't really there, like my life wasn't really happening. I had to get out of there.

I had recently been through a difficult breakup in May and had just filed for divorce. I felt a need to find something… animal or spiritual, I wasn't really sure, but something that I'd experienced on June 24th 2003 while descending off of Mount Rainier. The other reason why I felt compelled to go up there was that I had recently met a co-worker from Cambodia. We had discussed a series of dreams that I'd had been having for years. I'd dreamed that a Buddhist monk was trying to communicate with me about how to find true happiness. He told me that I needed to have a pure heart and, in order to do so, I must first understand "the three gifts". My co-worker told me it was very special to have such a dream and that I must remember more of what he said, or find him so he could tell me again. I thought Camp Muir on Mount Rainier might be a place to look.

I grabbed my pack, ran downstairs, jumped into my truck and left home at around half past three in the morning. The sound of my engine was all I listened to on the way to the Paradise parking lot. Climbing to the base camp on Rainier tells me what kind of shape I'm in. If I can get up there in two to four hours, I'm in excellent climbing shape; if it takes me four to six hours, good shape; if it takes me seven or more hours, I would not try summiting.

I pulled into the lot and shut off the engine. *I don't even remember the drive up here. Was I asleep?* I took a deep breath and began to put on my climbing boots. After one boot was on, I closed my eyes and took another deep breath through my nose then blew out through my mouth. A Reiki master taught me that this type of breathing is good for clearing your thoughts. The soft glow of the new day heightened the light enough so I could see the serrated outline of the trees. I slid on the other boot and, before I could tie the laces, the wind gusted and shook my 1994 Toyota 4x4. I paused until it stopped. *Do I really want to do this?*

Every time I've been to Paradise, there have been at least a hundred cars in the parking lot. Today, the lot was empty. I grabbed the door handle, swallowed hard, opened the door and jumped out. *Let's do this!*

It was cold. The temperature in the low forties and the wind made it feel like thirty—almost freezing. I opened the canopy, grabbed my parka and put it on. Then I put on my pack. It was uncomfortable at first. I adjusted my coat to keep it from binding under my pack straps. I looked around again to see if there were any cars anywhere. None. I locked my truck and began the hike up to the paved trails.

I had a weird feeling as I walked by the empty ranger station. I was the only one there. *This is not normal. Why are there no cars in the parking lot?* There was a soft glow on the upper section of the mountain from the sun rising. A gust of wind almost pushed me over. I started moving fast and practically jogged up the trail. I made quick time to Panorama Point. In another fifteen minutes, I was at Pebble Creek. I looked at my watch; it had been only thirty-five minutes since I left my truck. *I'm kicking ass!* The morning sun was on my back but it felt like the temperature was dropping. I stopped, looked at my freezing hands. *Shit! I forgot my gloves. Too late now, I'm up here and not going back.* I climbed on, only stopping when I came upon some large rocks that were still warm from the day before. I put my hands on them; it felt good to get them warm. I kept going up at a fast pace. *This is so easy,*

As I moved up to around 8,000 feet I started to wonder, *Where the hell are all the people? This is so weird to be up here and not see anyone.* I looked up, "There should be people at Muir, though," I mumbled to myself and kept on going.

At 9,000 feet, there's a giant rock to the right of the Muir Snowfield called Anvil Rock. I stopped and turned around there, and looked down the Muir Snowfield to see if anyone was on their way up. No one in sight. I could see the parking lot at Paradise. No one. Just the tiny dark green truck I'd parked there. I turned around and looked up. I could see Camp Muir in the distance. Normally you can see people walking around up there but I couldn't see anyone. *What the hell? I'm sure there will be some parties coming down off the summit by one or two.* My hands were getting numb so I stuffed them down into my pants under my long underwear to warm them up. Then I pulled my left hand out to look at my watch: 7:30. I'd left the parking lot at 6:05. I went from 5,000 feet to 9,000 feet in a little over an hour. It was almost like time was running backward. I began to hike up the rest of the way on the frozen crusty snow. In another twenty-five minutes I was walking up to the base camp. It took me two hours to get up there. That was a record for me. *I must be in really good shape!* Unfortunately, I could share that feat with no one.

The wind was blowing in gusts. The small buildings were empty. There was nobody there. *I've been here over seventy times and I've never been here by myself.* It was surreal—like an empty movie set. I began to question my grip on reality. I questioned my very existence. *Am I alive? Did I die in my sleep and is this the afterlife? Will I be on this mountain for all eternity?*

I began thinking about the friends I had climbed with. All of them are gone now. Either passed away or passed out of my life. I remember the feelings of excitement, terror, and all the challenges that we faced together. Some of those times were the best I'd ever had… and some were the worst. I remembered how climbing had interfered with other aspects of my life.

It's said that just before we die, our whole life flashes before our eyes.

"I think that's bullshit!" I said out loud, announcing my entry into the climbers' hut only to have my outburst fall on empty bunks. It felt like a walk-in freezer inside. I looked around. *So many memories.*

I went back outside and looked out at Cowlitz Glacier. Normally there are ten to twenty tents out there. Then I heard a banging noise that went on for one or two seconds over in the guide service hut. Anxious to see anyone, man or beast, I scurried over. It was locked from the outside. No one could be in there.

"The mountain is alive." That's what my climbing partners and I would say when we sat around and drank beer after summiting. "She chooses who she wants and lets the others go."

I sat down on a rock and took off my pack. I pulled out a power bar, tore off the wrapper, stuffed the wrapper into my pocket and took a bite. I contemplated the trajectory of my life: where it was going and where it had been. I still didn't understand the toxic hell of the past nine years. *Why did I choose that life?* I felt bad about hurting the people I loved. *When did it all start to go so wrong?* I began to think about my life and my roots. My beginnings. I had all the time in the world to think about things, so I thought about my childhood.

•   •   •

I spent the first ten years of my life on North Eighty-Second Street in the Greenwood area of Seattle, in one of the early houses built in the 1920s when

Seattle was growing and the homesteaders were getting pushed out. It was a house that had been remodeled a few times before my mom and dad bought it in the early fifties. It had three small bedrooms, one of which I shared with my brother John. My two sisters, Diane and Julie, shared the other bedroom upstairs. My oldest sister, Diane, was a bit obsessive-compulsive about cleanliness and order. My other sister, Julie, was not organized in any way. They fought constantly. They painted a line down the middle of the room and Julie was not allowed to step foot over it, but she did. Quite frequently. My parents' bedroom was downstairs. The house had a small front yard and an old rickety garage at the end of the gravel driveway. The roof of the garage was half roofing fabric and half cedar shake. I got to know the roof well because I would spend hours up there looking around the neighborhood and stealing pears from the neighbor's tree that hung over our roof. It was innately ingrained in me to kick steps into the rotten cedar shingles for better footholds. My dad was not happy about that. In the back yard of our house we had a large old cherry tree, probably thirty to forty feet high. It had been grafted to bear three different types of cherries which, in late summer, was pretty much all I ate. It was my favorite place in the world.

One summer day I came home from a neighbor kid's house and heard my brother and his friend Hutch up in the top branches. I yelled up there, "What're you guys doing?!"

My brother John yelled down, "Don't come up here Timmy! It's too dangerous!"

Well, that made me want to go up there more than ever. I waited for the two of them to climb down and as they were running off to Hutch's house, John yelled at me, "Don't go up there!"

Then I was alone. My mom was oblivious, reading one of her romance novels or talking to my grandma on the phone; my dad was at work. I looked up and began to climb. Higher and higher, slowly, holding on to the tiny branches, I finally reached the point where I couldn't go any higher. With my head sticking out of the top of the tree, I looked around the yard. I was so high! I looked out across the rooftops and saw what John and Hutch had been looking at, a glimpse of the top of the Space Needle.

It was a real challenge, hanging on to small branches and keeping balanced, but it was worth the effort for the view. Then something caught my eye to the left. I couldn't quite make it out at first, but there it was: the snow-capped peak of Mount Rainier.

I became obsessed with climbing up the tree and looking down on the world. The view was spectacular. On clear mornings I would sneak out of bed, slip out the back door, and climb the tree in my pajamas. From there I would just stare at the top of the mountain and wonder what it was like up there. Was it cold? Windy? I imagined myself on the summit. This was my secret hiding spot from everything. No one could see me spying down on them.

I built a tiny tree house from old scrap wood that I stole from the side of the garage and other places in the neighborhood. Using a rock as a hammer and nails stolen from an old mason jar in the basement, I fashioned a hideaway that was in no way safe. When my mom would come out looking for me, I just couldn't hear her A typical youngest child. My siblings tested my parents, but by the time I came along my parents were done and let me get away with almost everything. They'd just say "let him be a kid". Plus, with my oldest sister Diane, I had protection. She would always intervene when punishment was about to be given out. Nevertheless, my mom was pretty much oblivious. Or I was really good at pulling the rug over her eyes.

* * *

I never had a fear of heights. Looking down at nothing but air below me has always been exhilarating. As long as I have something to hang on to, or if I'm anchored with a rope, I feel very safe. I looked up at the mountain before me. *Strange... there's usually a plane flying by every twenty minutes from Sea-Tac, but today there's nothing but empty sky. Everything I am experiencing right now is...*

The wind blew hard for about ten seconds and I shielded my eyes from the tiny pumice particles that get blown into your face when it blows that hard. I look down at my feet. The toes of my boots sticking out of my gaiters. I remember the first pair of hiking boots I ever received. They were black with Vibram-type soles.

* * *

My tenth birthday was both a happy day and a sad day. It was the day I said goodbye to the old cherry tree. It was the day my family moved to the suburb between Lynwood and Edmonds, just north of Seattle. It was all so wonderful, moving into a large house with five bedrooms. My sister Diane was liberated from the abuse of a clothes-stealing sister. My brother could finally look at a Playboy without me asking what he was doing. I had a bedroom all to myself where I could arrange my mess however I wanted.

Having a bunk bed was awesome; I always slept on the top. From up there I could observe my mess. I would crawl out of bed in the morning, hang by my hands like a monkey and make my way along the bookshelf, then swing onto the dresser, almost knocking over the turtle tank. I could open the door and jump out of the room without touching my bedroom floor. What a feat!

I soon needed a new challenge. So I began climbing around the living room and family room without touching the floor My "indoor bouldering" drove my mom crazy. My dad would just say, "Timmy! That's enough!"

On the day I turned eleven, my dad decided it was time for me to join the Boy Scouts. I could tell because when I opened my birthday gifts, they all consisted of some type of Boy Scout paraphernalia.

At first I wasn't excited about Boy Scouts. My dad had signed me up with a troop at our church in Edmonds where I didn't know anyone. I hated going to the meetings, but the hikes were fun. I learned how to tie knots and set up tents. I also learned that I could carry heavy loads in the backpack handed down to me from my brother. It was an old Trapper Nelson with a wood frame and a canvas pack with canvas straps taped with sponges to them to make them less painful. It's amazing how many things you could tie to that thing with twine: pots and pans, tent poles, a sleeping bag, a shovel, a hatchet, and anything else that would dangle.

I was always concerned that we might run into a bear or a cougar on the trail, even though a marching band would have been quieter than this group of Boy Scouts. There was never an animal within a hundred miles of us.

After a year with the boys from Edmonds, I began to make friends and started to like going to the meetings. It was fun to sing songs, learn how to make cool stuff, eat cookies and drink Kool-Aid. But, a year later, my friends from school told me that they were in a scout troop that met at the elementary school close to home.

"You should transfer to our troop, Tim."

So I did. I discovered quickly that this new troop was not really into the spirit of scouting. They were just a bunch of brats that hung out every Tuesday night and played games. No one knew how to tie a knot or set up a tent. The only thing they knew was the game Capture the Flag.

The scoutmaster rarely made an appearance. He was not really the scoutmaster type. He smelled like booze and knew nothing about scouting. He would just let us do whatever we wanted while he talked with a couple of his buddies. He would always smile and wink at me; it kind of creeped me out. Usually, a father of one of the kids ran the meetings. None of the boys had ever gone on a hike.

About a month after joining the troop, after we had all gathered for our weekly Tuesday meeting, two Lynnwood police officers showed up looking for our scoutmaster. They questioned each of us privately. They asked me, "When was the last time you saw him? Did he ever invite you to his house?" I just stood there with a dumb look on my face and shook my head.

Then, the most confusing question of all, "Do you know of his whereabouts?

Whereabouts? What are "whereabouts"? Are they the clothes he was wearing, or maybe what he wore about? His wearabouts?

Hey, I was only twelve and I didn't read much back then. I was afraid to ask questions because I didn't want to look like an idiot. My mom must have really wondered about me though when I asked her one time if she could wash my *wearabouts*. "Your what?" she asked.

Anyway, the police were intently looking for our scoutmaster and it was a serious situation. I didn't fully understand what was going on, especially when one of the kids in our troop went missing. I don't know if they ever found our drunken scoutmaster, or whatever happened to the kid. It wasn't until I was older that my dad told me our scoutmaster was a child molester. After the incident, the parents in the troop were on the verge of disbanding it. I didn't care. I wanted to go back to my old scout troop. This one blew.

On the night of the parents' meeting, a decision about the future of the troop was made. They voted that we would continue if my dad took over as the new scoutmaster. That changed everything. My dad ran things like he did when he was in the navy. He was my brother John's scoutmaster, and my brother's troop kicked ass. At the first meeting my dad made us all stand at attention.

"From now on you will not show up at the meeting without wearing your scout uniforms, complete with hat tucked in your belt. Do you understand?" He barked out.

One of the kids said, "Yeah."

"I didn't hear you!" He demanded more conviction.

"Yes!" we all yelled.

He was scary. When we arrived at meetings, he held inspection. If we were missing any article of scout attire we were sent home to get it. We had knot-tying competitions and started working on merit badges. At first my friends were not too happy with the way my dad ran things, but it got better. We all became better friends. We worked together as a team, learned new things and started to go on hikes. After about a year, all the kids loved my dad. He was a great scoutmaster. He turned the troop around. We made and sold Christmas wreaths. We had a fireworks stand. The troop was making money, and we were able to buy tents and other camping items. Those were awesome times.

• • •

I listened to the wind whistle through my sunglass straps and thought about the lyrics to Cat Stevens song. "I listen to the wind, to the wind of my soul / Where I'll end up well I think only God really knows." I looked at my watch. It had only been a short time since I arrived. Time was going by slow. *I love this place.* There is no other place like it in the state of Washington—or in the world. I dream about it all the time. There is a webcam on Paradise that streams 24/7. I look at it almost every day, wishing to be on the other end of the camera. *Now I am here and I don't want to leave. At least not now, not until I figure out why I wanted to come up here.* Then I remembered the first time I ever really experienced being up on a mountain. It was when I was still a Boy Scout.

* * *

It was the early summer of 1970; I was fourteen. The troop went on a hike to Surprise Lake. There was still a substantial amount of snow up in the mountains. The trail was long and tiring, which made it very boring for a group of young boys with an overabundance of energy that we'd rather use playing tag and annoying the dads that had come along. As we hiked farther and farther toward our destination, we came upon a ridge top. The surrounding view was spectacular. My buddies Kelly and Pat wanted to climb higher, but we knew the dads would never let us. So we devised a plan.

"Let's wait back, tell them we're tired and want to rest a bit," I said.

Kelly jumped in with, "We'll tell them that we'll catch up in a few minutes."

The plan worked. They trusted us enough to leave us alone, thinking we'd catch up. So the three of us took off in the other direction. We came to a rocky area where there were few trees and climbed over the rocks. In no time, we hiked up to the top of the ridge. The sparse growth had opened up to a large, exposed cliff. We took in the amazing view all around us. It was more

14

spectacular than I could have ever imagined. Off in the distance, crystal-clear, stood majestic Mount Rainier. We didn't say anything, just stood there in awe. When we reached the lake my dad asked to see the three of us alone. He asked, "Where were you?" He looked stern and serious. I looked at Pat and then at Kelly and felt my head getting warm and the adrenalin was flowing fast. He knew we had done something dangerous that we were not supposed to do. He gave us a hard look and said, "Are you going to tell me? I don't know why but for some reason I felt I had to tell him, so I did. "It was beautiful dad, the mountains and all!" Kelly and Pat didn't say anything. He looked as though he was giving my words some thought and then he looked at me like he realized I was not a little boy anymore. It was almost like he didn't have anything to say and then, "Listen and always remember this guys. The human spirit has no limitations. It's up to you how far to let your spirit soar, but remember its best to soar safely and not without a plan. Now go and get out of here and have fun!"

I felt good inside. I believe it was on that very day, standing up there looking at the peaks and summits, something happened to me that I didn't fully understand. Though now I can explain it in a few words: In my heart, I am a climber.

Chapter 2

Avalanche Control

"If you want to climb a mountain, go up.
When there is no more up, you've climbed it".

THERE IS A FEELING YOU GET when you climb alone. When hiking on a trail, you periodically run into another hiker. Climbing is different; you might not see anyone for a long while—even a day or two. That's what I thought after putting on my pack again while contemplating my next move.

I thought about my new job. After having my own business for 5 years, depleting my retirement, and having no benefits I needed to find a new job. I was hired at a heavy equipment manufacturing company in Redmond. I was so desperate that I had lied about my qualifications. I had to ascend a steep learning curve as quickly as I could in order to assemble electronic components. I knew that if I was successful I could start building a future and find my way out of an unhappy relationship. I was successful on both of my goals and was finally on my own. *Now I need to rediscover myself. I need to make everything right. I need to know what the three gifts are. How do I do that?*

When I was in the Boy Scouts, I had a close friend named Pat. We lost touch after graduating from high school. A few years back he contacted me out of the blue via Facebook and we picked up right where we'd left off. I discovered after we reconnected that he had kept to the Boy Scout honor code and the Boy Scout laws: He was a devoted father, husband, and went to church every Sunday. He was what I tried to be but could never quite manage. He died from a heart attack shortly after we were reunited. I was devastated.

Then I thought about another high school friend. Alan was the key that unlocked the climbing world for me; he was my mountaineering cornerstone. Then was gone. Without him, I might never have started climbing mountains.

• • •

A senior in high school, I began attending a small church because of a girl. Phyllis was a "hippie chick" with long straight reddish-brown hair parted in the middle, big brown eyes, a small button nose and gorgeous legs. Church was not something I was really into, but I was attracted to Phyllis so I joined her. She made it fun. Unlike most Christian girls, she was a bit promiscuous. So, being seventeen, I was drawn to both the discovery of her and of her religion. Church was good for me; it kept me out of trouble. That's where I met Alan. Phyllis introduced us. I could tell right away that Alan didn't want to be there but, he went because his parents made him.

About my height with long shoulder-length dirty blond kinky hair, he was wiry but strong. As we shook hands the first thing he asked me, "Do you ski?"

"Yes. You?"

"No, but I'm looking for someone to teach me."

I smiled, then laughed out loud as I realized he was asking me to teach him how to ski. "I'll teach ya," I blurted out.

We hit it off right away and thus began a great friendship. I took him skiing and in no time he was as good, if not better, than me. After graduating from high school, Alan and I hung out more and our friendship became strong.

Alan came from a fairly wealthy home. His dad was an engineer who drummed it into Alan's head that if he wanted to ever become successful he needed to go to college and get a degree. Alan decided he wanted to be a doctor. So he took the college fund his parents had set aside for him and began attending the University of Washington in the fall after high school.

He also worked part-time as a gas jockey. With all the money he made, he could afford to buy whatever he wanted. His toys included a truck, skis, a dune buggy, motorcycle, climbing gear, and a VW bus. We spent almost every weekend together doing something. Hiking, snowshoeing, climbing, and skiing. We had many crazy mishaps that we called: "Tim and Alan Productions." Phyllis didn't really like all the time I was spending with my friend, so after a while she began seeing someone else. I was devastated at first, but I got over it.

I was working full-time as an apprentice carpenter at a door company, making three dollars an hour. Alan was making just as much working half as many hours selling batteries and tires. He was an amazing salesman. His boss loved him, so when he wanted to take time off he'd call me up and say, "Tim, let's go skiing!"

"Alan I can't afford it right now."

"It's okay, Tim, I'll treat!"

He was a good friend. We were alike in so many ways. We mirrored each other. We both had long hair, which was the style in the seventies. We were free-spirited and adventurous. I had a beat-up, blue 1957 Ford pickup; Alan had a beat-up purple 1957 Ford pickup. I had a beat-up 1971 Honda 350 motorcycle; Alan had a beat-up 1967 BSA 350. I had a beat-up green 1966 VW bus; Alan had the most amazing 1962 VW camper van, the likes of which I haven't seen since. It was dark metallic blue with chrome wheels and white-letter tires. It had an amazing stereo with an eight-track tape player and big speakers. It was always the vehicle of choice for our outings. We named his bus Magic.

In the middle of January, 1974, we were on our way up a chairlift at Stevens Pass, kicking our skis back and forth and arguing about which way we were going to ski down. We were high and singing "Que Sera, Sera," but we'd changed the lyrics. We thought it was funny; it really wasn't. When you're high and having fun, everything is funny. Alan began telling me about this crazy notion he had.

"Tim, I think that we should climb Mount Snoqualmie and then ski down the face. Whaddaya think?"

I sat in momentary silence listening to the sound of the chairlift hum and bounce over the cable track wheels. I finally said, "You mean, carry our skis up?"

"Yeah," Alan quickly responded.

"And boots?"

"Yeah!" he shouted back getting more excited.

"To the summit?!"

"Yeah!!"

Mount Snoqualmie is a 6,280 foot mountain located near Snoqualmie Pass in the heart of the Cascades. There is a lot of exposure all around it and it's in a very high avalanche area. Right next to it is a mountain called Guye Peak. Nestled below Guye Peak at that time was a cluster of tiny chalets and a very small ski resort called Alpental. Alan wanted to hike with our skis strapped to our packs from Alpental, then traverse across the front of Guye Peak toward Mount Snoqualmie at an uphill angle until we got to the base of the mountain. Then we would switchback up to the summit, put on our skis and boots, and ski all the way down to the parking lot at Alpental.

He said, "It will take us at least forty-five minutes to ski all that way. It's never been done!" We were always trying to find a way to ski as far and as long as we could.

Now, the thought of carrying my skis and boots all the way up the mountain to the summit didn't sound all that appealing, but with Alan as competition, I would try anything. Besides, it had never been done. We had adventurous pioneer spirits. I wanted to do it bad. I could tell Alan was just as pumped to do this. Everything was a challenge for us and we were always competing to see who could outdo the other. I thought about this crazy feat that we were about to undertake and wondered what I could add to make it even more daring. Then I said, "Hey, let's spend the night up there on the summit and ski down in the morning!"

It was the middle of winter and at night the temperature probably dropped to well below freezing on the summit. With the wind blowing, you're looking at twenty or thirty degrees below zero! All I had was an old, beat-up army surplus sleeping bag that was probably comfort-rated to at most forty degrees. Alan looked at me like I was crazy. I returned the look. Then he smiled at me and said what he always said: "Let's do it!"

That following Friday, we left Alan's house in Bellevue with all our gear packed. We drove off in Magic toward Alpental listening to the Doobie Brothers, both excited about our new adventure. We never worried about anything, even though maybe we should have....

When we reached the small parking lot at Alpental, the area was desolate, There were no cars.

"Hey Alan, where is everybody?"

"I don't know, who cares? Let's do it!"

So with nothing more said we headed out, skis sticking out from the tops of our packs, which were loaded with food and clothing for a week. With ski poles in hand, we started hiking through knee-deep snow angling to the left up the mountain.

In the mountaineering handbook, *Freedom of the Hills*, it says "Snow is considered excellent if the climber can stand on or near the surface, fair if he sinks to his calves; when immersion is knee-deep or greater, it is only good for 'character.'" This was a character-building day for us both.

After a few hours of trudging through the deep snow, we finally stopped to rest. It appeared hopeless but nothing was going to stop us from reaching our destination. Alan and I had no common sense back then. As we continued, the snow crust began to get harder the higher we climbed, making it easier to ascend. But things began to change very fast.

We had climbed to the upper slopes of Mount Snoqualmie and, as we switch-backed left of the summit at about 5,000 feet, we came upon a large cornice. A cornice is a very large snowdrift blown into an overhang by the wind. It was right above us on the ridge to the right of the summit. It didn't look that big from below, but when we got close to it, it loomed like a giant twenty-five-foot wall. As we headed around it to the right, there was an explosion down below us, echoing off the sides of the mountains all around. Then another explosion above us that echoed off in the distance. I stopped in my tracks and yelled at Alan, "What's going on?!"

He yelled back, "Avalanche guns!"

"Avalanche guns?" No sooner had I yelled when another loud explosion hit about 300 yards above us.

We hadn't considered that. The forest service periodically fired cannons at cornices so that they will avalanche down safely in areas where there are no people. You see, nobody is stupid enough to climb Mount Snoqualmie in the middle of the winter and ski down, at least not in those days. Nowadays it happens all the time.

"They're shooting at us!" I yelled, not knowing what to do.

Alan, never long on conversation, screamed at me, "RUN!!"

Just as he said it, the cornice broke loose and began to come down. I ran, tumbled, rolled, slid, jumped, and all the time I could hear the thundering avalanche behind me. I didn't take any time to see where Alan was or what an avalanche looked like up close, I just kept sprinting down the snowfield. My heart was pounding in my ears the whole way as I thought, *This is it, my life is over.*

The thundering finally stopped, so I stopped and waited for my breath to catch up. I couldn't hear anything. I dropped down on my knees, gulping for air. Once I gathered my composure I stood up, soaking wet, turned around and there stood Alan. He was nonchalantly cleaning the snow from his glasses, looking like a drenched rat covered in white. He looked at me with a silly grin on his face and said, "WOW! That was a close one!"

We looked up and saw chunks of broken up snow scattered all around where our tracks had been. My pack had opened up and spilled out some of my stuff. *Oh well, it was beat-up stuff anyway.* I walked over to the edge of the avalanche and looked up at the summit of Mount Snoqualmie. Turning around, I began to feel faint and sick to my stomach. "I don't think this is a very good day to climb, Alan."

He walked over, put his arm around my shoulders, looked up, swallowed dramatically, paused for effect, and said, "The weather's getting bad. There wouldn't be much of a view."

I smiled. "Yeah, and the snow is bad. It's not good for skiing."

Then we both let out a chuckle that became contagious. We started laughing hysterically. With tears in my eyes and still laughing I said, "What the hell were we thinking?!"

Alan replied, "People get killed doing stupid stuff like this."

I answered back with, "Thank God we're not those stupid people, right?"

We both started laughing again. I was a bit upset that we didn't make it, relieved that we'd lived, but mostly I was just really cold inside. "Let's get back down and get warm," Alan said as he grabbed my shoulders and shook me.

"I lost my sleeping bag," I said in a sort of joking way.

"I was going to tell you that it was a worthless sleeping bag, Tim. It's time to get a new one."

We spent the rest of the day skiing at Snoqualmie ski resort in the bad snow, singing our stupid song.

We headed home listening to an eight track tape that Alan had found in Magic when he bought it. It was a Judy Collins album that I can't remember the name of. The song "Clouds" came on and we both just listened quietly as we stared out the front window. I was thinking, *how did we manage to keep from getting destroyed by that avalanche?*

Chapter 3

A Mountain to Climb

"When he first came to the mountain his life was far away, on the road and hanging by a song.

But the string's already broken and he doesn't really care, it keeps changing fast and it don't last for long".

— John Denver

ALAN WAS AN AMAZING FRIEND. We spent so much time together. I miss him. "I climbed my first mountain with him," I said out loud as I took off my boot to adjust my bunched-up sock before heading back down. I heard another noise over in the guide service hut. I finished putting on my boot and walked over to the hut.

"Hello?" I yelled. "Anyone in there?" Nothing. I felt a shiver up my spine, like someone was watching me. I turned my head around quickly and looked up toward Gibraltar Rock. The wind gusted hard. I felt a chill, as if there were a presence there. Then a huge cracking noise erupted above—scaring the shit out of me. A huge boulder rolled down toward the Muir Snowfield. It was tumbling fast as it hit the frozen snow, then slid away out of sight. I stood there looking at what just happened taking it all in a then the memory of another time with Alan came back to me.

．　．　．

Alan was taking a basic climbing course. He would practice what he'd learned up in the mountains with me, even though the practice rocks they provided in the course were a lot safer than the real thing. Alan didn't concern himself much with what was considered safe.

The first lesson he gave me was on Guye Peak. It's not the type of mountain that you practice new things on. It has very technical rock faces. Before we headed up there I didn't even know what the term "belay" meant.

We left his house on a clear, crisp Saturday morning in April. We took Magic just in case we needed to stay the night. We arrived at the Alpental parking lot around seven thirty. John Denver was (appropriately) singing "Rocky Mountain High" on the eight-track. Alan was taking forever to get his gear together. "You won't need anything, Tim. I've got everything we need, including lunch."

We hiked up to the southwest side of the base of the mountain, and then up to the west side. We scrambled up to an area that cut into the mountain then walked into it. There was a giant ice chunk up where the two walls met. The chunk was about ten to twelve feet high and about eight feet wide.

It was cold, just above freezing, and the wind blowing slightly at our backs from the south-southwest made it feel even colder. I was wearing a flannel shirt, wool jacket, Levi's, leather hiking boots, gaiters and wool socks. Alan was wearing denim bell-bottoms, hiking boots, a denim shirt and a red down vest. Not the warmest attire but at least it was wool. As I stood there, shivering with cold and curiosity, I watched Alan pound in a couple of pitons. He looped the rope through a couple of carabiners and tied it off. He wrapped the rope around my waist a few times and tied a bowline knot. He ran the other end of the rope around my back and tied it to his climbing harness. Then he told me, "If I yell 'falling,' wrap the rope around your waist as hard as you can and don't let it slip. Hold on tight. Okay, ya got it?"

"Yes, Alan, I got it," I replied, sounding somewhat irritated because of his condescending tone. He then handed me a small rock hammer and said, "Use this to take out the pitons." It had a hole through the handle and a small leather strap with a carabiner attached to it. I clipped it on my belt loop.

I watched with curiosity as Alan began to climb up that big chunk of ice. In no time he was standing on top of it. He stood there scratching his head, looking for a good handhold, when it began making cracking noises. He gave me a look of utter astonishment, and then, CRACK! The ice chunk broke loose and came rolling out like the stone that came rolling out after Indiana Jones. It was rolling right at me!

It happened so fast that it was a bit of a blur. I'm not sure exactly how we both avoided being crushed to death. All I remember is Alan shouting, "Look out!"

It's hard to get out of the way of a two-ton slab of ice when you're anchored to the side of a mountain. I suddenly felt like a bowling pin. With no time to think, Alan jumped onto a rock ledge in front of him like he was Spiderman, while I turned myself into a pancake pressing into the rock wall in front me. The ice chunk brushed my back as it rolled by, literally shaking the ground as it headed toward Alpental. It fell off the side of the cliff and exploded thunderously into pieces as it hit the snowfield below.

Alan jumped down, walked toward me and gazed down toward the pieces of ice. He shook the snow off his hair, looked at me and said, "Wow! Did you see that?"

"No Alan, I missed that one."

"Well," he smiled. "Let's go, we've got a mountain to climb."

I was ready to end the whole thing and go home. I should have known that the ice chunk was a sign, an omen of what was to come. Alan resumed climbing up where the ice chunk had once sat, taking small lengths of rope with him as he scaled the rock. He slowly disappeared from sight. I kept staring down at the rope as it slid through my hands a little at a time. A cloud rolled by and blocked the sun, and for that moment the temperature dropped about ten degrees, or at least it felt that way. As I sat precariously, shivering, I realized that the rope hadn't moved for a long time and I couldn't hear anything but the whistling wind coming up through rocky crags. It had only been about fifteen minutes but it seemed like an hour. I heard Alan hammer in a piton. The rope moved about three feet, then it was quiet for what seemed like an eternity. I couldn't stand the silence any more so I yelled up, "You all right? Alan?!" Immediately the echo reverberated off the rock walls. Then, nothing but the wind. "Hey Alan!"

Just as the words left my lips, a rock broke loose from above and came rolling toward me. Then I heard Alan let out a painful, "Oh no! Oh shit!" It echoed off the wall, then a sliding noise that echoed, Then, nothing.

"Alan! You OK?" The echo followed… then again… nothing. I didn't know what to do. The rope was still somewhat slack and Alan hadn't yelled "falling" so I didn't wrap the rope around my waist and pull it tight as I'd been taught. Then the rope started to slide through my hands again. I heard some rustling noises above me.

"Hey, Lewis! Get your lazy ass up here!"

I looked up and there, about sixty feet above me, was Alan's smiling face looking down at me. I was so relieved. He quickly set up an anchor and belayed me. At first I climbed up like a bear was chasing me. Then I came to the first piton he had placed. "Pull those out on the way up!" he yelled down. I was having a difficult time using the small hammer he had given me. Hitting the pitons back and forth to work them out was intense, and I was using the rope to hang on. My arms were shaking along with my legs. When I finally got up to him, he explained what had happened. The rock that his foot was on had broken loose and he'd started to fall but managed to wedge his elbow into a crack and hold on until he could grab something else with his fingertips. "I knew it would have hurt if I had fallen because the last piece of protection was about eight feet down," he said as he munched on some trail mix. Then he handed me some. I wasn't hungry.

After a few more pitches we began to make our way around on a ledge from the west to the southwest face. I was getting more comfortable with climbing but was still quietly praying that we'd make it back. I thought to myself, *My mom doesn't know I'm up here, thank God. Wait a minute! Nobody knows we're up here. Not even Alan's parents.* I began to feel sick to my stomach. We set up some anchors, and off he went again up what appeared to be a dried-up waterfall. He was about twenty-five feet above me when more rocks broke loose and tumbled down. They just missed me as I jumped out of the way. Alan yelled down, "You all right?"

I looked up at him with a solemn face and nodded.

He climbed back down and said, "This isn't a good route." So we began working our way around on the ledge to find a better spot to ascend.

The summit wasn't more than sixty or seventy feet above. As Alan was tying up an anchor, we heard thundering and rock crashing sounds all around us. Alan looked at me wide-eyed and yelled, "Avalanche!" He grabbed me and we both pressed ourselves together into the wall as tight as we could while rocks and boulders thundered down right next to us. I can remember thinking, *This is it, our luck has just run out,* but it hadn't. The avalanche had come down where the dried-up waterfall was and if we'd kept climbing there, I wouldn't be here writing this story.

We eventually reached the summit and considered the climb a real success until Alan set his pack, with our lunch in it, down on a ledge and… off it rolled. The marmots got the fried chicken, and I'm sure some hungry varmints ate the rest. The best part of the climb was rappelling down. It took us about an hour to get down from what took us all day to climb.

I stopped on our way down, turned around and took a mental picture of Guye Peak. I felt like it was looking at me and saying, "I let you go this time." I was still vibrating from the excitement. Or maybe I was just cold. We were hungry and profoundly tired, but getting to the top had made it all worthwhile. This was my first mountain—what a way to start!

As we drove off in silence, the soft hum of the Volkswagen engine was the only thing we heard. Then Alan put in a mix tape that he had made and the song "Darkness Darkness" by the Youngbloods came on. I had never really listened to the words until then. "Darkness darkness, long and lonesome / Is the day brings me here / I have found the edge of sadness / I have known the depths of fear." My arms and legs were aching, I was cold and wet, but I was exhilarated. I thought to myself, *I have no more fear! I am becoming the mountain, the mountain is becoming me!*

After a few more climbs with Alan, including Mount Snoqualmie during the summer, my confidence increased. If we weren't up in the mountains being crazy, we were hanging around the newly erected climbing rock at the University of Washington. We spent much of our time there, and before the climbing wall project was finished we could climb all the faces and overhangs on it. People started asking Alan and me how to climb an overhang or one of the faces—as if we were the experts. We were like the gurus of the climbing rock back in those days. Alan was more skilled than I was only because, as a full time student there, he could spend much more time on the wall.

• • •

The experiences that Alan and I shared together remain clear as day in my memory. I'm still amazed at how we survived. I looked at my watch, then up at Cathedral Gap, then up to the summit. "Alan and I wanted more than anything to climb this mountain together," I said out loud, "It never happened." But, in addition to the crazy stunts we pulled in the early days, we also climbed Aasgard Pass and Little Annapurna in the Stuart Range in winter. I looked at the deep scar tracing the middle of my left index finger from left to right. Alan was all about challenges and it was easy for him to talk me into any challenge.

• • •

In December 1976, I was a full-time college student at Seattle Central. Alan was in his second year at UW. He called me one Friday and asked if I wanted to climb Aasgard Pass over the holidays. "Aasgard Pass?" I asked. "What's that?"

Aasgard Pass is a route to the upper Enchantment Lakes. Its true name is Colchuck Pass, but no one uses that name for some reason. It's known as the shortcut to the Enchantments. Short but not easy, it's over 2,000 feet of elevation gain in less than a mile. So basically—straight up. It begins from the southeast end of Colchuck Lake in the Icicle Creek area just south of Leavenworth. The plan was, we would drive in on Monday afternoon, sleep in my truck, get up and hike the four miles to Colchuck Lake on Tuesday morning, spend the night there, get up early on Wednesday, and climb Aasgard along with Little Annapurna and Dragontail Peak. It had not yet snowed at all that season. 1976 was one of the first of the "El Nino" years that we experienced in the Northwest. It was dry and there was no snow in the mountains. That was the main reason why Alan wanted to do this. Because we could.

Christmas was on a Saturday that year so we decided to leave Monday morning. Alan was having engine problems with Magic so we decided to take my truck. I had recently bought a canopy for it with a cozy bed inside. I picked Alan up at his house around eleven thirty. He still lived with his parents in a late fifties rambler-style house. "Why are you so late?" is how he greeted me.

"Couldn't find all my stuff."

We packed enough food for a month and by the time we were ready it was one o'clock. We got gas in Monroe and headed to Leavenworth. The weather was frigid and clear and there was no snow at Stevens Pass. We stopped at a place called the Squirrel Tree Restaurant by Lake Wenatchee and I had a hot turkey sandwich. Alan seemed distant and was getting more and more annoyed about everything. He wasn't himself. "This is way too late to be starting this trip, Tim," he said as were getting into the truck.

"We have all week, Alan. Hell, we could stay two weeks with all the food we brought."

He pulled out my Pink Floyd eight-track tape and threw it on the floor. "I'm sick of this." He put in Janis Ian. I was sick of that tape and he knew it. It was like he was purposely trying to piss me off. It was dark when we finally got to Leavenworth and very quiet in my truck cab. "At Seventeen" and the low hum of my 223 Ford six-cylinder were the only sounds.

Alan broke the silence. "Turn here!"

I slammed on my brakes and turned onto the road that leads to the Colchuck Lake trailhead. After a minute or so I asked, "What's wrong, Alan? You seem really pissed about something."

I could see him look at me even though it was almost dark. "I asked you to be at my house in the morning. You didn't get there until after eleven. Now we're driving up in the dark. That's what's wrong!"

I looked over at him. I could see the faint outline of his face framed by his huge head of hair. I looked back at the road as we hit a rather large pothole. "Alan, you could have been ready when I got there. We could have left at noon instead of one," I said rather sarcastically.

Keeping my eyes on the road, I could feel him looking at me. He said back in a low tone, "I wasn't sure I wanted to go when you got there."

I got really pissed, but before I could say anything my truck started to slip around the road as we headed up a steep hill. I changed my tone and said, "It looks wet."

We were coming up to a sharp corner and I was going fairly fast to keep the momentum going. "Slow down!" Alan shouted.

As I turned the wheel and we went around the hairpin curve, my truck started to slide out of control. I corrected and kept it going straight. The wheels started spinning as we kept climbing the hill. "This is not good," I said as we finally came to a stop. My emergency brake didn't work so I had to shut the truck off and put it in first gear. "I'll get out and see what's going on."

Alan didn't say anything. I left the lights on and grabbed my flashlight from under the seat. I opened the door and jumped out. The second my feet hit the ground they went out from underneath me and I landed on my ass. "It's solid ice, Alan! We're on ice!"

"Do you have chains?" he shouted back.

"Yeah, I do." Then I remembered that my chains were made for my old 16-inch wheels. I had bought new, fat off-road tires and wheels since and had tried the chains on earlier in the year to see if they fit. They were too small. I didn't want to tell Alan. It was so slippery that I had to grab ahold of my truck to pull myself up and inch around to the back. Just as I pulled on the canopy door to open it, the truck started sliding backward. "Holy shit!" I yelled.

Alan yelled out at me, "Do something!" The truck was sliding toward the edge of the road where we had made the turn. I was pushing against the back of the canopy as the truck was pushing me back. I was not going to lose my truck over a cliff. I just kept yelling "No!" over and over. Then one of the tires in the back hit an open rocky area about ten feet from the edge. My truck slid to a stop. Alan opened the door and got out. He walked around to the back where I was still holding on. I looked over at him and said, "Were you just going to sit in my truck listening to Janis Ian and go over the edge with it? You could have at least jumped out, you know."

He shined his flashlight in my face. "I knew it would stop," he replied with his arrogant tone. "Where are the chains?"

"There, under the bed, in the box marked 'tire chains.'"

"Let's get them on and get the hell out of here."

I didn't say anything. Alan went and found a large rock to chock the front tire. I pulled out the box, pulled out the chains and separated them, hoping the tires had worn down enough to make them fit. He took one and I took the other. I wrapped mine around the tire knowing full well that it wouldn't fit. I could hear him over on the other side working away. I pulled each side tight and somehow the chain latch hooked onto the last hole on the other side of the chain. They were as tight as they could possibly be, but they fit.

"These chains are really tight!" Alan shouted at me.

I walked over to him and shined my flashlight on him. Then it all hit me. I started laughing. "Alan, these chains didn't fit last summer."

He looked at me. "You mean to tell me that after you bought these four-wheel-drive tires for this two-wheel-drive truck,` you didn't buy new chains to fit them? What the hell!" He was not happy with me.

"You were always jealous of these tires," I said accusingly.

"Jealous? Do you know how dumb it looks to have a two-wheel-drive truck with off-road tires on it?"

We kept going at it, back and forth; we were out in the middle of nowhere arguing about my stupid tires. It finally ended with him saying, "Let's just go back home."

"No, Alan. We're doing this. Get in, let's go." I really didn't want to try to turn my truck around. I didn't say another word, just got in the driver seat. Alan reluctantly got in.

My lights had been on the whole time and Janis Ian's voice was subdued. She sounded a bit manly. I shut the lights off and pulled out the tape. I glanced at Alan, took a deep breath and turned the key. The motor barely turned and then quit. The starter relay started clicking. Alan shouted out with a voice that could be heard clear to Leavenworth, "Shit!!"

I didn't say anything. *Oh no, we are fucked.* Then, in a low voice, "Maybe we should pray…."

Alan had his head in his hands but he wasn't praying. It was dark and quiet. We just stared silently out the front windshield at a million stars that taunted us in the dark. After about ten minutes, I said a little prayer, *Please help us God,* closed my eyes, held my breath, and turned the key again. It started. I looked at Alan and he at me. I put the truck in gear and let the clutch out and we started going up. We made it to the trailhead in no time. I parked and shut off the engine.

"I'm sleeping in the cab!" Alan barked out.

"Fine. More room for me in the back," I said back as I smiled at him.

He looked at me, "You know, you can really piss me off sometimes, Tim."

"It could have been a lot worse, Alan. You could be at the bottom of a ravine listening to 'I learned the truth at seventeen…'" I sang.

He started to smile. Then he let out a chuckle. Then we both started laughing. Then we broke out in chorus together.

Friends again, Alan decided to sleep in the back too. Even after all that had already happened, I was a bit apprehensive about the climb. It was so cold that the inside of my canopy windows had ice on them.

The morning came fast. After only about four hours sleep, Alan was up getting ready. I looked at my clock. It was 4:26 a.m. "What's going on, Alan?"

"I'll tell you what's going on. We got to get going. That's what's going on!"

He sounded mad. I was still a bit disorientated. "It's still dark outside."

He answered back quickly, "It will be light when we're on the trail. Come on, let's go!"

I got up and began getting ready. He was packed in no time and boiling water. He had just purchased an MSR stove—one of the best mountaineering stoves ever invented. Alan was infatuated with it. We ate instant oatmeal, finished packing, and began walking up the frozen trail at about five.

It was impossible to stand on the ice wearing heavy packs in our hiking boots. Our snowshoes had little built-in ice grips, so we put them on. They worked amazingly well. We arrived at Colchuck Lake around eight thirty. It had taken us three hours to get there, negotiating switchbacks with snowshoes and heavy packs. The lake was completely frozen and it had a dusting of powder on it. Dragontail Peak loomed forebodingly at the south end of the lake. There was no sign of anyone having been there in a long time. It felt desolate.

We found a small crude shelter at the north end of the lake. Someone had built it using logs and plastic tarps. It was makeshift but felt safe, so we decided to spend the first night in there. It had a dirt floor but there was plenty of room for the two of us and all our gear.

We dumped out our packs and began getting our gear together for the climb. I had brought the Arctic Expedition coat that I had ordered out of an Alaskan gear catalog. It was rip-stop nylon, goose down–filled and had real animal fur on the hood. Wearing that coat was like wearing a sleeping bag, it was so warm. Alan had a similar type, but his was an Eddie Bauer. Our wardrobe had improved since we'd first climbed together.

Lake Colchuck is surrounded by mountains and in the winter the sun is gone by three o'clock. After a good meal of beef stew and tea, we turned in, keeping the stove fired up to help keep us warm. It wasn't but maybe an hour after we crawled into our sleeping bags that the wind started blowing hard. We got up to stuff our extra clothes in the holes of the shelter and anchor the door better with large rocks. In the distance, the wind howled as it came down off Dragontail Peak. It hit the lake which would, in turn, let out an eerie cracking noise. It was like no noise I'd heard before or since. Then it would hit the shelter like a maelstrom. It started snowing and blowing into the shelter from under the tarp. It was like something out of a movie. We came up with an idea to wrap the bottom of the tarp with a large stick and tack it down with tent stakes. Fighting the wind, it took us a while to do it but it worked. We were finally safe from the storm, so we hunkered down into our bags like frightened children to wait it out. Soon, the wind began to subside a little but the snow didn't. We finally fell asleep.

I was awakened suddenly by Alan screaming, fighting to get out of his bag. "What's wrong, Alan?" I yelled.

"There's something in my sleeping bag with me!" He was freaking out.

I grabbed my flashlight out of my sleeping bag and shined it on him just as he scrambled out frantically. I shined the flashlight on his bag and out ran a big pack rat.

"We can't stay in here tonight, Tim!" he yelled.

"We're going to have to. We don't have a choice right now. It's snowing hard and we could never get the tent down and set up somewhere else in this blizzard."

He relaxed a bit. We could hear snowflakes hitting the plastic tarp door and what sounded like something walking around outside. "What do you think that is?" I asked, afraid to hear the answer.

He didn't say anything right away. "It sounds like an animal."

"That's just great!" I said loudly, hoping to scare it away. "What's next? Bigfoot?" I didn't feel very safe with just a sheet of plastic between me and some unknown creature. Whatever it was, it left and only the sound of heavy snow was heard as it piled up outside and pushed against the door of the shelter. Needless to say we didn't sleep much.

When I woke up, Alan was asleep sitting up with the drawstring of his sleeping bag tight around his neck and his balaclava pulled down over his head so that you could only see his eyes. The sun was shining through a small hole and it was cold—I mean like below-zero cold. Everything was frozen. There were condensation icicles hanging off the ceiling. It took some time to get Alan's stove going and then for it to get warm enough to entice us out of our sleeping bags.

We had to literally crawl out of a hole that we made at the top of the door to get out. It had snowed around three feet through the night. Outside was a winter wonderland. The sky was a dark, beautiful blue and the lake was covered with snow, but you could still hear cracking sounds echoing off of it.

Alan and I discussed what time we were going to begin what we thought might be the first winter ascent of Aasgard in history. And for all we knew, it could be the first winter ascent of Little Annapurna and Dragontail too. We were excited about our mission. We spent most of the day preparing for the next morning's expedition. We had a rope, crampons, ice axes and some anchors, but no ice screws.

By two o'clock it was already starting to get dark. The wind was picking up and it sent a chill through us. We had our tent all set up and were ready for what had to be a better night's sleep. I was still a bit nervous about what kind of animal might have been walking around outside our shelter the previous night. We ate a delicious dinner of lasagna, shared a joint, and crawled into our bags around five.

We didn't have the type of headlamps then that we have today. Alan had a calcium carbide head lantern. We drank tea while Alan read out loud from *Ice Station Zebra*. I had seen the movie years before but the book was better—at least the first chapter was, before I fell asleep.

I was awakened suddenly by Alan pushing me. "What?"

"Shh," he whispered. "There's something out there."

I was still in a sleepy state and didn't really care… but then I heard it walk right up to the tent. The snow squeaked as it walked around to the other side. It sounded like a large four-legged animal. The adrenaline was pumping and I shakily whispered, "Where are our ice axes?"Alan whispered back, "I think they're out there.""Shit!"

Whatever was out there was really curious about us; It was sniffing around like a dog. It started pawing at the side of the tent that Alan was on. He jumped on me and we both screamed like a couple of babies. "AAAAAAAAAHHHHHHHH!!"

With that—we scared the shit out of whatever it was and it took off. Poor thing, it was probably more scared than we were. After gathering our composure, we put on our jackets and crawled out of the tent. Shining the flashlight on the snow we saw hundreds of bobcat prints all around the tent. We'd been close to being his "mountain stew."

Alan shut off his flashlight and said, "Tim, look up." There were billions and billions of stars, so bright that they lit up the snow. It was incredible. Alan got his camera out, set it on a large rock and took a time-exposure picture of Dragontail Peak. I wish I had that picture today.

We finally settled down and tried to get back to sleep. But I started thinking about the bobcat. "Hey Alan?"

"What?"

"I bet that bobcat is in Leavenworth by now having a beer."

"Or taking a big shit."

We both started to chuckle. Soon we were all-out laughing.

"You know Alan, the avalanche on Snoqualmie Peak didn't scare you, the giant boulder on Guye Peak didn't scare you, but the packrat and little bobcat made you scream like a girl.""That was when I thought it was a Bigfoot!" he said with tears in his eyes."Which one? The packrat or the bobcat?"

Between fatigue and pot-induced hysteria, I thought I was going to die laughing. We finally settled down and slept, until Alan woke up in a rage. "Tim! It's five o'clock! We should be on our way by now!"

We scrambled and got our gear on in record time and left about five thirty. Alan was leading the way with his headlamp on. He was afraid to cross the lake because he wasn't sure if it would be frozen enough this early in the season. Not wanting to risk it, we walked around the lake on the west side with our snowshoes. It made for quick travel to the base of Aasgard. After arriving at about six thirty, we stopped and looked up the pass. It looked a lot farther than it did from the other side of the lake. It was just getting light when we got there and I was feeling really good. We rested for a bit and ate some hard candies. We took off our snowshoes and put on our crampons.

I grabbed the shaft of my ice axe and held it as if it were something I'd never seen before. Alan grabbed it from me and said, "You hold it like this!" He wrapped his right hand around the head of the axe and held it out for me to see the pick protruding out of the back. "If you fall, stick the pick into the snow and it will brake you. You got it?"

It reminded me of when he taught me how to belay.

My feet were numb after about an hour of working our way up the pass. It was slow going. In some areas there was little snow and solid ice, in others there was waist-deep powder. I had no idea how to use an ice axe. We managed to work our way toward the middle of the pass, then off to the right side next to Dragontail Peak.

"Shouldn't we rope up, Alan?" I asked.

"We could never stop in this powder if we tried to team-arrest."

I thought about what he said as we made another switchback to the left toward the top of the pass. Then I stopped for a second; it didn't make any sense. "So, you're saying that if we rope up and one of us falls we couldn't save each other?"

"Yes," was his simple reply.

"So what's the point of the ice axes? Shouldn't we be roped up putting in anchors?"

Alan stopped, quiet for a moment, then said, "Tim, we only have a few hours to do this, we don't have time to be setting anchors. Just don't fall, okay?"

Just don't fall? I looked at him and thought about all the anchors he was carrying and the rope that I was carrying. So I yelled up at him, "Then why are we carrying up all these anchors and a rope?!"

He looked back at me like he was really pissed off; he looked up to the sky like he was thinking, *help me, Jesus.* Then he looked back at me and said loudly, "JUST. DON'T. FALL! OKAY?!" His words echoed off the two peaks on either side of us, twice, then faded. It was quite a dramatic moment.

I didn't have much to say at that moment, but I began to analyze the situation. *Let's see… We're standing on a steep hill in the middle of nowhere, in the darkest time of winter, it's probably fifteen degrees, we're both sleep deprived, and Alan is mad at me because I'm asking too many questions. Hmmm…well, I hope I don't fall.*

I turned around and looked down. It was really steep. The lake looked beautiful with the wind-blown snow in drifts and spots where the aqua color of the frozen lake peeked through. Off in the distance I could see our tiny tent and all our tracks around it. We were about halfway up and I couldn't feel my toes and fingers. But I kept going. Alan was making small switchbacks up the middle of the pass. When we were about three-quarters of the way there, I finally started to feel my toes and fingers again. It was eleven forty-five when we reached the top. It had taken us almost six hours.

We stood there, side by side, and looked around. I'm not sure if I can accurately describe what we saw when we reached the top. The white granite, the snow, the blue frozen water, the dark blue sky with the winter sun illuminating it all. Just Alan and me… the only two people in the world experiencing this.

We stopped by a large rock and took off our packs. Alan fired up his stove and cooked some chicken noodle soup. It was delicious. Everything tastes better when you're outside and you've worked for it. I had some hard French rolls and a giant block of cheese that I kept slicing off with the buck knife that I had permanently borrowed from my brother. By the time we finished eating, packed up and began heading toward Little Annapurna, it was twelve thirty.

"We gotta hurry Tim, we don't want to be going down in the dark," Alan barked at me.

I didn't say anything, just followed along.

We were traveling fast at first. We walked right across the center of Isolation Lake and started heading up. We ran into problems when we traversed across to the right, toward the summit. Ice everywhere. Alan's crampons had no toe points and they were getting trashed as we tried to sidestep our way up ice and granite. Between our heavy packs and the steep terrain, it was awkward trying to make our way up. Time was running out, But we were both driven to climb this mountain no matter what. It was probably after two o'clock when we finally reached the last three hundred yards to the summit.

There it was, you could see what seemed to be the summit, but we kept climbing and climbing and never seemed to reach it.

"Where the hell is the summit?" I yelled at Alan.

"It's around here somewhere!"

At two thirty-five we walked onto the summit. There was a cliff in front of us and everywhere else was down. There was powder snow everywhere. It was incredible to be up there in the dead of winter with the sun shining down all around, Mount Stuart right there and mountains as far as you could see. There were some dark clouds to the north that seemed to be heading our way. We took our packs off and sat for a while, looking off into the distance. "We should probably get going, right?" I asked Alan.

He turned and looked at me. "Probably." But we both just sat taking in the view and a well-deserved rest.

I suddenly realized how hungry I was. I pulled out my block of cheese. I took off my wool mittens and grabbed my knife to carve off some frozen cheese for the both of us. The cheese was so hard that I couldn't get the giant hunting knife to pierce it. My hands were shaking from the cold as I kept pushing hard. Then, in an instant, the cheese flipped out of my hand and the knife sliced my finger to the bone.

"Shit!" I yelled.

"What's wrong?" Alan asked.

I didn't want to tell him. I didn't want to look at it. I pulled my blue scarf from around my neck and wrapped it up as tight as I could, applying pressure to stop the bleeding. I slid my wool mitten back over it. Fortunately, Alan remained unaware of what was going on.

"What are you doing?" he asked like he was annoyed.

"Nothing." I think that because it was so cold, and my fingers were so numb, it wasn't bleeding as bad as it would have if it were warmer.

"Well, we better get going if we want to get back down, right?" I said as I calmly put the cheese and the knife back in my pack. I was in a hurry to get going and had lost my appetite. I was feeling sick. Alan quietly got up and put on his pack.

We started heading back down the same way we had come up, and it wasn't long before we ran into the frozen snow and rocks. It wasn't easy trying to climb down. It was difficult to get a good foothold on the ice. I was slightly ahead of Alan, using my ice axe to keep myself balanced, when my right foot slipped out from underneath me and I came down hard on my right side. I immediately began sliding fast. I rolled onto my belly attempting to self-arrest. The pick of my ice axe caught a rock and I stopped. Pulling on the shaft of the ice axe with my left hand caused excruciating pain in my cut finger. I let out a large yell. I could feel the blood running down my hand inside my mitten. I rolled over on my back and closed my eyes in pain. I could hear Alan approaching.

Stunned, I just lay there thinking about what my mom had said to me on Christmas Day. She had overheard me tell my dad and brother what Alan and I were going to do and she said, "I don't want to hear about what you and Alan are doing, just let me know when you get home safe."

I hope I get back home safe.

"Are you okay?" Alan asked.

"Yeah… I think so." I slowly got up. We were close to the bottom of the mountain and could see the tracks we'd had made earlier across Isolation Lake. I looked up and saw that I had probably slid one third of the way down the mountain.

"What the hell is going on with your hand?"

My mitten was almost soaked red from blood. "I think I might have cut my finger earlier."

"Let's take a look at it," he demanded. He was studying to become a doctor.

I pulled off my mitten and slowly unwrapped the bloody bandana bandage. We inspected my badly cut finger. "Holy shit, man! You need stitches!"

He took off his pack and pulled out his first aid kit. He grabbed a bottle of something out of it and began to treat my cut. I was feeling nauseated. "You better sit down, Tim." He cleaned the wound and put on a butterfly bandage, then wrapped it with gauze and tape. "When did you do this?"

"When I was cutting cheese back on the summit."

"Did you ever get any?"

"No." I was feeling weak and didn't want to talk or move.

"Let's get down to level ground by the lake and warm up, okay?" He helped me get up. When we got down to the edge of the lake, Alan pulled out his stove and heated water for soup. We got warm and I began to feel alive again. It was dark by the time we were ready to get going.

My flashlight was starting to lose its charge and it wasn't long before all we had was Alan's headlamp for light. When we finally reached the edge of the pass, it started to snow. "This is not good," I said when we began to head down, "When did these clouds move in?"

"I don't know, probably when we were getting warmed up." He sounded worried.

It was slow going. We were trying to follow our tracks from earlier, but it wasn't long before we lost them. We knew we just needed to go down, but we couldn't see anything and were feeling a bit disoriented. Little powder flakes were falling harder and not sticking to anything. My down-filled coat was wet on the inside from perspiration and I would freeze every time we stopped—which was about every fifty feet. I could tell that Alan was getting nervous by the way he was swearing at everything. "Shit!" he yelled out when his headlamp began running out of calcium carbide.

"Do you have any in your pack?" I asked.

"I might. But I can't see anything." He took off his pack and began rummaging through by feel. I remembered that I had an old metal lighter in my pack—something else that I had permanently borrowed from my brother. I took off my pack and began searching through the top compartment. I found it, flipped it open and tried it; it worked. We had enough light to see if Alan had any more calcium carbide. He did. He refilled his headlamp and we were in business again.

I followed him close, a foot behind him so I wouldn't lose him in the snow. He began to slow down and it seemed like he was losing confidence. "What's wrong, Alan?"

"I can't see anything." Just then a rock broke loose under his foot and he started to fall off the edge of what looked like a cliff. He let out this, "Ahhhhelp!!" all in one word. It happened so fast that all I could do was grab the top of his pack and lean backward. I don't know how I did it but I stopped his fall as I fell on my back, still holding on to his pack. I felt the cut on my finger tear open again and warm blood started to flow inside my already blood-drenched mitten. Most of Alan's body was hanging over the edge while I kept a death grip on his pack. I had just enough strength to pull him about twenty inches and then I had to rest. He was trying to reach back but couldn't get his ice axe in the snow because he was on his back and his pack was on my legs. My ice axe strap was around my wrist and there was nothing I could do but hold on. Alan then tried to roll over and I yelled, "Don't move!" I could feel us both sliding toward the edge when he moved.

I dug my feet into the snow underneath his pack and felt my foot contact a rock, which gave me a better foothold. Using what was left of the strength in my legs, I pushed hard while holding on to his pack. I managed to pull him up about another twenty inches and yelled out in pain. The sound echoed off in the distance. It was just enough for him to turn around and get a knee in the snow. He rolled off me and took a big swing with his ice axe, anchoring it enough to get away from the edge. He looked over at me, flashing his headlamp in my eyes. "I can't see, Alan!"

He looked down, then rolled over on his back. "Wow! That was close, wasn't it?" he said as he let out a huge sigh. We both just lay there allowing tiny snowflakes to melt on our faces.

"You really have a way of summing it all up, don't you? 'That was close'? How 'bout, 'Thanks for saving my life, Tim!'"

He was quiet for a minute and then said, "I think that goes without saying. Both ways."

We both just lay there for a few minutes. Then a realization came over me. I wasn't scared at all. I just knew we were going to make it back. Was it faith? Calmly, I got up.

"Alan?"

"What?"

"It stopped snowing!" I could see the stars through the breaks in the clouds. Looking toward Colchuck, I could see the faint outline of the lake. At the end of the lake, there was a light. "Look! There's someone down there at our camp!"

"It looks like they have a campfire going," Alan said as he got up.

We were looking directly down the middle of the lake. Something wasn't right. "Where the hell are we?" I asked. "Shouldn't we be more to the right of the lake?"

"Oh my God!" Alan gasped, "We're on Dragontail!"

Yes, when we became hopelessly lost in the snow, we had ventured out onto what appeared to be part of Dragontail Peak. "No wonder we're on a cliff," Alan said. "We gotta get out of here!"

I led us back the way we'd come. It took a while to get back to the pass and we started heading down. There was still a long way to go. The clouds had cleared out, making it easier to see our way without Alan's headlamp. As we descended, I kept taking off my mitten and putting snow on my cut to numb it. When we reached the lake, Alan wanted to redress my wound. Doing so probably helped save my finger.

It took us an hour to get around the lake because Alan was still not confident enough to walk across it. I was ready to drop when we finally reached the campfire of the unknown hikers. The three of them didn't hear us at first when we approached because the fire was snapping loud. One of them turned around when he heard us, he backed up and let out an "Aaah!" He was scared shitless. "Oh my God, you scared me!" he said after he realized we were human. My fur-trimmed hood was up and my beard was covered with icicles. I must have looked frightening in the firelight.

"You must be the owners of this tent," one of the other climbers said.

All I could do was stand in front of the fire and let the icicles melt off my face. I was too tired to say anything, but I felt relieved that we made it back and that we had company. Alan did all the talking. I don't remember much of the conversation but I do remember him telling them a bit of what we had just experienced. They were going to try do the same thing in the morning, so Alan spoke like he was an expert. I just smiled listening to his voice and thinking, *It's not as easy as Alan is making it sound.* We turned in after about an hour and I slept hard until after nine.

Alan made pancakes for breakfast and they were delicious, even though they weren't fully cooked. It didn't matter. We got to the truck around one o'clock. It was a quiet trip back. We couldn't agree on what to listen to, so I put in a Led Zeppelin mix tape. He didn't say anything. For some reason, the song "That's the Way" was the only song I remember hearing.

Time went by fast and then we were at Alan's house pulling things out of the back of my truck. I didn't say much to him when I left except, "Well, it was fun. Talk to you later?"

He just said, "Yeah, later," and I drove off.

I went over and over the trip in my mind as I drove home . We could have died at least two times, maybe three. It was a miracle we didn't. I felt distant from Alan like we really aren't friends anymore. What happened?

A few days later I went to my parents' house to wash my clothes. As I came through the door I yelled out, "Hi Mom, I'm back! Made it safe." She was happy to see me but later she knew something was up when she folded my clothes for me and saw my mitten.

Chapter 4

Petting the Sow

"Spent the last year Rocky Mountain way, couldn't get much higher."

— Joe Walsh

I LOOKED AT MY WATCH AND couldn't believe how fast I'd made it up here.

I made it up here in two hours! Damn. The first time I came up here. it took me eight hours. Eight hours! I must be in really good shape.

I thought about when our family would come up to Mt. Rainier during family vacations. We all crammed into a 1953 black Oldsmobile and drove up to Paradise. My dad used his 8mm movie camera to capture memories. Years later, he had them converted to VHS. After watching them over and over, I could locate all the areas on Mount Rainier I had been. I could see the Muir Snowfield the way it looked back in the sixties. *I never knew I would climb Mount Rainier someday, let alone guide people to the summit.* After looking around at the empty buildings, I sadly realized, my brother had never been here. I began to think about how important my brother's influence had been in my life…

• • •

When you're a kid, having a brother six years older is a mixed blessing. For the most part, I was somewhat jealous of John and all the cool toys he had, so I would break them. Not necessarily on purpose, mainly because I was fascinated with how things worked. We would sometimes get into arguments, but they would always end up with me swinging at air while he held his hand on my head at arm's length and laughed at me. He was a very tolerant big brother.

After John graduated from high school, he went up to Sitka, Alaska, for most of the summer and I really missed him. When he came home he started college and moved out with some friends, so I didn't see much of him. Every now and then he would take me for a ride in his 1956 Chevy Bel Air. It was a two-tone blue and white convertible and it kicked ass. Hanging out with my cool big brother was so amazing.

In the spring of 1969, John had to report to the draft board. I think for the first time, as a 13-year-old kid, I understood what was going on in the world and I was worried about him. I didn't want him to go to Vietnam.

He ended up joining the navy. I would see John when he would come home on leave, Christmas, for a week in the summer, and it was, somewhat ironically, during those few times we became very close. After he was discharged, my sister Julie and I flew to Virginia to meet him and drive back to Washington in his new BMW. We visited the Smithsonian in D.C., visited with family in Ohio, saw Joe Walsh in concert at Kent State, and visited a pig farm in Wisconsin.

John had a navy buddy named Charlie who lived on a pig farm in Mount Hope, Wisconsin. His dad (I don't remember his name so I'll call him "Scooter"), a real redneck farmer, enthusiastically offered to take us on a tour of his farm, which for hippie, West Coast city folk like us was an interesting change. In the barn were the biggest pigs I had ever seen in my life. They were the size of small cattle. Tied up in a pen was a gigantic sow. She had ropes tied to all four legs and around her neck so she couldn't move. While Scooter explained why she was in quarantine, my ADHD mind began to wander. I was not paying attention to anything he was saying. I stared at the sow and she stared back with her soft brown eyes I heard Scooter say something about "killed her piglets" but it went in one ear and out the other. I just kept staring into the eyes the sow. She raised her head and opened her mouth like she was in pain. She looked so sad. Scooter just kept on sounding serious about something in his midwestern drawl. I looked deeper into her eyes and then reached out my hand toward her head. Scooter spoke out, "You ought not be pettin' that sow"! I didn't hear him and for some reason I can't explain even to this day, I pet her on her head.

Holy shit!!! That sow went out of her mind! She screamed so loud it was deafening. Jumping up and down like a bucking bull, slamming herself into the side of the pen out of control, she broke two ropes. Scooter yelled out, "GADDAMIT SON!! I TOLD YOU NOT TA TOUCH THAT SOW!" He threw a blanket over her.

John raised his voice, "Tim! Didn't you hear a word Scooter was saying?"

Scooter yelled, "Get the hell out of here!" The pig was still screaming like she was in agony. It was all surreal.

We took off down the road, leaving that place in our dust. We left Wisconsin soon after that and I couldn't wait to get back to the Northwest.

• • •

The wind blew in my face as I thought about the sow. I never talked about that experience with anyone, but ever since, when I find myself in a situation that could turn out badly, I warn myself, *Don't pet the sow, Tim*. It has sometimes saved me… but not always. "Don't pet the sow," I said out loud, shaking my head. I have pet the sow many times in my life. I can still see that sow looking at me.

My brother was so mad. He's been upset with me a few times, but we always worked it out somehow. There was that time I thought I could take him to the summit of Glacier Peak and not tell him that it was my intention. I wasn't sure he would want to go up there so I didn't tell him exactly where we were going.

•   •   •

I was twenty-one. John still seemed so much older and wiser than me back then. It was early February, 1977, a month after Alan and I had climbed Aasgard and Little Annapurna. I was hanging out one night at Alan's and watching a slideshow of our trip, and he showed slides from his climb up Glacier Peak from the previous summer. As I watched the slides with great interest, I felt I had missed out on something. I'm not sure if it was jealousy or if it was just seeing the summit of Glacier Peak that intrigued me. I'm not sure why, but over the following weeks, I became obsessed with climbing it. Maybe by myself or with Alan, but Alan wasn't interested in going up there again. He did tell me about how to get up there though. I had a dream about climbing it and then I couldn't stop thinking about it. I thought maybe John would go with me since we had been doing some hiking together and I didn't really think it would be that big of a deal because I had just climbed Little Annapurna. I didn't think Glacier Peak would be any harder.

I called John a few days later. "Hey John, I'm thinking of going on a hike?"

"A hike? This time of year? Where?"

"Kennedy Hot Springs. There's no snow there, John. We can hike into the hot springs no problem." I had never been to the Glacier Peak Wilderness Area before, and Alan hadn't given me a lot of details about the hot springs or where they were located. So I embellished a bit and made it sound like it was a place of enchantment. "It's a really cool place, John. There's these big hot springs that bubble out of the ground into a clear pool, like a hot tub. We can sit back and relax after we hike in. And, no one knows about it… it's a secret place." *Ha! No one knows about it? That was no embellishment; that was an outright lie. He bought it.* He got excited and couldn't wait to go.

We prepared our packs and\ that Friday after work, we climbed into his '67 Dodge pickup and took off, listening to Joe Walsh's "Rocky Mountain Way."

Glacier Peak is one of Washington's smaller dormant volcanoes. Located in the North Central Cascades, it's a little over 10,000 feet: not a mountain that you just hike up. I didn't fully understand what I was getting us both into, but I knew that to climb the mountain we would first have to hike into Boulder Basin. I didn't have a clue where Boulder Basin was. After we put on our packs and hiked five miles in the dark, we became lost.

We found an area flat enough to set up John's tent and cook a can of chili. After settling down, the chili gas began to take effect and, between the both of us, we scared away every animal within a five-mile radius.

The next morning, we found the trail in the daylight and headed for the hot springs. John had developed some rather large blisters and was limping slowly behind me. As we walked up to the hot springs, I was the first to stand and gaze in amazement. It was a cesspool. I gasped at the foul odor. I began unsuccessful attempts at blocking the view of the hot springs from John with my pack, but it didn't work.

John was incredulous. "This is it?"

"Yes, John, this is Kennedy Hot Springs," I replied with authority, as if I had once visited the place and was still enchanted by it. In reality, it was a small, six-by-six–foot hole, about five-and-a-half feet deep, barely bubbling with brown sulfur–smelling, slightly warm water. And it was packed with people! So many people that it resembled an open pack of cigarettes. It's the one place where you can fart all you want and nobody would even know. There were brown dirty socks and underwear hanging from tree branches, because when you got into that stinkpot it turned everything brown—including you.

We looked around and didn't find a single campsite. "This is what we hiked all this way for?" John blasted out at me with the look he'd use when I'd just busted one of his toys.

I defended myself. "Well,… we could hike up to Boulder Basin."

"Where's that?"

"Oh, it's not very far. And the view…!"

John blasted again, "How far?"

I looked out the sides of my eyes for a second, then back at him. "Just a few miles."

Alan had told me that Boulder Basin was the base camp for the Sitkum Glacier route up to the summit, but I didn't want John to know that. So I lied again and said, "Alan and I came up here just last year."

"If you and Alan came up here last year, why did you tell me that the hot springs was a clear bubbling pool of enchantment?"

He had me there, I really had to think. "Well, John, it's winter, and it gets muddy in the winter." I had pulled off another good whopper, I think he believed that one. I then proceeded to tell him that if we traveled about three miles per hour, we'd make it in about an hour. He agreed to go, so off we went.

We hiked up the trail, down the trail, over the trail and through the woods, and up back-killing, blister-burning switchbacks. All the time John kept saying, with sweat pouring down off his forehead and his neck bright red, "Tim! We've gone more than a few miles!"

I would confidently say, "It's just around the corner, John," knowing full well I had no idea where we were going or how far it was.

The weather was beautiful, not a cloud in the sky, and we just kept on forging forward. The majority of trees in that area are old growth, and we'd stop now and then and gaze up in wonder at a tree over two-hundred feet tall and maybe twenty feet around. I kept his mind off the trail by talking about the injustices of our childhood, like how our sister Diane had a pair of shoes for every day of the week and we just had one pair of patrol boots that had to last us until the summer when we got our Converse high tops that had to last us until fall. He finally stopped me and asked, with a Clint Eastwood edge to his voice, "Do you really know where we're going? Punk?"

I looked at him and said with the same tone, "It's just around the corner, John!" I knew that he knew that I wasn't sure where we were going. I don't know why he let me get away with it.

We finally ran into a group of climbers getting water at a creek by the base of a hill. John stuck his head in the creek, drinking like a horse that had just walked out of Death Valley. With a quiet, embarrassed tone to my voice, I asked one of the climbers, "Uh… do you know how to get to Boulder Basin?"

The guy looked at me like I was an idiot and pointed up the hill. "Straight up!" he said in a loud voice that John could hear.

John looked up at me quickly with eyes that could kill. I looked at him and just said, "Come on John, it can't be that hard." Hiking uphill with a full pack was a new experience for him. The trail literally felt like it went straight up. We were hanging onto roots, and part of the time we had to crawl on our hands and knees it was so steep, but we finally made it up to Boulder Basin—blisters and all.

The view was fantastic. The well-forested hill gradually opened up into small alpine firs with about two to three feet of snow on the ground. It was wide open all around with a spectacular view of Seattle, Mount Rainier, and the other surrounding mountains. Glacier Peak loomed in front of us, glistening. It looked as if the summit was not even a mile away. The air had a faint pine smell, fresh and crisp, and the sky was a deep indigo.

Normally at this time of year you couldn't even get to Kennedy Hot Springs, let alone Boulder Basin. There should have been about fifteen to twenty feet of snow up there. We set up our tent and I started talking about the possibilities of climbing the mountain. "We made it this far, John, we could go for the summit in the morning."

John was so caught up in the excitement and rapture of the novel experience that he was somewhat agreeable. He took a series of photos in succession to get a wide angle. We took off our shirts and lay out in the sun. This was the place of enchantment. We had a delicious dinner, drank some wine, smoked some pot, and sat back and looked at the stars.

"Is this what climbing is all about?" he asked. John was changing from a hiker into a climber. I finally confessed to him that I had never been up here before and the truth about why I was so obsessed with climbing this mountain. He understood I think. I feel that there were times he questioned my sanity, but I also felt as though he understood me more than anyone. We crawled into our sleeping bags and slept like babies.

The following morning came with a blast of wind that shook the tent and woke us up abruptly. John got out of the tent first and then was quiet.

"What's going on out there, John?" I asked.

He said, "Wow, Tim, you need to see this. I don't think we'll be climbing anything today."

I crawled out to witness something I had never seen before: A dark purple and brown front was moving toward us. We knew it was going to get ugly fast. It hit just before we finished packing up our stuff. It started with light snow but quickly turned into a whiteout. Blizzard conditions with gale force wind. We ran most of the way down. By the time we reached the area where we had met the climbers the day before, it was raining hard. We stopped to talk to some other climbers who narrowly escaped the storm, and John noticed one of the climbers had a unique cook stove called a "Phoebus." John was intrigued. We hiked out in the rain and by the time we reached his truck we were soaked. We drove home listening to Elton John's "Yellow Brick Road." He couldn't stop talking about how amazing it was up at Boulder Basin on Saturday. I smiled and felt I had successfully turned John on to mountain climbing. At the Big REI Spring Sale, John bought a Phoebus stove, a new pack, a sleeping bag and together we bought a mountaineering tent. I wanted to tell Alan about my attempt of Glacier Peak but when I called I learned he had moved out of his parents' house. I was able to get his phone number from his mom. I called and went to see him at his tiny apartment in Seattle. He had given up on the idea of being a doctor and started working at a steel mill. He was doing coke and was a mess. He had sold Magic and his truck and bought a 1972 Jaguar XKE and a Suzuki 1000. He was not the person I knew anymore. We lost touch after that. When I began to write this book, I wanted to reconnect and tell him. So I called a mutual friend to find out where he was and he told me that Alan had died in a motorcycle accident. I was devastated. I loved Alan; Alan loved climbing. He was an amazing rock climber, skier and friend. He taught me so many things and I miss him.

Chapter 5

Settling down? Maybe.

"Every summit is obtainable. Find your route, follow it, don't look back,
and eventually you'll be on top of the world".

I LOVE THIS PLACE. I'VE BEEN UP HERE, *what, about seventy-five times?* I
began to count the times I'd made the trek up to Muir. *The snowfield has*
changed so much in the last thirty years. There was only one area that rocks
were exposed in the late summer. The "Moon Rocks," as they were called,
were all laid out in the shape of a half-moon. You knew you were close to
8,500 feet when you reached them. It was always a resting place. Now you
can't even find them. It's mostly rocks all the way up here in early fall. Rocks
and ice fields. I felt lost for a few minutes.

I am living in an attic that someone converted into a mother-in-law
apartment in Sammamish. I once had a home, a family, and a wife who loved
me. Now I am alone. This is what I wanted for so long. Now I have what I
wanted—to be alone. Am I happy? In 1978, my life was complete. I graduated
from Seattle Community College where I'd met Debbie while I was interning.
I had toned things down a bit with the climbing and settled down.

The love of my life, and mother of my children, is now my ex-wife. How
did that happen?

• • •

I met Debbie while working a summer job in a large electronics company just northeast of Lynnwood. I was learning how to operate the reproduction equipment when I heard someone behind me ask a question. I turned around to see this goddess. She handed me a form and asked, "Could I have this printed in the next hour? I need it right away. And it must be the best quality!" She sounded irritated.

I took it out of her hand and clumsily dropped it on the floor. We bent over to pick it up at the same time and bumped heads. Embarrassing. I looked at her sheepishly and smiled. "I am so sorry, I'm new at this," I said.

She didn't say anything for a few seconds, and then, "I need the best quality!"

Wow! She's not just beautiful, she's feisty! Her long brown hair touched her beautiful behind. She looked like a model. She was wearing an expensive, colorful blouse and long yellow pants. I noticed her dainty, red-polished toes peeking out of her open-toed shoes. I was instantly in love. I was not in any way a prize. I had let my hair grow long to my shoulders and had this gross handlebar mustache. I realized it would take a miracle for her to be interested in me. I was just a crazy art student at a community college. There were top engineers that wanted to go out with her.

I worked hard at trying to win her over, or at least be friends. By August, I was successful. We became friends and then finally went out on a date in September. She told me she liked to hike, so the very next morning we went on a hike together. She drove us to Taylor River in her MGB Roadster listening to Stephen Bishop's "On and On." We hiked to a quiet, secret area that only she knew about.

She'd brought a blanket and a picnic basket. We sat by the river's edge, drank wine, and ate cheese and crackers. It wasn't much of a hike. In fact we really didn't hike at all. We talked for hours. I was head over heels infatuated with her. We went back to her townhouse where she made me the best dinner I had ever had. The way to this man's heart was definitely through his stomach.

We were a good fit together, and by January I moved in with her. It all happened so fast. I graduated from college in May. With a little prodding from my mom, Debbie and I married on Memorial Day weekend. I think Mom thought that having a wife and family would instill a sense of responsibility in me that would keep me off the mountain. It was a small ceremony with just my best friend Garry and my sister Julie as witnesses. We went out for dinner afterward and left the following morning for a quick honeymoon in Seaside, Oregon.

Debbie's father, a successful engineer, was not exactly warm to me at first. Like any father, he was probably hoping all three of his daughters would marry someone top caliber. I was a renegade in his eyes. I tried to play the part of the educated college grad, devoted husband and hard worker, but I did not play that role well. Most of the time he seemed annoyed with me.

Debbie's parents owned a rather large Tudor-style home in the foothills of Issaquah. The house was on a large lot with a view of Mount Rainier. At first, I felt like an outsider when I went to my in-laws' house, but things got better as time went on. I landed a great job shortly after graduating and was finally making decent money. I sold my restored '57 Ford truck for a substantial amount and we made a down payment on a house in late June. For the most part, I was happy with my new life. Was I settling down? Maybe. I missed being in the mountains. And I felt deep in my spirit, they were missing me.

Debbie and I hiked together, and it was fun for me but not for her. She hated bugs and didn't like to sweat. Plus, I always pushed her to go faster and it made her resent hiking. By no means did she want me to climb again after I told her of my adventures with Alan. I couldn't tell her that climbing is who I am. I couldn't let go of it…

Debbie got pregnant in April of 1979. I felt like I had to climb Glacier Peak before we had our first child or I would never climb it.

Late one afternoon I had a long phone conversation with my brother John. I began telling him how much I wanted to climb Glacier Peak before it was too late. I was panic-stricken and was desperate to climb that mountain. Before we finished our call, John said, "Hey Tim, we can do it. We'll have to climb some smaller mountains first and then go do Glacier." That was all he needed to say. Seconds after we hung-up, I began to make plans.

My best friend Garry wanted to go with us. Garry was my oldest friend. We met in the seventh grade and within two weeks after meeting we began to play tag and it didn't stop even into adulthood mainly because we were both so competitive. Garry hated being "It." There was a time when I saw him at the grocery store but he didn't see me. I sneaked up behind him and tagged him on the back of his head, then took off running. He took off after me, chasing me clear out to the parking lot, knocking over people and displays. People were yelling, "Stop him!" thinking I was a crook. He didn't get me though, and he was "It" for a few days until he stopped by my work and asked the receptionist to call me to the lobby. He knew I couldn't chase after him there. He greeted me with a slap on the arm, smiled and said, "You're It!" Then he left. I gave in because I knew how much he hated to be "It" even though it was just a dumb game.

Garry married my sister Julie and I was his best man in the summer of 1975. While we were standing at the altar watching my sister walk down the aisle with my dad, Garry and I were tagging each other back and forth like "Dumb and Dumber."

My somewhat controlling sister, Julie, did not in any way want Garry to get into climbing. The following Friday after work, Garry, John and I got together for a beer. As we sat next to the fireplace and sipped our beers, I initiated the idea of mountain climbing.

Garry asked, "You mean like Mount Pilchuck or something?"

"No! I mean like Glacier Peak. Well?"

John knew I was still deeply obsessed with that mountain. Garry really didn't care, he just wanted to go. But he didn't want Julie to know about our plans. "She'd kill me if she knew we were going climbing," he said as took another sip of beer. Garry really didn't like beer that much.

"Just tell her that we're going on a hike together and we're not sure where," I said just before I gulped down the last of my beer.

John was in agreement mainly because his wife didn't care so much what he did. So I convinced them that if we climbed Pilchuck and another medium-sized mountain, we could get ourselves ready for Glacier Peak.

Since I was the most experienced, and driven, I took on the leadership role. It took some convincing but an agreement was made to climb it in early June.

I didn't tell Debbie of my plans at first . I was afraid of her reaction. I only told her that Garry, John and I were going on a short hike.

•   •   •

That was the beginning of the communication issues between us. I thought to myself. I looked up at the blue sky and the small clouds then I looked around all the emptiness that surrounded me at Camp Muir. *This foreboding, frozen, lifeless place is who I am. Yet, this is my strength. How can I love someone so much and yet love something that conflicts with that person so much, that it tears me apart inside?* At that moment, a little bird landed at my feet looking for something to eat. It took my mind off of Debbie and for some reason I thought about an old friend that I once climbed with. Dave.

•   •   •

He was wearing an apron that said "Seattle Times" on it when we were introduced.

"Hi, I'm Dave," he said as he shook my hand. He had a good firm handshake. I liked him from the moment I met him. He was the camera operator and worked in the darkroom. He would come out squinting after hours of developing film. He was enthusiastic about everything. We became good friends in a very short time. He's half Italian and half Irish. His overbearing father expected Dave to be an overachiever like his brother, whom Dave lived in the shadow of. He got married young to a conservative, but outspoken, woman. Dave seemed to want to break the chains when we went to lunch together. He would invite the cute young girls from the bindery to join us. We would stop at the local mini-mart, grab a bottle of wine, and drive down to Edmonds Beach where we would proceed to drink the bottle. All the while, Dave would be flirting with the girls. I didn't hold back either. We never crossed the line with these girls but I always felt a bit guilty after those lunches.

Dave and I talked about climbing and hiking, and he continually asked me if I wanted to go up and do some climbing. He didn't have any real climbing experience but he wanted to learn. I think maybe he wanted his dad and his brothers to view him as a strong mountaineer so he could brag to them, "Hey, look at me, I'm a mountain climber." I wasn't too sure about taking him with us at first, but I decided to teach him like Alan had taught me—the "Tim and Alan Productions" method, or... learn as you go. I really didn't know what the hell I was doing, but I thought I did.

Dave was careful, confident, fun and funny. After clearing it with John and Garry, he became the fourth member of our group.

In late spring, we all chipped in and bought a climbing rope together. We thought we were ready for anything. I wanted to teach Dave a few things like how to rappel off a cliff, Tim and Alan style. So, one sunny day at work during lunch hour, we climbed up on the roof of our company building to the "Tim Lewis School of Rappel." It was about thirty feet down, and kind of... not safe, but we made it down. We acted like daring climbers while our co-workers all came out to watch two men act like idiots. We were feeling quite full of ourselves, especially when the cute girls from the bindery were so impressed. I can't believe how stupid I was to attempt such a foolish act. A person would likely get fired for doing something like that now.

I finally talked to Debbie about our plans. It was difficult. At first I could sense the resentment in her silence. Then she let it go. She smiled and said, "I don't care, just be safe." It was hard to tell if she was really okay. I was young and immature, naïve to think that everything would be fine.

A week later, on a sunny Saturday in early June, we set out to climb Mount Pilchuck in Garry's 1970 Ford van. The album, *Breakfast in America* by Supertramp was the music of choice that day.

We headed up the long, steep, winding two-lane highway toward the mighty peak, which, I might add, has a fairly easy trail all the way to a lookout on the summit. When we arrived at the parking lot, we encountered a little more snow than anticipated.

I had recently bought a new 35mm camera and thought of myself as an instant professional photographer, as well as an exceptional mountaineer. I was taking so many photos that it took us about two and a half hours to reach the summit. The view was worth it.

We glissaded down on our asses the whole way, screaming like school kids. In a rocky area just above the parking lot, there was a spot that produced an awesome echo. So I began yodeling—loud. It echoed back perfectly. Another climbing party approached us laughing and asked who was making that God-awful sound. My face must have been tomato red.

After reaching the parking lot, we took our packs off and leaned against Garry's van, drinking water. I glanced across the valley at Three Fingers and said, "Well you guys, that's our next challenge: Three Fingers." This time John seemed more excited about climbing a mountain than ever before.

The climbing guide said Three Fingers is 6,870 feet high. It looks higher than that. It also said that it is an unmistakable sight from the Puget Sound basin. The south peak summit is obtainable in five hours from the road. We thought we could do it even faster if we went up on a Friday night and hiked into Saddle Lake, a small lake along the trail, spend the night there, get up early the next morning, and summit. We figured we would be home by two or three o'clock at the latest. It's funny how plans can sound so smooth…

Garry called me late on the Thursday night before the climb and told me he was bringing his little brother, Joe. I really didn't like the idea of bringing a seventeen-year-old kid along, but Garry felt confident about him so I agreed. The climbing guide did not recommend a rope, only an ice axe, so we left the rope behind. That was a mistake…

It was late on a Friday afternoon in late June when John, Garry, Dave, Joe and I all left from Garry's house in his green Ford van. We headed up the long, extremely bumpy and dusty logging road. On the drive up, I was starting to get sick. "Radar Love" by Golden Earring kept fading in and out on the radio. John was eating Starburst candies and Garry kept threatening to stop driving unless John gave him one. If he didn't, Garry would let go of the steering wheel. Just before we headed over a cliff, John would throw him a candy and Garry would grab the wheel and turn at the last second, laughing the whole time. It was sort of funny in a scary way. Dave and I knew Garry wouldn't drive over the cliff. We also knew John would always throw him a candy.

We made it to the trailhead all in one piece and started hiking up to the lake at around seven. It was starting to get dark when we reached the lake, and trying to find a place to camp was difficult. We had not anticipated all the snow remaining that late in the spring and weren't prepared for snow camping.

I kept John awake all night with my shivering and my constant moving around. It felt like there was a rubber knife stabbing me in the back where I was lying in my sleeping bag. John kept getting annoyed with me. About every hour, I would shine my flashlight on my watch to check the time, but somehow always managed to shine it in John's face. "Tim! Go to sleep!"

The morning didn't come fast enough, and when I finally got warm and started dozing off, it was time to get up. When I crawled out of the tent I saw the reason why I was so uncomfortable. Not only was I sleeping on a small tree but the tent was covered with ice, as was the lake.

"It wasn't like that when we got here last night," John blurted out in his deep morning voice.

Meanwhile, Garry did his usual start-a-campfire-and-fry-up-some-eggs routine. While Dave and I gnawed on our frozen granola bars, we watched Garry and Joe struggle trying to light a fire, blowing on some ashes underneath wet frozen wood. John, on the other hand, was busy organizing his pack again after eating oatmeal and drinking coffee that he'd heated on his Phoebus.

We got a late start and immediately ran into deep snow on the way up the trail. We needed snowshoes. It was difficult to find the trail. Every now and then we would find a blaze on a tree or some frozen footsteps that let us know we were heading in the right direction. The weather was mildly overcast with sun breaks. At times the fog would descend and we couldn't see at all. Other times it would be clear and we could see the top of the mountain. I was taking pictures like a fashion photographer at a bikini shoot. Good thing I'd brought two rolls of film with me.

It took us hours of trudging through snow and backtracking to get to Goat Flat—just above the tree line. We finally took a break there, and figured out a plan of ascent. It was already noon. We got our ice axes out and began climbing straight up toward the summit. We'd climb up one hill and encounter a cliff, then we would have to backtrack back down and try another route. It took a long time. The clouds kept rolling by.

I realize now how foolhardy we were to do this without being roped up, but we were very inexperienced and didn't really know the dangers. Well… I kind of did, but I thought we were safe enough. Unexpectedly deep snow, not having the right equipment, and changeable weather conditions can turn an easy climb into a dangerous one. Number one rule: Be prepared for anything.

We finally reached the last snowfield leading to the summit at around two thirty, and there was no turning back. We followed frozen footsteps the whole way up. Stopping and looking up, we could see the small lookout cabin on the summit; it gave us incentive.

The lookout was built on a flattened spire in 1932. The forest service also installed a series of ladders that are strapped with cables to the rock on the west side of the spire to make the lookout accessible. It's very exposed: one slip in any direction could result in a fatality. There are two sections of ladders that rise the last fifty feet, and at the top there's an old tugboat rope to hang on to for the last ten feet to the lookout. Anyone with any kind of fear of heights could not go up there because on the east side of the summit there is a two thousand foot vertical wall and no guardrail.

We reached the end of the snowfield and began heading around to the west side of the summit, following frozen footsteps. We were excited and couldn't wait to see the ladders that the climbing guide described. We kept saying, "We made it! All right! We made it!" As we rounded the corner to the southwest side, we all stopped cold and stared in silence. We were gazing at an almost vertical snow wall about twenty feet high between us and the ladders. Whoever had made the footsteps had turned around at this point. Dave broke the silence. "I'm not going up there—no way!"

We looked at each other and Garry said, "I think we need a rope." The snow wall rose up into a rock wall where the first ladder was. To our left, the small snowfield sloped down about fifteen feet to a cliff that dropped straight down to a glacier a hundred feet below.

"There isn't enough room to self-arrest," I said with a quivering voice, because I was freezing.

John took off his pack and pulled out a little 5mm hemp rope that was about thirty feet long. "I brought it just in case," he said.

We really wanted to go up there after all we had been through, except Dave, who said he would wait for us right there. Garry volunteered to go first. We decided we would makeshift belay him up to the ladder and he would anchor the rope to it. He tied it around his waist and we all hung on as he began digging in his ice axe and kicking steps in the frozen crust. When he was about halfway across I started thinking about what would happen if he fell. He would probably pull all of us down with him. Adrenaline began to rush to my head. Garry kept going, and just before he reached the base of the ladders, we ran out of rope. So, Dave, Joe, and I let go of our piece and John held on, and we held on to John. We all held our position as Garry reached up for the bottom of the ladder. It was intense. We let out a collective sigh of relief as he grabbed the first step. He untied himself and tied the rope to the ladder and began going up. I was next. John held the rope as I crammed my boots into Garry's footsteps, which were already starting to freeze. Holding on to the rope with my left hand and digging my ice axe into the deep snow with my right, and with sweat rolling off my forehead, I carefully took each step and made sure my ice axe was buried deep up to the head before I took another step. My heart was pounding so loud I think the sound was echoing off the rocks next to me. When I finally reached the ladder, I relaxed. I turned around and said, "Come on, John, it's a piece of cake," in a tone that sounded like it didn't faze me a bit. I then carefully climbed the series of ladders as my ice axe, hanging on my wrist, banged on the rock and wood making a sound like a gong.

When I reached the tugboat rope, my hands were shaking and my palms were sweaty. As I walked into the doorway of the lookout, I was happy to be in one piece, but concerned about how we were going to get down, and the time... "Holy shit!" It was already past three and we still had to go back.

64

There was no fast way down, and I'd told Debbie we'd be back by three or four at the latest. *This was the first of a series of miscalculations that I would make that would bite me in the ass.*

The inside of the lookout was like a time capsule from the 1930s. There were old magazines and items you would find in a museum. Garry was out on the east side of the summit checking out the view. I started to join him when I heard someone coming up toward me. I looked out expecting to see John, but to my surprise, there stood Dave with a big grin on his face. I managed to muster, "Dave! You made it! What made you change your mind?"

He just looked at me and said, "Your brother talked me into it. And I'm glad he did."

I was proud of John for doing that, and I wanted to tell him, but when he showed up all I could say was, "We gotta get going."

John looked at me like I was crazy. "Tim, we just got here. Let's enjoy our triumph."

All I could think about was what Debbie would be thinking right about now. But there was nothing much I could do on my own. We were a team. We hung out for a while, looking at other mountains and calling out their names. We found a 1935 edition of Cosmopolitan and signed the summit register. We lay on our bellies and looked down the back side. It made my toes curl in my boots to look down there, but it was exhilarating. Then we began our descent.

I think the hardest part was when Garry came back across the snow wall with all of us hanging on to the rope. I took a picture just as Garry was coming down, and when he heard the shutter go off he said, "Don't let anyone see that picture—especially Julie!"

We glissaded almost the whole way down, maintaining control with the shaft of our ice axes. By the time we got to Saddle Lake it was about six o'clock We ran all the way out to the trailhead and Garry drove like a wild man because he knew Julie would be upset, too. Julie was happy to see us but was showing some resentment when we arrived. When I got home Debbie was not happy. Not so much because I was so late, but mostly because I did not communicate well with her on my arrival times. She asked me to not give her a specific time the next time I climb. "Just call when you can, that's all I ask," she said.

Later that summer we attempted Glacier Peak but we never made it past Kennedy Hot Springs. I thought I would have to give up on my obsession to climb it, but I didn't.

That October our first daughter, Melissa Joann, was born. I didn't mention climbing for a while to Debbie. I focused on being a father and not a climber… for a while.

Chapter 6

Man-Eating Marmots

"Climb the mountains and get their good tidings. Nature's peace will flow into
you as sunshine flows into trees. The winds will blow their own freshness into
you, and the storms their energy, while cares will drop away from you like the
leaves of Autumn."

— John Muir

CAMP MUIR IS SUCH A DEAD PLACE. *Nothing grows here.* I looked down
as another little bird flew down to my feet. Delicate birds in a hostile
environment. *Why here? They could be down at the campgrounds getting fed*
by the campers. Why do we choose to come up here to climb a mountain? I
feel a bit like this delicate bird in a hostile environment—taking a risk every
time. *Maybe my soul is seeking to be fed.*

I was sweating profusely and began to get cold. My heart was thumping
because of the altitude. It made me think of the time Dave got altitude
sickness so bad that I had to go down the snowfield and help him get up
here. He was so driven, so hungry to climb, that he wasn't going to let a little
sickness hold him back. There must've been a tiny soul-bird in Dave looking
to get fed, too.

•   •   •

Dave and I made plans early in 1980 to climb a bunch of mountains once the weather got warmer. I started jogging every day at work during lunch to get in shape, and by spring I felt ready.

On a beautiful day in May, I ran into James while hiking with Debbie and our daughter Melissa. James was an old friend from high school. I'd been the best man at his wedding but hadn't seen him for a while.

Back in my high school days, James was on the wrestling team. One time I met him in the gym after practice so we could shoot some hoops and then go get something to eat. I told him that I had been a pretty good wrestler in middle school. I challenged him to a quick match thinking that, since he was smaller than me, I could easily take him. He agreed and told me to say, "Go!"

"Ready, set… GO!"

Now try to imagine this scenario: First you have me, with my long shaggy hair, wearing bell-bottoms, white socks, and tee-shirt with "Atlantic Records" silk-screened on one side and "Led Zeppelin" on the other, wrestling a guy in a wrestling outfit complete with a buzz haircut. It was a quick match. Unfortunately for me, a couple of cheerleaders just happened to walk into the gym and saw James turn me into a pretzel in a matter of seconds. After struggling on my back, and grunting I then let out a huge fart, as he pinned me. Then he let me go. I immediately jumped up, pulled my shirt down from around my neck and said, "Nice work man! You know, wrestling is really not my sport, basketball is my sport." I glanced at the girls who were giggling at me. It was a good thing they left before they saw me lose five out of five games of one-on-one.

He never really grew out the buzz haircut, which worked out real well for him when he joined the Army and became an M.P.

James, his wife Denise and daughter, Megan, were at our house for dinner one night when I told him I was going to climb Three Fingers with John, Garry and Dave. He asked if he could come with us. I thought about it and asked John, Garry and Dave and they were fine with bringing him along. I planned the climb for the second weekend of July, but something came up for John and Garry and they couldn't go. James turned out to be a good person to take climbing because he added a lot of what I call "minus" personality. Between Dave and me there's too much personality, so having low-key James with us helped to even it out.

On a warm Friday night, Dave, James and I took off toward the mountains in my new truck and camper. We started out on the trail early on Saturday morning after spending the night at the trailhead. There were no cars in the parking lot that morning so we knew we would be the first ones up that day. We made it to Saddle Lake in no time; I was surprised to see how different it looked without snow. We didn't stay long, we just kept hiking. The trail eventually opened up into beautiful meadows with little freshwater tarns and beds of colorful wildflowers.

"It looks a lot different without snow," said Dave as we reached Goat Flat.

Just before heading up a long series of switchbacks that led to Tinpan Gap, we stopped to get a drink from the stream. I heard James say in his monotone voice, "What are those varmints on the rocks?"

I was gulping "Tim gulps" but managed to blurt out, "Where?"

James pointed to the rocks just above us and said, "Right there. Are you blind?"

I had never let anyone know that I am slightly nearsighted; I squinted up at the rocks and saw what he was pointing at. They were furry critters about the size of a medium-sized dog. "I… think they're—" I paused for a minute, thinking. "Why, those are—" I wasn't sure. They were light brown and slightly resembled a badger. They seemed so aggressive. One was running down the trail toward us. As it got closer I began to get panicky because in all my hiking and climbing adventures, I had never seen an animal come running toward me. I knew that only one animal other than a bear or cougar was aggressive enough to attack. "IT'S A BADGER!"

I took off down the trail with Dave right behind me, asking, "Are they vicious?"

"Yeah, they can tear you apart!"

I turned around to see if the badger was chasing us and noticed James was not behind us, so I stopped abruptly. Dave practically ran me over. As we both lay there all tangled, along came James walking down the trail toward us saying, "Tim, I don't think those are badgers. I think they're marmots." He sort of smiled and said, "I don't think they are man eating".

He was right. I realized it as I got up slowly with a stupid grin on my face, all the time thinking up something intelligent to say so as not to lose the confidence of my climbing party. "Well, ya know James, I think you're right. But marmots and badgers look a lot alike and many people make the same mistake. They were very tame marmots looking for handouts."

I think Dave bought it, but James just gave me that look like, *Yeah... you also once told me you could wrestle and play basketball.* But luckily for me, he didn't say anything. I'd already had just about all the humiliation I could take for one day.

We hiked back up past the man-eating marmots and threw them some food. We couldn't find a place to set up camp at Tinpan Gap so we decided to continue on until we found a good spot.

On and on we kept climbing until we came to the ridge that leads up to the summit. Dave and I knew that there wasn't any place to camp except in the lookout. The only problem: one bed. "Well, there's also the floor," I said to James.

He scowled back at me. He didn't like the idea of staying in the lookout, but Dave and I were very convincing. We let James think that he would get the bed.

We reached the top of the snowfield and I pulled the rope out. After experiencing the conditions the first time we were here, I didn't want to take any chances. When we rounded the corner toward the ladders, Dave and I were astonished to see what lay before us. There was no snow between the trail and the ladders. If we had come up here last year at this time, it would have been a piece of cake.

We brought a deck of cards with us and played poker—winner gets the bed. I was the lucky winner. In all the climbs I've been on, this one stands out as having the most spectacular sunset. The visibility was incredible. We could see ships on Puget Sound and details of the Olympic Mountains which are normally obscured by smog. I took lots of pictures. We read a story about a fatality that happened back in the 1960's on this very mountain. They never found the body. Not a good choice of stories... it scared me a bit. We also read, in the summit register, about a pack rat that lived up there in the lookout. "Didn't see any pack rats 'round here," James said.

James's emotion was nonexistent, I don't think he laughed. Ever. Always serious. I swear he could step on a burning log with bare feet, walk away, and in a couple of days say, "Ouch." Maybe.

After the sun had completely sunk into the horizon, we turned in. James closed the door and asked us if he should lock it since it had a small dead bolt. "We don't want any pack rats gettin' in here." I think he was trying to be funny, but Dave and I were never quite sure.

Dave and James slept on the floor and I slept comfortably on the old moldy mattress. If you combined the aroma of the bed with the smell of Dave's and James's gas, you get something that could remove the varnish off old furniture.

I was awakened rather abruptly at around eleven or twelve o'clock when the wind started to pick up. It was howling like a banshee. The window shutters started banging like gunshots. It was like something out of a horror movie. Off in the distance, the howl was getting louder and louder until it hit the lookout and shook it like it was trying to empty out its inhabitants. My teeth were chattering like castanets. On top of all that, I kept hearing a sound like someone was walking around outside. At first I thought it might be James or Dave outside taking a leak or something. So I sat up and looked to find them both asleep on the floor. I decided the best thing to do was hide my head in my sleeping bag. It must just be my imagination.

It got quiet for a few seconds, then started howling again. I swear I heard footsteps tromping on the crushed gravel outside the lookout. There is no mistaking the sound of boots on gravel. It stopped, then, started heading for the door. The hair on the back of my neck began to rise. All I could think about was that guy who died up there. Is it him? At that instant, out of nowhere, Dave jumped up and yelled, "THERE'S SOMEBODY OUT THERE!"

I jumped straight up from the bed. All I could see was Dave's silhouette and the whites of his eyes wide open with fear. The wind hit the lookout and the door blew open. I didn't want to look. I kept thinking that the ghost of that guy might be standing there, his decomposing body staring at us. I yelled at Dave to shut the door but he was deep in his sleeping bag, shaking. Things were flying around inside the cabin from the wind. "DAVE! SHUT THE DOOR!"

He finally peeked out, eyes huge, got up to shut the door and locked it. We both looked out the window but there was no one there. I don't know how James was able to sleep through all the commotion.

After a while, the wind died down and we finally got some sleep. The next morning brought us another surprise. When Dave unzipped his sleeping bag, out came a pack rat, all refreshed after a good night's sleep, leaving behind a few turds.

I never hear from James the cop anymore, but I'm sure he must think of me from time to time as he remembers the frozen footsteps we made together that weekend.

Chapter 7

On a Small Mountain and Falling Big

"There are no small mountains, only oversized egos."

I LOOKED DOWN. There was a tiny piece of paper on the pumice by my feet. I reached down and picked it up. It was a piece of notebook paper that had been torn out with the letter "M" on it. It was old and looked as though it had been there for a long time. *Words and names beginning with the letter M... hmmm... Morgan?* Morgan was a great friend, at one time we were very close. We met as co-workers and became friends almost immediately. He drove a little yellow Chevy Luv pickup, and we would drive around at lunch listening to Billy Joel, Genesis, and this obscure band from England named Camel. I loved Morgan and I'd made a promise to take him climbing. So I did.

Morgan is unique. He loves life. He's intelligent. Always a 4.0 student. We didn't always agree on everything, but we were compatible. We liked the same music and we both liked to drink beer.

In a way, he was like a little brother—he could be an ass at times. We got away with a lot at work with the practical jokes we would play on each other. One time he sneaked up behind me with a squirt bottle and when he said "Hey, Tim," I turned around and he sprayed it point-blank in my face and took off running and laughing. His laugh was contagious, but I wasn't catching it that time. I wanted to get him back in a major way, so I filled up a two-gallon bucket with water and tried to catch him off-guard. I sat and waited for him to return, hiding behind a stack of paper boxes. He came into the room cautiously, looking around. I jumped out from behind the boxes and he took off like a rat. I ran after him with the heavy bucket, stopped and threw the water out after him just as he ran through double doors. The water missed him but it got our manager, who was standing close by. I had a hard time explaining that one.

One day a few months later, he came to work and told us all that he had joined the Nuclear Navy. "You didn't ask anyone about this before you signed the papers?" I asked in anger. I was not happy with his decision. I tried desperately to talk him out of joining the Navy, but he wouldn't listen. "We've got to go on that climb I promised to take you on before you go," I said, thinking to myself, *maybe I could work on him some more and talk him out of the Navy.* I decided we would do Liberty Peak, a small mountain located south of Three Fingers, but not as challenging. Or so I thought…

The climbing guide made it sound easy enough. Morgan was excited about going on a climb with me. I told Debbie I was taking Morgan up Liberty Peak and she asked me if I had ever climbed it before. I told her no. "It's an easy mountain" I said confidently. She said, "I was just curious because you have told me that before and it didn't turn out that way. I keep thinking about your "Tim and Alan Productions" and it scares me a little."

"Don't worry, Debbie, I'll be fine".

That night we sat down after putting Melissa to bed and she began to ask me questions.

"When did Alan take the Mountaineering climbing course?" I told her, "It was in the spring of 1975."

Then she asked, "Why didn't you take the class with him?" I didn't have an answer for her. I knew it would just be an excuse.

"I don't know," I said and took a deep breath, thinking about Alan. "I really don't know why. Maybe I should have."

I was looking at the fireplace and could see her in my peripheral vision looking at me, not saying anything. Then she said, "Maybe you should."

I finished packing and threw my pack in Morgan's truck as he was checking his oil. Debbie was standing by the front gate with Melissa in her arms and the camera in her hand. I yelled out, "I won't be too long, and I really don't need the camera!"

She said, "Oh, take it along anyway, you may see some wildlife." She held it out and Morgan grabbed it.

"See ya in a few hours."

"Be careful!" she said back. "I don't like the feeling I'm getting…"

Off we went, never giving any thought to what she'd said. We were flying around corners on the logging road that leads to the trailhead, listening to Jackson Browne's "Running on Empty." We were spraying gravel all over and I was gripping the "oh shit" handle above the passenger seat. Every corner brought a different surprise. We came around one corner, and, standing before us in the middle of the road were five deer with a large buck. Morgan slammed on the brakes, turned the wheel, started weaving around and spraying gravel all over, and choked out the word, "Deeeer!" The deer took off to the sound of my heart pounding.

Just as my heart started to slow down, we rounded another corner and standing in the middle of the road was a big black bear. It was almost the same scenario as we'd had with the deer, only this time I was able to get my camera up and snap a shot before the bear ran into the woods.

We finally reached the trailhead—or what we thought was the trailhead. We jumped out of the truck, put on our packs, and started hiking what we thought was a trail. It ended, rather abruptly, in a bunch of blackberry bushes and devil's club.

Morgan asked, "Are you sure this is the way?"

I looked around and replied, "It has to be. Come on, let's just head up to that ridge then maybe we can see where we are."

So we beat brush, hacked at stickers with our ice axes, tore our clothes, walked through streams and rivers, and periodically grabbed a prickly devil's club stalk with our bare hands, all the time saying, "The trail has got to be around here somewhere." When we finally reached the top of the ridge, with sweat dripping off the end of my nose, completely saturated and covered with scratches and mud, I realized I forgot to bring water and a compass.

Morgan kept saying, "Wouldn't a nice cold beer taste good right now?"

I kept saying, "Shut up, Morgan!"

It was getting late and we still had a long way to go. We began climbing the ridge that led to the summit, and I felt like I had tangled with a cougar. My feet were feeling a little chewed up too. We rock-scrambled up to a flat area right below the summit. I looked up and said, "There's the summit, Morgan, it's just a hundred feet away. Let's stop here. We've got to eat some food." I was getting weak. We were both starving and thirsty. I could have drunk a gallon of something wet. So we sat down on a ledge overlooking the valley and ate. While we were sitting there, I kept grumbling about how was I going to wash down a dry, smashed, peanut butter and jelly sandwich. Then, Morgan reached into his pack and pulled out two icy-cold beers and handed me one. I was speechless.

"Morgan, you rat! You had these all the time and didn't tell me?"

After we ate and drank, I expressed the need to head back down. "Let's summit this thing and get the hell out of here."

We packed up our stuff and just as I put on my brown felt Stetson, the wind picked up and blew it off. It went straight down and landed about seventy-five feet below us on a ledge. "I can't leave without that hat Morgan, it's my lucky hat." I took out my rope and instructed Morgan on the "Alan-style" quick hip belay. He couldn't have learned it that quickly but I didn't care. I wanted that hat. I tied the rope around my waist and began to climb down to my hat, which was hanging by a string and fluttering in the wind. It looked like it was going to fly away any moment. Morgan wasn't sure what he was doing and, as I was descending, he wouldn't let out enough rope. I kept having to tug on it to get him to feed me more rope.

When I got to my hat, I was careful not to knock it down and so reached for it very slowly. Just as I was about to grab it, it flew away down about another twenty feet and stuck into a little group of rocks. I yelled back at Morgan, "I need more rope!" It was getting intense.

Morgan yelled down to me, "Did you get your hat?"

"NO! Damnit!" I yelled back, "It went down farther!" I had to get that damn hat. I kept going until I ran out of rope. "Morgan! I need more rope!"

"What?!"

"I. NEED. MORE. ROPE!!" I couldn't yell any louder.

"There isn't any more rope!" he yelled back.

So I did something really dumb. I untied the rope, climbed down another ten feet and grabbed my hat. I stuffed it into my shirt and then as I rock climbed back up to the rope I thought, *What in the hell am I doing?* I was probably on class 5.9+ rock, unroped, risking my life for a stupid hat. I was really not in a rock-climbing frame of mind. The rope was too far out of my reach. I didn't want to let go of the rock long enough to grab it. My hands started to tremble and a foreboding feeling came over me. I knew I would have to do something, so… I let go of the rock and grabbed the rope. I fell and yelled "FALLING!!"

It was all Morgan could do to hold on and keep the rope from slipping and burning his hands. He stopped me. I climbed up far enough to tie the rope around my waist again. I took a deep breath and thought, "This is a small mountain and I'm falling big". I took another deep breath, looked at my scraped, bloody fingers on the rock and then started to climb back up to him. When I made it, he just looked at me and didn't say a word. I stared at him for about ten seconds and finally said, "Thanks, buddy."

Everything started to change at that moment. I was insecure about the climb and wanted to get down fast. We were in over our heads but I didn't want to tell him. I wanted to go down a different way, since the way we came up was brutal. "I think I see a better way down, Morgan. We can make time."

There was a snowfield just below us, and if we could hike down to it, we could glissade to where I thought it turned into the river. He agreed. So we headed across the face until we reached the top of a small cliff. The bottom of the cliff met the top of the snowfield. I told Morgan we would have to rappel down to the snowfield. He gave me this "you've got to be kidding" look as he pushed his glasses up his nose.

"I've never rappelled in my life," Morgan said with a "help me" look on his face.

"Well, you've never belayed before either but you did it. Right?" I said in my best Michael Douglas–type voice. I fashioned a makeshift harness out of nylon webbing and put it around his waist. Then I pulled out my harness and got myself prepared to rappel the only way I knew.

"You had that harness when you went after your hat?" he asked… already knowing the answer. "Why didn't you use it?"

"I was in a hurry and I didn't want to waste time dealing with it."

"Really?" He was starting to question my climbing knowledge.

"We need to do this, Morgan. We need to rappel down to the snowfield and get the hell out of here!" I wanted to build my confidence (and his!) back in a bad way. I threw the rope down after wrapping it around a tree, then showed him how it's done. "Just slowly let the rope out one hand and use your other hand as a brake to slow you down." I let go and went rappelling down Hollywood-style, the way Alan had taught me.

Then it was Morgan's turn. He started down OK, but when I looked down to take my harness off, he had flipped over upside-down and was coming down head first. He righted himself slightly before he landed, saving his head, Once again, my heart was pounding rapidly, and I'm sure his was too. Thank God he was all right. He just looked at me and smiled ruefully like, "you asshole!"

I put the rope away and we headed for the snowfield. We glissaded down and made good time until we ran out of snow., The safe way down didn't turn into the river like I had thought. At the bottom of the snowfield was a six or seventy foot waterfall that dropped to the river, and there was no way down. So we had to go back up the snowfield and head off into the bushes again.

Then it really started getting ugly. We were hopelessly lost and it was getting late. It was mostly quiet, just the sound of breaking branches and much cussing. We sort of sensed the way we should go, but it was hit or miss. The truck was parked in a very obscure place at the end of a logging road—no trails and no landmarks. I had a sick feeling in the pit of my stomach as we rambled through the forest for hours. Neither of us had a watch or a compass or a map. It was getting dark, we had no food and no extra clothing, and it was getting colder. On top of it all, it was starting to rain. We were wearing shorts and our legs looked as if a cat had used them as a scratching post.

We were screwed. I stopped and said, "Morgan, I think the only thing we can do is pray," in a joking kind of way. He looked at me like he wasn't in a joking mood.

We eventually came to a creek that was muddy and full of skunk cabbage. I remembered crossing something like it when we came in, but all creeks look the same when you're lost and it's dark. We walked through the water and Morgan said, "I think we should go right."

I said, "No. We should go left."

He didn't argue, just followed me like a loyal dog. We could only see the faint outlines of trees and stumps. As we walked through the ankle-deep, muddy water, I began thinking what a strange feeling it was to be lost and wondered if we would make it back that night. When I had gone through the Boy Scout's "Order of the Arrow" ritual, one of the requirements was to be in the woods by yourself with just a blanket. I had spent a cold night freezing in the dark curled up next to a large sword fern. *Was this what we were about to do? At least I have Morgan to curl up next to.* Not a good thought. I would much rather have Debbie. *Debbie! Oh my God, she is going to kill me! Why is it, when I am in a possible death situation, I always think that the person who loves me the most is going to kill me?*

The Boy Scouts had pushed "be prepared" down my throat. Once again… I wasn't. I had broken every rule in the Boy Scout Handbook. I began whispering to myself, "help us God, please help us." I think every climber gets to that point at one time or another. Praying was the last desperate act I could think to do.

As we were walking through the creek, we both stopped out of exhaustion. We looked up at the same time, and there, faintly visible, was Morgan's truck. Right in front of us, not more than fifteen feet away. It was a welcome sight. "Yes!" I yelled out so loud that any wild animal within five miles was running for its life. A feeling of great relief came over me as my eyes began to well up, but I held back the tears. *Thank you, God…*

We threw our packs in the back of the truck, jumped in and drove like madmen. Debbie was glad to hear my voice when I called her from a phone booth in the small town of Granite Falls.

It wasn't an experience I can be proud of. I failed to get my friend to the summit of a mountain—a rather small mountain; a mountain that I would have no problem climbing today; a mountain I have no desire to climb today.

But, after that day, whenever I feel lost in my life, I remember that climb and know that I can resort to prayer as a last-ditch effort to find my way.

Chapter 8

Fulfilling my Obsession

"The mountain decides whether you climb or not. The art of mountaineering is knowing when to go, when to stay, and when to retreat."

— Ed Viesters

I LOOKED AT MY WATCH AGAIN as I sat there. It's eight thirty in the morning, only twenty-five minutes since I arrived at Camp Muir.. I began to think about what happened after the Liberty peak climb with Morgan. *Oh yeah, I finally climbed the mountain that I was obsessed with.*

• • •

I'd put together a plan to climb Glacier Peak at the end of summer in 1980. I'd ran up Pilchuck a couple of times and felt like I was physically ready when the time arrived. The forecast was for rain, wind, the usual crap we seem to get on Labor Day weekend. Debbie did not want me to go. My daughter was just ten months old. Did I feel guilty? No, nothing was going to stop me. I had to climb that mountain. A week before the climb, Dave told me that he couldn't go and since Morgan had a week before he was to report to basic training he was begging to go with us. John and Garry were fine with him coming with.

On a rainy Friday afternoon on August thirty first of 1980 I climbed into Morgan's pickup and we took off to the Glacier Peak Wilderness Area.

It rained all the way to the trailhead. Morgan and I listened to Jackson Browne's "Hold On" and Alan Parsons' "Pyramid." We were to meet John and Garry at the trailhead at four, but we were running late. It was raining at the trailhead, and it rained all the way to Kennedy Hot Springs.

Morgan and Garry, both alpha males, began to argue the minute they started hiking together. I had to separate them on the trail. They shared a tent together and it was not a pleasant first night at the hot springs. They argued, just for the sake of arguing, over the dumbest stuff. So I got into the hot spring pit. It felt good to sit in the warm, stinky water where I couldn't hear them while it poured rain. I felt revitalized. Early Saturday morning when we got up, it was raining but I didn't care. It rained all the way up into Boulder Basin and we pressed on. Then it finally stopped.

We set up base camp and tried to stay warm and dry. Morgan and Garry kept bickering and calling each other all sorts of names. They needed a break, so I took Morgan to do some rock climbing while John and Garry took a nap. I taught Morgan how to rappel a bit better after we climbed the wall.

Then it began to get foggy, very foggy. We hiked back to camp. In no time, Morgan and Garry were back at it, calling each other names and throwing out each other's smelly socks and underwear out of their tent.

We got up Sunday morning at around six and saw other climbers heading up, so we decided to go too. We roped up using nylon webbing as harnesses and only one carabiner to tie the rope to us. We began hiking up with our ice axes in hand and crampons tied to our boots like we were real experienced climbers, off into the fog. We let Garry lead the way with Morgan after him, then me, and John was last. The other climbers' frozen footsteps came in real handy because the snow was like cement. After about an hour of climbing, it began to snow and blow. John was getting pretty angry with us because we were going too fast. "Do you guys know what rest-stepping is?" he shouted out.

We stopped, turned around and gave him our usual blank stare. The three of us turned back around almost simultaneously and began climbing again at the same pace. Then I felt a real hard tug on the rope behind me. I stopped, making Morgan and Garry stop in turn. We looked around again to see my red-faced brother unclip himself from the rope. The three of us looked at each other sort of like, *What should we do?* So we kept on going, I mean, we had a mountain to climb! If he wanted to stand there mad, and wait for us—fine; we were not going to stop. He began yelling at us, which was quite a feat in itself because the wind was howling so loud. I could hear his well-constructed sentences, so I tugged on the rope. Morgan stopped, then Garry. We rested for a while so John could cool off.

When it came time to start going, we got up, put on our packs, and Morgan, he fell into a crevasse. He slipped right down into the small crevasse without even a warning. Fortunately he stuck his ice axe in before he went in over his head and was able to hang there. I had no idea how to rescue him. John and Garry looked at me like, "you're the experienced climber, what do we do?" So, I yanked hard on the rope until he could crawl out on his own. We were very lucky.

As we continued up, we met some climbers coming down and they told us that it was clear at the summit, you could see Mount Rainier. We were excited at that point. We kept on following the frozen footsteps in the snow until we reached Sitkum Ridge. We followed the ridge up in the driving snow until we ran into a traffic jam at the bottom of what appeared to be a very steep rock face covered with ice. There were about three climbing parties heading up, and one of the climbers had freaked out. She wouldn't go up and she wouldn't go down, she was frozen with fear. The wind was howling and it was so foggy that we couldn't see more than twenty yards ahead. We were starting to get very cold just standing there waiting. The ice was brittle and no one could get a good foothold in it. We decided to go around the situation, but we couldn't get an axe in deep enough to dig in. The brittle ice made it impossible to kick a step in. I was wearing the same type of crampons that Alan had borrowed on the Aasgard pass climb: no toe points. I knew that if one of us slipped and fell, none of us could stop and we would all probably perish. I was using the pick end of my axe and crawling on my hands and knees to keep from sliding. With no toe points on the rented crampons, I kept jamming the side of them into the ice and digging in the pick of my axe. I couldn't tell how John was doing, and I couldn't see Morgan or Garry ahead of me, but I could tell by how slow the rope was moving that they were having a rough time of it too. As we slowly passed the woman who was stuck, I could hear her crying and shouting, "I can't move! Help me!"

There were a couple of guys next to her but it was so foggy I couldn't see what was going on. It was an extremely intense hour of climbing. At the top of the face, unknown to us, was the summit. We reached it thinking there was more to climb until one of the climbers sitting down looked up at us and said, "Congratulations, you made it!"

"Made it? Made it where?" was my first response as I stuck my hands under my sweater to get the feeling back into them.

"The summit," he said.

"This is the summit?" Morgan asked. "How can you tell?"

I was so relieved. Not long after we had reached the summit, the woman who was having such a hard time on the ice face emerged with her party from the fog, her tears still frozen on her cheeks.

After signing the register, I looked at the dome top of Glacier Peak. This was it. The mountain I had been obsessed with climbing for years. I fulfilled my obsession and I was finally standing on the summit. I remember watching Alan's slideshow of the summit and wanting so bad to be here. After my short but sweet victory, I was ready to go down. "John, we really need to go back down! We're running out of time"!

John looked at me and said, "Why do you always want to leave? We just got here!"

I didn't say anything to him, just thought about the fact that we had barely made it up there. Garry and Morgan were wearing Levi's and cotton shirts with ski parkas that were frozen stiff, and no gaiters. John was wearing Morgan's stinky socks on his hands because he'd forgotten his gloves. I was stressed to the max. We were in a cloud, it was snowing, we were out of time, and John was asking me "What's your hurry?"

We ate peanut butter and jelly sandwiches and got ready to descend. I was relieved when Garry began to lead the way. Going down the steep face was about as easy as coming up, and it took us about as long. It was getting later and later, and we were not making good time. When we reached base camp, it was four thirty and we still had a long way to go. John and Morgan wanted to stay another night, but Garry and I knew our wives would be freaking out. So we talked them out of it. We pushed hard down the trail to get out before dark, but when John developed a bad case of shin splints, he could hardly walk.

We were traveling at a slow pace coming out of Kennedy Hot Springs. The trail was mostly flat as it followed the White Chuck River. A long and tedious five miles.

As the bats began dive-bombing us, I thought of an Alan Parsons' song. "Don't look back, you got one more river to cross…" I pulled my collar up over my neck. *I told Debbie that we would be home at around four o'clock. Why do I always give her specific times? I hope these aren't vampire bats.*

We made it back to Garry's house at midnight. My sister had called search and rescue and they were getting ready to head out and search for us in the morning. After we called off the search and told them we were home and safe, I headed home. I came in through the garage door and I stood in the kitchen. Debbie was there waiting for me, in silence. She looked troubled. I said, "I'm sorry, Honey." She didn't say anything at first, she looked me right in the eyes and surprised me by saying, "If you're going to climb mountains, learn how to do it right!" I didn't know how to react to what she said. It was bittersweet.

In the early spring of 1981, I joined the Mountaineers and enrolled in the basic climbing course.

Chapter 9

Feel the rock and feel its energy. Have respect for it.

To Learn, Read; to Know, Write; to Master, Teach.

— Unknown

"Climb if you will, but remember that courage and strength are nought without prudence, and that a momentary negligence may destroy the happiness of a lifetime. Do nothing in haste; look well to each step; and from the beginning think what may be the end."

— Edward Whymper

THE MOUNTAINEERS WERE FORMED in 1909 in Seattle. A group of explorers decided to put together a nonprofit climbing club that offered training and a vision toward the future of preserving the outdoors. They have one of the most comprehensive programs in the United States. Alan had graduated from that program. I was eager to follow suit. I knew that it would be good to learn to the basics of mountain climbing from professionals. Dave, Garry, John, and I all enrolled in the course together.

The experiences I had there were some of the best in my climbing career. The instructors pushed hard to teach us all of the basics of climbing—fundamentals, proper procedures, safety, first aid, and crevasse rescue techniques—and most importantly, the execution and proper use of an ice axe, using either hand, over and over until you can stop yourself on a glacier or snowfield with your eyes closed. We had to take a CPR class as part of the Mountaineering Oriented First Aid (MOFA) course. The training took one whole weekend and it was not easy, especially for John. One of the instructors, Page, gave a group demonstration on how to do a thorough check on an injured victim. She volunteered John as her practice dummy. We all gathered around him as he lay on his back on the grass. Page instructed him to close his eyes, and while explaining the scenario, straddled his hips and began feeling his neck gently. John opened his eyes, quickly studied the situation, and looked at me questioningly. Page was very attractive and John was feeling a bit uncomfortable with her feeling him up. While she was explaining what she was doing, sounding very professional, Garry knelt down next to John and whispered in his ear, just loud enough for all of us to hear, "Slide, John, slide." It was an epic moment, John immediately rolled over on his belly and started laughing, along with everyone else except Page. She didn't find much humor in it, but it kind of broke up the stress from the seriousness of the training.

Weeks after MOFA was over, and somewhat forgotten, it was time for the snow cave field trip on Mount Pilchuck. We were required to build snow caves and sleep overnight inside them, then do our ice axe training in the morning.

Garry, John, Dave, and I were together. After having worked all night, Dave was not in any kind of condition to be digging a snow cave, so we wrapped him up in Thermarest pads and sleeping bags after we got there. He slept through the whole day while we dug the most unbelievable snow cave ever dug by any group of mountaineering students in the history of the Mountaineers. Our snow cave was the size of a living room in an average house. It had four sleeping chambers built into the wall, one for each of us. It had a huge pillar from the floor to the ceiling, with shelves for candles. A stairway, complete with handrails, led from the entrance down to the main floor. From the main floor you could see the upper level where the sleeping chambers were. It was like something out of "lifestyles of the rich and famous climbers." I don't think anyone who toured our snow cave will ever forget it.

Snow caves only have one purpose: to keep you from being exposed to stormy weather. Sleeping in one is like sleeping in a giant walk-in refrigerator. The next morning, after a sleepless night, we began learning self-arrest and team-arrest techniques. It was a beautiful day, and the snow had a four- or five-inch deep frozen crust. We headed to the upper part of the snowfield in groups of five. We began by learning how to do a "sitting glissade" by sliding down on our butts and inserting the point and shaft of the ice axe into the snow to slow down. The third or fourth time down the hill, Dave flipped over onto his stomach and did a self-arrest, but his foot caught a frozen footstep, forcing his leg to jam right into the point of his ice axe. I immediately slid down to him and asked what had happened. It was a freak accident. I don't think he was initially aware of how bad the puncture wound was.

The next field trip, Rock 1, is held every year at Camp Long, which is nothing more than a large city park with a manmade climbing rock. It's a prerequisite for the Rock 2 field trip, but I don't think that anything could have prepared me for the Rock 2 weekend at Mount Erie, just outside of Anacortes. It's a good mountain to train on because you can drive to the top, set up a secure anchor and be top-roped, rappel down, and climb back up.

After the field trip leaders got things sorted out, I found myself with a bunch of people I didn't know. My brother and Dave had gone one way, and Garry had gone another. As I was busy taking pictures of the great view from the top, they told me it was my turn. It was the first time in a while that I had rappelled down a vertical rock wall, and I was going too fast. Upon arriving at the bottom of the wall, I listened to a lecture on the dangers of rappelling "Hollywood-style," as they called it. The way that Alan had taught me. My next assignment was to climb back up what I had just came down. It was about sixty or seventy feet up to the top. I figured since I was such an experienced climber, and the instructors had left me to my own devices, I would start climbing without their help. The instructors had focused their attention on an exceptional rock climber, climbing to the left of me, that was making moves up the rock face like I had never seen before. He was amazing and I felt somewhat jealous. Standing alone I looked up the rock face and I yelled up to my anchor man, "ON BELAY!" I listened in silenced.

I heard a faint, "Belay on!"

So, I yelled, "CLIMBING!" and listened to the silence. I yelled it again, louder. "CLIMBING!!"

Finally a faint response, "Climb on." So I started climbing.

I was doing great at first, but when I was about halfway up, I ran into trouble. There were not many handholds, and I didn't realize that I had deviated from the correct route because of my impatience and foolhardiness. Once again I, alone, had put myself in a tough situation. I was stuck and couldn't move; I couldn't go down and I couldn't go up. I wasn't confident enough to reach up and grab a handhold that was just two feet above me. Nobody was there to help me. Looking at the fifteen feet of slack rope below, I thought if I fell it would be a long way before the rope caught me, so I tried to yell "Up rope!" but I didn't have enough breath. Then, my hands and feet started to shake involuntarily. I couldn't hang on any more and I let go. I tried to yell "Falling" but I was out of breath. I could only whisper it. I fell about twenty feet before my belayer felt the rope slip through his hands and caught me. The rope stretched another five. At that point all the instructors focused their attention on me. I was bouncing up and down like a bobber, banging into the wall beside me, then dangling limp. They had turned their attention from a really good climber making incredible moves up an overhang to an imbecile making some really dumb moves up an easy face.

I was lowered back down and told the correct route up the face. I pulled my sleeves down over my cuts and bruises, regained my composure after being thoroughly embarrassed, and realized I wasn't such a great rock climber after all. I had a lot to learn.

I climbed back up the wall and made it all the way, but I was changed after that. What I learned from my experiences with Alan didn't compare with what I was learning on Mount Erie. "Study the rock, look at the features, be one with it," one of the instructors named Ken, said to me as I put my hands on the rock face looking up the route. He continued, "Feel the rock and feel its energy. It's been around for millions of years, so have respect for it." I felt at ease, like I was home. I was now just beginning to become a real rock climber and had taken it one step further from what I had learned from Alan. He would have been proud.

There was much to learn that weekend. I wrote down the things that happened and then called my mom when I got home. I told her about learning how to rock climb. I remember her asking me how Debbie felt about it. She was surprised to learn that it had been Debbie's idea for me to join the Mountaineers.

After finishing the classroom study, the field trips, and the final exams, I was required to make three climbs with a climb leader in order to receive my diploma. One glacier climb and one rock climb, and the third climb could be either. I climbed Columbia Peak in the Monte Cristo Range and Mount Baker. John came with me. Both climbs were executed flawlessly. My third climb was a bit different, though.

It was a club climb; anyone who was a member of the Mountaineers could participate.

Del Campo Peak is a rock climb, not too hard, and it started off really well. The climb leader, Dick, was a guy whom I looked up to very much. He was a big guy, dynamic, with a brash personality and a deep voice. If you couldn't keep up with him and his rules, he'd let you know he was disappointed in you. He had climbed mountains all over the world: Russia, South America, India. I wanted to lead my climbs like he did—everyone ready on time, everything done on schedule.

The climbing party consisted of Dick and his girlfriend Lynn, John, Roy, Ruthann, and another Tim. We all met at a parking lot in Everett and headed up the Mountain Loop Highway to the Weden Lake trailhead.

The climb started out as most climbs do, me leading the way getting ahead of the party, with John behind me and the other Tim right on John's tail. It didn't take long for it to turn into a marathon. The weather was great: blue sky, light breeze, hot spring sunshine. As John and I stopped to rest, Tim kept going on up the trail. Well, I was not going to be outdone by this guy; I couldn't have another Tim competing with me. So I kept right on his heels, trying to pass but to no avail. John was right behind me telling me to slow down. "We've got all day, Tim!"

Ha. Not me. I am going to pass this guy, get in front of him, and prove something. I'm not sure what I was trying to prove, other than which Tim was better. On we went, and all you could hear was stomping boots and heavy breathing. Our climb leader was at least a mile behind us, but we didn't care. It was a race to the top.

Upon arriving at Weden Lake and resting awhile, we realized that Dick and the rest of the party were not behind us. John said he remembered that Dick mentioned a shortcut. It's funny, I didn't remember Dick talking about a shortcut. We decided to leave Tim at Weden Lake and backtrack down to try to find Dick.

The weather was starting to blow and clouds were rolling in as John and I raced down the back-breaking switchbacks that we had just painfully climbed. After about a mile or so, we realized that we had definitely lost Dick and the rest of the party. So John and I decided to head back up to Weden Lake. It was on the way back up that my actions revealed how much I was not thinking with a clear head.

I decided to take a shortcut up to the lake. I thought it would cut time off the switchbacks. It was probably the dumbest thing I did all day, including the competitive stupidity with Tim. There was a rather large rock wall beside us and I thought if we climbed up the wall, the lake would be right there. I began scrambling up and got myself into quite a situation. As I hung there with no handholds and no energy, I looked down at John with a "don't just stand there, do something" expression. John just stood there watching me with his arms crossed, a disgusted look on his face. I began to climb back down with my tail between my legs, so to speak. As I approached him, he finally said what he'd wanted to say to me all day: "What in the hell are you doing?" He continued with, "That was really stupid!"

Well, that really got me worked up. Then he said, "Is this what you learned in the Mountaineers climbing course? To be an idiot?"

Then I was pissed! There we were, lost, separated from our party, tired from racing up a mountain, the weather was turning bad, and my brother was helping me to see myself for the idiot I was. All that justification didn't stop me from saying words that I regret to this day. I felt my head burning and I wanted to hit him. Instead I just lost it on him. "You fucking know-it-all! You always think you know everything! I'm surprised you don't try to show me a better way to blow my nose! You're critical of everything I do! I'm sick of it! Why don't you just leave me the fuck alone?"

Silence. Just silence. After that, we quit talking to each other. When we reached Weden Lake again, we found our climbing party there waiting for us. Tim had hiked over to Foggy Lake by a different trail and found Dick and the rest of the party. I had failed. Not only did Tim beat me up to Weden Lake, but he went and found Dick, whom I was trying so hard to impress. After getting chewed out by Dick, and I mean really chewed out, we started heading for the summit. Two members of our party, Roy and Ruthann, decided to head back down because of the changing weather conditions.

The weather was starting to get ugly; it was starting to snow. There are two different ways to approach the summit: I went to the left with Tim, no longer caring that he'd beat me to the summit, and John went to the right with Dick and the rest of the party.

John decided to deviate from his group and got himself into a tough situation that required my help. He was within reach, so I extended my hand. He looked at my hand for a second but didn't want to take it; he kept looking for another way to get up to me. But there was no way. I didn't say anything to him, just kept holding out my hand. He finally took my hand and I pulled him up. He kind of whispered out a "Thanks," but didn't look at me, just kept on climbing.

By the time we reached the final pitch toward the summit, the snow was coming down so hard we could barely see anything, maybe ten feet in front of us. It was a whiteout. Tim was only fifteen or so feet away from the summit when Dick decided to stop the climb and go back down. All I could think about was, *I just need one more climb and I can graduate. We're so close, we can't turn back now.* Common sense leaves me at high altitude, but Dick was right. I would have done the same thing if I had been leading the climb.

So we headed back down navigating by map, compass, and altimeter. The trip taught me how to navigate in those conditions. Once we got to the trail, it started letting up and we could find our way much easier. We were cold, wet, tired, and had accomplished nothing. But I learned a great deal about strengths, limitations, and how competitive behavior has no place in mountaineering. It was a while before John and I were on speaking terms again, and things were never quite the same between us, climbing-wise.

Dick took me up Mount Stickney so I could meet all the course requirements and graduate. It took us longer than we thought it would. There was no marked route and it was a complete bushwhack. It was hard to see where we were going and where we had been, but we made it and I became a climb leader. Garry and Dave never finished the climbing course. Garry and my sister broke up and divorced and he went up to Juneau, Alaska to start a new construction business. Dave got through the climbing course up to the final exams but was working so much he never was able to get his three peaks in.

John and I went to the graduation ceremony and received our diplomas together. We both were graduates of the basic climbing course and were both given the climbing leader status which only 5 out of the 15 graduates were given. We both were very confident in our climbing abilities—enough to climb any peak. John and I got very involved with the Mountaineers, committing ourselves as instructors on field trips. We helped out in the Basic class, and then led club climbs. We were very thorough. We did everything by the book. Even though we climbed many of the easier mountains, I always kept one eye on Mount Rainier. It was my goal—reaching the summit of the highest peak in Washington. It became a burning desire: to stand on that summit and look out at the world. I was obsessed. It was as if the mountain was alive and beckoning to me. I started making plans.

Chapter 10

My Little Lion Man

"Great works are performed not by strength but by perseverance".

— Samuel Johnson

I LOOKED UP AT THE TOP of the mountain for a moment and thought about the number of times I'd looked at it from that cherry tree in our backyard. The tree is gone now but the memory is always there. My childhood friend Sean would hang out with me in my treehouse and we would eat cherries until we were sick. He didn't like to climb up to the top branches. It scared him too much. He didn't have it in him to risk everything to see the view and be on top.

Then I thought about Rob, my climbing partner for so many years. I influenced him, taught him and brought him into the world of climbing; he was my strength. And he did whatever I asked him to—like a loyal dog. I hadn't realized what a good friend he had been to me. "He was the best!" I said out loud as I began to get emotional, maybe hoping somehow he'd hear me and accept my delayed acknowledgement.

• • •

Shortly after Morgan left for the Navy, our department hired a replacement. I liked Bob the minute I met him. He was short, but built, a handsome ladies' man fresh out of high school. The first words that came out of his mouth as we were shaking hands were, "Hit me! In the stomach, as hard as you can."

I laughed. "I'm not gonna hit you."

The harder he squeezed my hand, the harder I squeezed back until we were both squeezing as hard as we could. He laughed, let go, and said, "That's a good handshake."

I ignored him at first, since I was already 25 and he was just a kid. Our supervisor's name was also Bob, so the new guy was renamed Little Bob. It was appropriate. Little Bob didn't like it, but he was new, so he let it go... for a while.

I had just climbed Glacier Peak, and Dave and I had climbed Three Fingers that summer, so every day Little Bob would sit quietly and listen to Dave and me tell our climbing stories. Little Bob would listen intently, piping in now and then with something like, "My brother and I go camping all the time with our parents" or some other random thing. Dave and I would just look at each other and roll our eyes. Little Bob was always trying to impress us. He would follow me around asking me if I needed anything. I would just laugh and say, "No, go away." I learned later that he had an identical twin brother, Mike. They'd had a troubled childhood. Little Bob was trying to turn his life around.

While Dave and I were in the Mountaineers program, Little Bob kept asking if he could go on a hike with us. So I took him up Mount Pilchuck. He surprised me. I taught him how to self-arrest with both hands backward and forward. He did well and learned quickly.

"He's smart!" I told Dave at work the following Monday. When Little Bob walked in I barked at him, "Little Bob!" He looked at me, surprised. "Name all the parts of an ice axe."

He smiled and rattled them all off. "Pick, adze, carabiner hole, shaft, ferrule, spike."

"That's awesome, Little Bob!" I said back. Then I pulled out a gift for him. It was my old first edition of the Mountaineers' handbook, *The Freedom of the Hills.* Alan had given it to me years before. I'd bought the newest edition when I went through the basic climbing course. I handed it to Little Bob. "Here ya go, it's all yours."

He looked at it like I had just handed him the holy grail.

"Read it, study it, and learn!" I said as he flipped through the pages with a look of amazement on his face. He gave me a giant grin and simply said with a shaky voice, "Thanks!"

Little Bob read that book over and over. He was obsessed with learning about climbing. I watched him mature. In the summer of 1982, John was leading a Mountaineers club climb up Three Fingers. I asked him if I could bring Little Bob and John said okay.

The first weekend of August was one of the hottest that year. Little Bob had just bought a new pack, new boots, and an ice axe. I spent hours showing him how to pack a pack, explaining what to take and what not to take. He was so excited. "Remember the story of you and Morgan climbing Liberty Peak?" he asked.

"Yes, of course."

"What kind of beer did he take up and surprise you with?"

"Miller High Life. Not my favorite beer, but it was delicious up there."

"What's your favorite beer?

"What's with all the questions?"

"Well," he smiled, "if I ever buy you a beer, I'll know what you like."

I looked at him and said, "You're not old enough. You've got a year to go before you can buy me a beer. And you owe me a beer! So, I guess it'll be a Lowenbrau." It was one of the more expensive beers back then.

There were four of us—John, Little Bob, another program graduate named Randy, and me. We left early Saturday morning. We got to the Saddle Lake trailhead at around eight thirty and it was a quick hike up to the lake. John and Randy wanted to rest for a while, so I asked John if Little Bob and I could go ahead to get a good camp spot at Saddle Gap. John was cool with it, so off we went.

Little Bob was in incredible shape. We practically ran up to Goat Flat. It was a long and hot climb up the switchbacks to Camp Saddle and sweat was pouring down my face. When we reached the top, there was snow all around. The light breeze felt good. We sat down to enjoy the view. As Little Bob took off his pack, he said, "Wouldn't an icy cold beer taste good right now?"

"Knock it off, Bob." I said. "Don't torture me like that!" I started to drink down the last of my semi-warm water as he reached in his pack and pulled out a large plastic bag with ice and something else in it. He opened up the bag and pulled out a frosty Lowenbrau.

"Here ya go," he said.

I just stared at it, in shock. All I could muster was, "Little Bob! You…" I didn't know what to say. The only thing I could think of was, "I can't believe you did this! Oh my God!"

He opened it up and handed it to me with a smile—so proud of himself. I grabbed it and started guzzling like I was dying from thirst. It was gone in a matter of seconds. Little Bob was watching me like he enjoyed my drinking that beer more than I did. "Did you bring one for you?" I asked.

He smiled and said, "I brought twelve! There's enough for all of us. But I only put four in the ice bag."

"I can't believe you carried all that weight up here!" I said, realizing what a great friend he was. He handed me another, and we sat together on a rock and drank beer together absorbing the view in silence.

"This is amazing," he said. "The best damn day ever."

It was a great day. We put the rest of the beer in the snow for John and Randy and set up camp. They arrived dripping with sweat and breathing hard. "Hey guys," John said between gasps as he was taking off his pack "Been here long?"

"Nah," I said, "just a couple of hours." Then I laughed. "Hey, Little Bob brought you something I think you might like."

Little Bob let out a chuckle. I walked over to the snow and pulled out two ice-cold Lowenbraus. The look on John's face was priceless. Randy was in awe. They looked like baby birds when the mother comes back with a big fat worm. "What? Where…? Who in the hell brought these?" John asked excitedly.

I laughed and said, "Little Bob!"

My brother grabbed the beer and looked at Little Bob. "Little Bob! You are awesome!"

I handed Randy his beer and the opener. They both gulped them down almost as fast as I had. We finished setting up camp and got ready for the summit.

The snow was hard on the south face heading up to the summit so we had Little Bob kick steps for us. He was a workhorse. He was a little man with the heart of a lion. We climbed the ladders and were in the lookout by midday. It was a spectacular view. We signed the summit register and had a group picture taken of us by a fellow climber. We got back to camp at around five o'clock and began making a hardy dinner. The four of us ate steak and potatoes, watched the sun set over Puget Sound and drank our ice-cold Lowenbraus. It was the perfect end to a perfect day.

The following day, we headed out on the Three Fingers Glacier and did team-arrest techniques with the climbing rope. We taught Little Bob how to stop all four of us from falling. At one point, we pulled him off his feet into the air. He landed on his back, flipped around and stopped us. "He's a natural," John said, and we headed back up the Three Fingers Glacier. We had successfully launched Little Bob into the world of climbing.

During the winter months, Little Bob's brother Mike got into bodybuilding. Not to be out done by his extremely competitive brother, Little Bob followed suit. In no time, he was rock solid—not so little anymore.

In May, Little Bob called a meeting with all the staff, including the supervisor and manager. We all wondered what he was up to. As we sat there in anticipation, he said, "Hey guys." He smiled nervously. "I know you all know me as Little Bob," his voice was shaky, "but I want my name to be changed to..." He paused and looked around. "Rob. Are you all okay with that?"

We all looked at each other and one of the women laughed. I looked at him and said, "Yes, Rob." Then the rest agreed, and Little Bob became Rob.

I decided the end of June would be a good time to take my first expedition up Mount Rainier. I figured the Emmons-Winthrop Glacier route on the north side would be the best route, as it was the easiest. I thought about whom I should take after filtering through all the people that had called.

I narrowed my list down to John, Dave, Rob, and Don who was friends with Dave, and my boss Bob. Since he was eager and I was trying to earn points with him, I made the mistake of including him. It was a large party, and three were not experienced but three of us were.

John and I left Everett Friday at around two in the morning and drove south in my truck with Rob and Bob in the camper. We listened to Journey, Bob Seger, and Christopher Cross—what a combination. The plan was to meet Dave and Don at the White River campground, stay for the night, get up around four or five, hike up to the base of the Inter Glacier, gear up, and climb to Camp Schurman. We would arrive at Camp Schurman around noon. Camp Schurman is the base camp for the final ascent to the summit on the north side of Mount Rainier. It's located where the Emmons and Winthrop glaciers split into two glaciers, and tops out at about 9,500 feet.

We reached White River around five, and found that the campground was closed about two miles below the trail head, so I knew we would get to Camp Schurman later than we planned unless we left earlier in the morning.

After eating, we played cards to see who would sleep in the camper and who would sleep in Dave's car. It worked out that Bob had to sleep in the Toyota with Rob. He didn't like the idea at all.

Bob was in no shape to be climbing anything. He was about thirty pounds overweight and didn't really have the strength to climb. It takes conditioning, determination, and endurance to climb a mountain. You can't just climb on a whim. I sensed this was going to be a problem… but he was my boss.

After a restless night of the fart band with Dave and Don on tuba, we overslept. It was about seven o'clock by the time we were ready to leave. Bob was complaining about having to sleep in the car. The weather was not looking good and neither were we. We were traveling at a slow pace with Bob about a mile behind us traveling at a turtle's pace. We finally made it to Glacier Basin at around eleven and we stopped to rest awhile. I realized Bob was not going to make it when he showed up wheezing after having hiked up just the first part of the trail. He was pale and showing signs of overexertion on his pained face. Bob felt bad that he was slowing us down. He decided to turn around and go back, saying he would stay in the camper until we got back. I had to let him make that decision on his own. It was a wise decision.

We reached the start of the Inter Glacier at about twelve thirty and roped up: John and me on one rope with Rob in the middle, Dave and Don on the other rope. We started heading up the glacier at around one. It had become hazy but I could feel my face burning. At three o'clock, the weather was starting to deteriorate. It was getting late and we should have been a lot farther along than we were. John kept complaining that we were going too fast and then we all started grumbling at one another. Every time we stopped to rest, Don took out his stupid stove and started melting snow. I got sick of hearing that thing hiss. We stopped for a quick bite then started off again, slogging up the glacier. It turned from hazy to foggy and we were having a hard time navigating. "Are you sure this is right?" John asked.

" I'm following some footprints!" I yelled back.

At five in the evening, Dave and Don were alongside of us as we headed for what looked like the top of Steamboat Prow—a large rock formation that resembles the front of a steamboat. I could barely make out what looked to be a huge rock with some people standing around. Forty-five minutes later our party reached the large rock, which is an area called Camp Curtis. Dave and Don immediately took their packs off and began talking to the other climbers. Then I could hear the hissing sound of Don's stove in the background again. It was irritating. Although I was leading this climb, I felt that Dave was trying to take control of the leadership. Camp Curtis is no more than a gigantic rock on top of another gigantic rock. There is enough room under the rocks for several people to get out of the weather.

The other climbers were from Canada and were contemplating whether to go on or head down. After a quick bite, we headed up toward the top of the rock formations. Snow was starting to fall and we couldn't find the route because of the fog. I had to make a decision whether to keep going or not. We got together and took a vote. The majority wanted to keep going. I shouted in the howling wind, "We can stay in the shelter at Camp Schurman." I felt that if we headed down now, it would be dark before we got to a safer place. Camp Curtis is too small for all of us and doesn't really provide adequate protection from a storm. So I said, "Let's try to find Camp Schurman." I roped up with Dave and Don and led the way through the blizzard-like conditions down from the top of Steamboat Prow through loose rock, ice, and deep snow. We had to keep stopping because I wasn't sure of the route. I was feeling strange; my body was freezing while my face was on fire.

After a precarious, cautious, and tedious climb down from the top of Steamboat Prow to Winthrop Glacier we made it to Camp Schurman. Fortunately, the door to the shelter was open and we had a warm place to stay. Immediately, the hissing sound of Don's stove could be heard throughout, and I was about ready to throw that thing out in the snow. Rob stayed out in the storm and tried to set up camp, but to no avail. The howling wind and blowing snow chased him back through the door looking like a Yeti.

We tried to settle down as more and more climbers kept showing up. There were about fifteen of us crammed into the little building, which resembles a tiny metal army barracks with cemented stones covering the outside. With five or six stoves all going at once sucking the oxygen out of the air, I could hardly breath. Every time the wind gusted, the door would blow open and snow would come flying in. It was like some kind of "B" horror movie.

As I lay on this smelly mattress, trying to sleep, I kept thinking about my experiences on Three Fingers. This was almost the same scenario.

We had to get up at around two in the morning to make the summit, and I couldn't sleep because I was so stressed thinking that I wasn't going to get enough sleep. As I listened to the howling wind and the rustling of all the people, I was getting more concerned that we would have to head back down in the morning. I lay awake, getting up periodically and checking the weather, but the snow didn't stop. Two o'clock came; it was still a blizzard outside. I didn't want to wake the guys and tell them that I had decided that a summit attempt was not in the cards for us; I just let them sleep. It was very disappointing for me. The mountain had won the game… this time.

The weather finally started to settle down and high pressure was starting to prevail. Around six, John woke up and asked, "What's going on? Why didn't you wake us up for the summit attempt?"

I just looked at him and said, "Sorry John, it was blizzard conditions. I decided it would be better not to go."

He looked angry for a minute, then thought about it and agreed. "Probably better that we got some sleep. Your face doesn't look too good," he added as he started climbing out of his bag.

My face was on fire. I ran my fingers down the right side from the bottom of my ear to my chin. It felt numb and blistered. When I heard Don's stove start up again I couldn't temper my tone, "Do you have enough fuel for that thing?!" I went over to John as he was sorting through his perfectly organized pack and said, "I will never let anyone talk me into bringing someone I don't know on a climb again."

John looked at me, smiled, and said, "We learn something new every time we climb, don't we?"

I nodded. We finished breakfast and I was chomping at the bit to get out of there. Rob brought the frozen climbing ropes in from outside. They were unusable. I made a great decision to use Don's stove to heat them up. He was resistant.

"Can't we use all of our stoves?" he asked.

"No, we need the other stoves for emergencies." I shot back.

So he got out his stove and began to heat up the ropes. My idea worked. In no time, he ran out of fuel. We finished thawing out the ropes with John's Phoebus. Weary from fatigue and exposure, we were a somber group as we packed up our stuff. My face was so burnt, and I was in such pain, that I couldn't enjoy anything. I was mean and barking at everyone.

The sunrise was incredible as it rose above the clouds at 9,000 feet. This had been only our first attempt to climb Rainier, so we didn't get discouraged. The important thing was to make it down safely, and now we were more experienced for the next time.

When I got home, I peeled my lips off, literally, in two pieces. My face was never the same after that climb.

Chapter 11

The Holy Mountain

"I will climb that holy mountain in the hours of the day, let it break my sturdy body as it may, I have worked long and hard to weave this magic from my dreams, and I will not run from it, till I'm laughing from the summit, and if my life should end that moment, let it be, Lord, let it be."

— Michael Tomlinson

I WAS CONSTANTLY THINKING about my failure to climb Mount Rainier. The following spring, I trained hard and spent a lot of time instructing and leading field trips. I began planning another expedition up Mount Rainier, but this time I would be better prepared. I bought new equipment, I jogged and worked out almost every day, running up steep hills with a pack full of weights.

Debbie was pregnant with our second child and needed my support, but I was too self-absorbed to care. I was on a mission. I'm amazed she didn't leave me—I'd become obsessed with climbing. I was, once again, an asshole. I can't count the number of times I left her standing at the front door of our little house crying, holding Melissa and looking like she had a watermelon under her shirt. We were struggling financially and couldn't afford the enormous climbing expenses. Yet there I'd go, driving off and waving good-bye like nothing was wrong.

After helping Rob through the climbing course, I planned some club climbs. The first was Mount Baker on the third weekend of May. Unfortunately, when I advertised for climbing members, the only climbers that were interested were the women in Rob's climbing class. My climbing party consisted of Rob and five women. The women felt comfortable with me, but I was very uncomfortable with the idea of taking five women up a mountain and so was Debbie. She was due any time, and there I was, taking off to spend a weekend climbing with five young women. It's not that she didn't trust me, it was just the idea. I trusted myself... so off we went.

We all met at the trailhead and started heading up, but the weather began to change soon after we'd started. Feeling very uncomfortable about the whole situation, I was relieved to use bad weather as an excuse to turn around. Rob wasn't happy with my decision until he found another party to go up with. I had really wanted to go, but I just felt strange about the whole thing. When I got home Debbie was so happy that she gave me a hug and cried on my shoulder. I didn't pet the sow this time.

When Rob came back, he told me how lucky I was that I hadn't gone. "Tim! An avalanche came down on us and we had to run down the glacier or get buried," were the first words out of his mouth.

I knew what he must have felt like going through that ordeal, having been through one myself. He looked like he'd lost ten pounds. I just said, "Well, you'd better be ready for Rainier."

When June started, time was becoming more essential because of Debbie's due date in July. I planned every hour of the climb to the last detail. I think my friends liked having me as a leader because I was strict and did things by the book. In the second week of June I had my first successful climb of the summer.

Rob and I had talked about doing all the summits of Three Fingers in one day. Rob brought out that adventurous spirit I thought I'd lost after my days with Alan. Rob and I were trained, and not quite as foolhardy... maybe. Two weeks before the Rainier climb, we made a plan to do it. The day before we left, we went to our favorite outdoor store and bought a few articles to take with us. Talking to the cashier about the conditions on Three Fingers, we learned that the bridge had been burned out about sixteen miles before the trailhead. We considered not going, but then I came up with the idea of riding our bicycles up the road with our packs on our backs. "It's only sixteen miles, Rob. We can do that in forty-five minutes." I was not to be defeated easily.

Rob thought we could do it too, so we left the next day after work in his '72 Chevy Blazer with the four-inch lift kit and worn-out shocks, listening to The Cars' *Greatest Hits*.

After a bouncy ride, we arrived at the burned-out bridge about five thirty and immediately began getting ready. Rob was wearing white long underwear and doing ballet kicks and pirouettes all around while I laughed uncontrollably.

We proceeded to put on our packs with our overnight gear. We got on our bikes and tried to pedal. It was hopeless. Then we tied all our stuff to the frame of our bikes and wore our day packs with our essentials. It was a lot easier going. After a while, though, we were having a hard time pedaling with our sleeping bags tied to the main support bar on the front of our bikes. We had to pedal bowlegged and the seats were rubbing our butts raw. About halfway up, we got off and started to walk our bikes. Dusk was approaching and we weren't making good time. As we walked along, talking about how long it had been since we'd seen anyone, we heard a loud thump in the bushes next to us. It shook the ground, it was so close.

Rob gasped, "What was that?"

I whispered back, "It's gotta be a bear!"

At that point, Rob threw down his bike and started running, yelling, "Get my ice axe. Quick! Get my ice axe!" Making such a commotion, thinking that his ice axe was his only source of defense, he scared the huge buck and his three does out of the bushes and right at us.

"LOOK OUT!" I yelled, scared out of my mind.

Four giant animals ran past us, as scared as we were. I had to dodge to get out of their way. It was like being in the middle of a stampede.

After the dust settled and you could hear the galloping hooves fade off in the distance, we looked at each other and started laughing out of control. We ended up walking the rest of the way to the trailhead in the dark. We found a flat place to set up the tent about sixty yards from the trailhead and, as we were setting it up, we heard the strangest sound. I'd never heard anything like it—some kind of crying or screeching, coming from just inside the woods. It didn't really scare me that much, but Rob was not too experienced with strange sounds.

"Wha-what was that?" he said with this horrified look on his face. Rob is not one you would think, by looking at him, to be the wimpy type.

"I'm not sure, Rob, but it could be either a screech owl or a—" Another loud screech interrupted me. Then there was silence.

"Or a what?!" he snapped back as he unholstered his ice axe and held it stoutly in his right hand.

Another long screech—like a baby's scream—erupted and the sound was getting closer. I stood in silence, holding one of the tent poles, while my head started to tingle and my heart started pounding. "Do ya think it's gettin' closer?" Rob whispered.

Then we heard a twig snap no more than a hundred feet away. "Wow! Whatever it is, it's not far away!" I exclaimed. "Maybe we should build a fire."

"Why?"

"Well, because animals are afraid of fire."

Rob immediately started running around like a member of a pit crew working on a race car at the Indy 500, grabbing everything that was burnable. He soon had a roaring bonfire blazing about ten feet in the air. I finished setting up the tent. He just kept gathering logs and bushes that he had pulled out of the ground and throwing them on the fire. He'd be gone for about five minutes and come back rolling a log the size of a garbage can right into the fire. We never heard any more from the strange animal.

When I was crawling into my sleeping bag, he was still putting wood on the fire. "Hey Rob, are you going to sleep tonight?" I shouted.

"Yeah, I'll be there in a few minutes," he shouted back over the roar and crackle of the fire.

I fell asleep listening to the breaking of sticks and the crackling fire, but I didn't sleep very well because I kept thinking Rob was going to burn the tent down. When I awoke, I was alone in the tent. The sun was just coming up as I stuck my messy bed-head out of the tent door and looked at the smoldering coals of what was once a giant bonfire. Sleeping next to it, in his sleeping bag all curled up like a dog, was Rob. He had kept that fire going all night. I looked at my watch; it was after six and we had three summits to climb before four o'clock. I had dinner reservations at seven and I was not going to let Debbie down this time.

We packed up our stuff, left the tent and our bikes hidden in the bushes, and began jogging up the trail with just our essentials: rope, ice axes, harnesses, and crampons. We made record time, not stopping until we reached Saddle Lake. I think it took us just under an hour, but our butts were sore from riding those bikes so there was much complaining. You have to just ignore the pain. We rested for a while at the lake and then began running again. We ran through Goat Flat, and when we started for the switchbacks I felt my groin pull and then I was in agony. I lay down on my back and looked up at the sky, thinking to myself, *Why do I do these things?*

Rob then came into my view looking down at me, chewing on a breakfast bar. With his mouth full, he mumbled, "Why are we doing this?"

He annoyed me when he chewed with his mouth open. Pushing the bad etiquette out of my mind, and holding the inside of my leg, I said in a rather matter of fact voice, "Why are we doing this? Let's see, Rob... We're going to climb three summits in one day, and we're in a hurry because I'm taking Debbie out for dinner tonight."

It was all starting to make sense. I was trying to do something that was impossible by anyone's standards, and it was turning into something unobtainable. I sat up and ate a quick bite, not saying anything. Rob looked at me like a puppy that had been reprimanded. "Do you still want to go?" he asked.

I felt bad. I looked at him and smiled, and said, "Hell yes! Let's do this!"

I got up and we took off. As I limped up the trail we talked about our upcoming climb on Rainier. It took us about thirty minutes to get to Tin Pan Gap. When we got there, we looked out to the south at Mount Rainier, then at each other as if we'd read each other's mind, and said, "Let's go for it!" "Let's climb this Holy Mountain"!

We roped up and took off across the glacier, literally running, then up to the approach to the north summit. I was thankful that the route was marked. On the east side of the ridge to the summit of the north peak, there were some yellow paint marks on the rock. "This is it, Rob," I said. "Why don't you lead? Okay?" My groin was killing me and I didn't want him to know.

Rob started up the rocks with authority. We could see the summit about sixty feet away. I belayed him, thinking it was not really the best way to do it but it was safe. He put in two anchors on the way up about 10 feet apart. It was more of a scramble than it was vertical, but there was some class 5. He did a fantastic job of setting anchors and doing everything by the book. I was proud of him as he belayed me to him.

He then quickly scrambled to the summit, set an anchor and belayed me up. The summit was very small and precarious. We looked out and enjoyed the view for a minute and I said, "We gotta go!" He laughed at me. "You don't waste any time do you Tim'? We put a sling around a rock and each repelled down.

We didn't even sign the register, which was in a small brass cylinder. In no time we were down and then, off to the middle peak. We were there in about forty-five minutes. I went first. We didn't have to get the rope out because it was just a quick scramble. We were on the summit by one o'clock. We began laughing hysterically as we ran back down to the glacier. I think the adrenaline was keeping my pain at bay. On to the south peak. We ran up the ladders, ran through the cabin and lay down on the warm rocks behind the cabin.

"Who does this stuff, Rob?" I asked, while I rested and looked up at the sky. *Why was I doing this? It's all like a dream.*

It took us a total of four hours to conquer all three summits and get to Goat Flat. We ran all the way down to the trailhead. As we were tying our equipment on our bikes, I asked Rob, "You know what? Someone needs to come up with a bike with bigger knobby tires, a stronger frame, and higher gear ratio to handle this kind of terrain." If only I had worked on developing such a thing! We finished strapping our stuff to our bikes and flew down the road.

I did go out to dinner that night. I was an hour late, and in extreme pain, but I was really good at acting like I was fine.

Chapter 12

Don't Let Go, Just Hang On

"If you see yourself as trying to beat the mountain, eventually the mountain will win. You don't conquer mountains, you cooperate with them."

— Stacy Allison

THE UPCOMING MOUNT RAINIER CLIMB was a club climb, and a lot of people were interested in going. The phone rang constantly and it got to the point where Debbie would pick up the phone and hand it to me without saying hello. She wasn't happy with me at all. By the end of June I had chosen the people I wanted to take: Rob, Tom and Linda from Rob's mountaineering class, and John. I felt very comfortable about my party this time. The climb was planned for the third weekend of July, but because of Debbie's pregnancy I decided to make it earlier.

It was the first weekend of July, 1984. We left work early. The weather was looking good. John, Rob, and I arrived at White River campground at around five. We didn't hesitate; we put on our packs and started up the trail. We reached Boulder Basin and set up camp. Tom and Linda joined us at around seven and we ate dinner together. I told everyone that we would be getting up around four in the morning to get a good start by five. They all sort of grumbled except Rob. "I want to reach Camp Schurman by ten so that we'll be acclimated by Sunday morning." I sounded like an officer giving orders to a bunch of recruits.

We got going about five thirty. "We have to make up for lost time," I barked, as Tom and Linda were putting on their packs.

We reached the lower part of the Inter Glacier and roped up around six forty five. John was not going fast enough for me, as usual, and I was really pushing him. I put him on the front of the rope, Rob in the middle, and I was on the end. Tom and Linda were together on the other rope.

The weather was perfect, and I was feeling very good about the climb. John was keeping a good pace as we ascended the Inter Glacier. Everything looked different to me this time because the sun was shining. When we were about two thirds of the way up, we could see buildings in Seattle. Off in the distant north, the Cascades, and looking left, the Olympics.

It was starting to get very windy as we approached the place just below Camp Curtis where we would head down to the Emmons Glacier. Clouds were starting to form and it was getting colder fast. We stopped to eat and put on our foul weather gear. When I took my pack off, the wind blew it over and it started to roll down the ridge. I had to chase after it. I didn't want to tell the others that I thought the weather was falling apart and we might have to head down.

We made it to Camp Schurman and set up. John and I had a tough time setting up the tent because the wind was really blowing hard. The weather was definitely falling apart, and John wanted to head down. I wanted to wait it out. We argued for a while and he finally agreed to wait it out. He got really quiet after that as we sat around waiting for the night to come. We listened in silence to the howling wind. John kept organizing his stuff and he would answer questions with a simple "yes" or "no" when I'd ask him something. I decided to leave him in his silence and go visit Rob's tent.

It was snowing at that point and not looking real promising. I brought my Walkman with me so we could listen to a Mariner game. Rob made me some hot spiced cider, took one earphone and I had the other, and we listened to the staticky broadcast of an exciting game. Mariners 8, Blue Jays

4. Rob had filled the inside of his tent with rocks with just enough room for him. So I left there with rock prints on my ass.

I headed over to Linda and Tom's tent in the now gale force wind. I crouched down because the wind was blowing so hard I couldn't stand up. I yelled, "You guys okay"! Tom yelled, "Come on in!" I unzipped the door and entered the tent just in time to see Linda topless and not really caring that I was gazing at her breasts—one of the perks of climbing with open-minded women. We talked about the chances of making the climb as we listened to the sound of frozen rain hit the fly. Then a loud crash of thunder with simultaneous lightning. It was right over head.

The whole time I was gone, John was trying to tie our tent down better. The wind was blowing so hard that it kept lifting the tent up and pulling the stakes out. By then it was midnight. The storm was unforgettable—moving through us with all its crashing thunder and lightning strikes, and snow blowing fiercely. Our tent was bending over from the wind and the ceiling was nearly touching us. Then the wind lifted it and almost blew it over. John crawled out to try to tie it down when another gust hit and filled the fly up like a sail, with me in it. John held onto the straps as the tent was literally coming off the ground. I was screaming, "Holy Shit!" I was at least two to three feet off the ground. "Don't.Let.Go. Just.Hang.On"! I yelled as ....as what??

People all around were yelling, boulders were breaking off of the Willis Wall and crashing down, thunder was rumbling as lightning was flashing, the wind howling with snow blowing everywhere. It was a nightmare.

The storm lasted a couple of hours and John and I were silently praying that the tent would stay on the ground. The wind finally subsided around two thirty. It was just a light powder snow falling. I immediately went to check on my party members. Tom and Linda were okay. Their tent was damaged a bit. Rob was okay. He was smart to fill his tent with rocks or he would have ended up in eastern Washington somewhere. Our tent was toast, the poles were bent and the ripstop nylon was ripped. But John suffered the most. I think he thought we were doomed. We both tried to get some sleep but it was impossible. When the sun finally came up and we could see, we decided to head down as quickly as possible. The weather was not improving; it looked as if we were between storms. So we left, depressed, in a quiet somber march down to the parking lot. I tried to keep spirits up by saying we would try again in a couple of weeks, but John didn't show much interest.

John hung up his ice axe and never attempted Rainier again after that. We did a few hikes up Pilchuck later but he lost his desire to risk his life on the mountain. He became more focused on sailing—he had experience at holding down sails—and then he started a family. I missed him.

• • •

I took a deep breath and as I slowly let it out, I whispered, "My life changed, too, after that climb. I went in the opposite direction from John. I lost all fear. I became so insensitive. When I led a climb, if the members couldn't keep up, I thought of them as weak. Rob was the only one I felt had equal climbing ability."

Debbie never knew what happened that weekend. I felt it was better to keep her in the dark. She was due to have our next baby any time and I didn't want her to get stressed. I looked out at Mount Adams and thought about Amanda my daughter who eventually became my climbing buddy. She has climbed Mount Adams; I never had a desire to climb it.

Funny, I remember when Amanda Jane was born. It was July 21, 1984, but don't remember much of the time when she was a tiny baby; all I remember was that I wanted to climb Rainier. *Who was I? No wonder my relationship with Debbie was never the same.* All I could think about was climbing this mountain. I kept failing, and changing that outcome became more important to me than changing the outcome of my failing marriage. I knew the next time I climbed Rainier I would go for the summit no matter what. No storm nor wind was going to stop me, and because of a request from the deceased, I finally made it.

Chapter 13

A Final Request

"Following the shadow of the Eagle as he flies
By and by, on my way back home
Telling all the stories, of a people that I love,
By and by, on my way back home
Through the eye of the Eagle,
Take me home."

— Kenny Rankin

MORGAN WAS STATIONED at a Navy facility in Idaho. He called out of the blue one night to ask me how I'd feel about taking his friend Brian up Rainier. At first I had no interest. Morgan gave me Brian's phone number anyway. Morgan went on to say that Brian had only one reason to climb it: He wanted to take the ashes of his deceased grandparents to the top and throw them off. It was their dying request. At first I thought, *I don't think so,* but by the time I got off the phone with Morgan, I had decided to do it.

I had Brian and his wife over for dinner and we discussed what would be required of him. He had just finished his accounting degree at Edmonds Community College and taken a job in Omaha. This would be the last thing he'd do before heading to one of the flattest states in the U.S. He had never climbed a mountain before, so I knew this was going to be a challenge for all of us—including Rob, who would be the third member of the climbing party. Brian had taken some mountain safety classes because he was originally going to go up with guides, but they wouldn't allow him to disperse human remains off the summit. That's where I came in.

Brian and I spent a Saturday on the slopes of Mt Pilchuck learning how to use an ice axe and how to rope up. I did feel somewhat okay about his abilities, but still questioned him about crevasse rescue techniques, prusiks, and anchors. I showed him how to use chest and foot prusiks, and by the beginning of August 1984, I was feeling good about the climb. Rob and I did more climbing throughout August and by early September we were ready.

This attempt started out very different from the other two. The weather wasn't good when we started. The plan was to be at Paradise Friday afternoon by five, head up to Camp Muir that evening, and be fully acclimated by Saturday morning. Brian had to work late, so we were delayed right from the get-go. We couldn't put anything in the trunk because it was rusted out. So the three of us were crammed into Rob's '76 Celica with all of our equipment like sausages in a pot of jambalaya.

Rob drove like a man possessed, passing long lines of rush-hour traffic on the shoulder. There was a line of stopped cars heading into Puyallup that must have been two miles long, and we passed them all on the shoulder going forty-five. Just as we approached the traffic light that was causing the backup, the light turned green and we cut everybody off. I'll bet even to this day there are people in Puyallup looking for a silver Celica with shotguns in hand. The mad driving didn't stop in Puyallup. In Graham, a construction worker attempted to hold a "Slow Construction" sign in front of us but had to dive out of the way as we drove over his sign. All this to climb a mountain?

Brian sat quietly in the back seat with his eyes closed, pretending not to notice Rob's maneuvers. I had my fingers stuck in his dashboard. We did eventually make it to Paradise around seven. We got geared up and were ready to go right at dusk. I took one quick picture of us leaning on Rob's car with the mountain in the background.

Brian was carrying close to ninety pounds on his back, counting the ashes of his grandparents. I gave Rob both ropes since I was carrying a ton of equipment. When we reached the Muir Snowfield it started to snow, and it continued to snow harder as we went up. We couldn't see where we were going; there were no wands with florescent tape to mark the route. The snow was covering up any footprints made by other climbers.

After a few hours had gone by, I became extremely tired. I don't mean slightly tired, I mean exhausted. I have never experienced fatigue like that before. Rob was feeling the same way. Brian kept getting ahead of us and then running back down to us and saying, "What's taking you guys so long?" We were in the clouds and could hardly see each other, let alone the route. The snow was blowing in little powdery flakes. I can deal with fog and snow, but it's the wind that can kill you, so thank God it wasn't windy. In fact it was rather mild. Rob and I were practically sleepwalking, resting about every fifty yards. At one point we both lay down on our packs and fell asleep. Just before I fell asleep, I felt tiny snowflakes hitting my face and I didn't care if I froze; I didn't care if Brian got lost in the fog; I didn't care if we even climbed the mountain… as long as I could sleep. It was the strangest thing.

I woke up rather abruptly to Brian yelling at us, "You call yourselves great climbers?! Do you guys even want to climb this mountain?! Here we are lost, and you guys are sleeping?!"

I looked over at Rob, who looked like the cowardly lion in the Wizard of Oz. His knees were sticking up and he was covered with snow—just his face showed. I must have looked the same way to him. We both got up, shook the snow off and pulled out our map, compass, and altimeter. We put on our headlamps and pinpointed our exact location without saying a word to Brian. We looked like professionals. He was quite impressed and didn't say another harsh word to us after that.

After I had taken that nap I felt alert and stronger. We would climb for about thirty yards and then take another compass reading, and begin climbing again. Eight hours after we'd left Paradise, the fog was starting to clear and we could see the lights of other climbers at Camp Muir in the distance. We were not setting any records; three turtles with broken legs could have made it faster than us.

We reached Muir at three forty-five. There's a rock shelter up there that holds about fifteen people. It has a long table in the front with bunks along the back, all connected together. The place was full of climbers and there was nowhere for us to sleep. There were three climbers who were thinking about leaving for a summit attempt as we arrived, but they couldn't make up their minds, so I made up their minds for them. I said, "Quit being wimps and go climb the fucking mountain!"

They actually laughed a little, looked at each other, and decided to go. I had woken up everyone in the shelter. I didn't care. I was tired and desperate to lie down. The trio grabbed their gear and left, making just enough room for the three of us. Rob and Brian had already grabbed the two spots in the lower bunks and were headed to dreamland. I went out with the three climbers that I had just insulted and went over the route with them. One of the climbers went back into the shelter while I was talking to the other two. I thought he was just getting some extra stuff to take with him. The weather was clearing and I told the guys that they had a good chance to make it if they left right now.

I was so tired that I didn't even look up at the spot on the upper bunk that I had intended to take when I walked back into the shelter. I took off my gear and pulled out my sleeping bag. As I was about to throw it up on the bunk, I noticed that the other climber had not come in here to get more stuff. No, he had changed his mind about going and guess where he was? In my spot in the top bunk. I wasn't feeling real warm toward this guy and I think he could see that I wasn't real happy. I started to growl at him. He said, "Hey bud, we can work this out."

So we woke everyone up and asked them to move closer together so that I could fit in. I mumbled out a "Thanks" and crawled into my sleeping bag. I was asleep before my eyes were shut and dreaming about operating a chainsaw.

The next thing I knew, everyone in the place was saying, "Throw that guy outta here!" I guess I was snoring so loud that they could hear me on the other side of Camp Muir.

Morning came with a lot of commotion, and I felt like I was hung over from a night of drinking whisky. The other climbers were getting ready to go back to Paradise. Rob and Brian were up, talking to the climbers that I had talked into going to the summit. They hadn't made it. They'd turned around when they got to Disappointment Cleaver. The wind was blowing them over.

It was about ten thirty in the morning and the weather was lousy. The two climbers told us that they were about halfway up the Cleaver when the weather started getting really bad. I apologized to them and explained that I hadn't been myself when we'd come in earlier in the night. They both just laughed at me.

Later that morning, I decided to sleep out in my tent alone so I wouldn't be disturbed. Rob and Brian didn't really care. They wanted to get some sleep without my snoring.

While we were fixing an afternoon snack and watching a storm pass through, I listened to the Huskies game against Michigan on my Walkman. I really didn't think we were going to have a chance to climb; the weather was not conducive, and I really didn't care this time. I told them, "If the weather changes, we climb it. If it doesn't change, we don't."

Brian didn't like my attitude. He didn't like the fact that I wasn't serious about anything except the fact that the Huskies were up by nine points in the fourth. I must have looked like a fool, with my balaclava on over my headphones jumping around and screaming whenever Washington made a good play. Brian would ask a serious question and I would start to give him a serious answer, then look away and start dancing around, high-fiving everyone in the shelter. The Huskies won and, almost immediately, the sky started to clear and I was feeling alive again.

Rob, Brian, and I went out and hiked around. By early afternoon the weather was improving. We checked out the park rangers hut. The new solar-powered outhouse wasn't working yet, so we had to use the old one. I still didn't really think we were going to climb the mountain, but I tried to stay positive. The plan was to get up at one o'clock and leave by two.

I crawled into my tent at six in the evening but couldn't sleep. I lay there thinking about Debbie, my daughters, the safety of this trip, all the other climbs I had been on, and how this one was so different from the rest. Normally the weather starts out good and gets bad. This time the weather started out bad and was getting better. The only sound was the wind blowing and shaking the tent. I wasn't afraid of blowing away this time because I had filled my tent with rocks. I kept trying to find a weather report on my Walkman, but all I could find was country music. I fell asleep listening to Roy Rogers singing "Tumbling Tumbleweeds" and awoke from a deep sleep abruptly when Brian shook my foot saying, "It's one o'clock, Tim. Let's go."

I wasn't sure what was going on for a second, but it all came back to me when a rush of cold wind filled my tent and made me shiver. I had to convince myself to climb out of my bag and get my foul weather gear, climbing boots, crampons, climbing harness and wool hat on. I wasn't motivated. I sauntered over to Rob and Brian, quietly talking in the dark. Rob was setting out the rope for me and getting Brian ready to rope up. I looked up to the sky—alive with billions of stars. I thought deep and hard, swallowed, and said, "I don't like the weather, do you? Think we should try?"

They looked at me with their mouths open like I was nuts. "I think there's a good chance, Tim," Rob spoke delicately so as not to upset me. "It's clear and not that cold. I think we can at least rope up and climb for a while and see how it goes."

He sounded like he was talking to a four year old. He made a lot of sense and I couldn't argue with him. I barked out, "Okay, I'll lead. We'll put Brian in the middle, and when we get to Disappointment Cleaver, you can lead."

Nothing more was said while we roped up. Disappointment Cleaver is a massive, rock-covered mound that divides the Emmons Glacier from the Ingraham Glacier. After you cross the Ingraham Glacier, you reach the path that heads up the Cleaver and you must gather up the rope and hold it as you hike about half a mile up the pumice-covered bulge.

We finished roping up and began following the frozen footsteps of the hundreds of climbers that head up there every day. We crossed the Cowlitz Glacier very fast and headed up Cathedral Gap. We slipped through the gap that leads to Ingraham. As we walked down from the gap and onto the glacier I stopped, turned off my headlamp, and gazed into the surrounding darkness. Ingraham Glacier lies right below one of the most massive rock formations on Mount Rainier called Gibraltar Rock. Standing below that rock is like nothing I had ever experienced before. Even in the dark, the light reflects from the snow and lights up the side of the gigantic ice wall that rises next to Gibraltar. All three of us stood there staring straight up in amazement. Just below our feet, buried in ice, were the bodies of eight climbers who had died in an avalanche just four years earlier on Father's Day. I felt like I was standing in a graveyard.

We hiked across Ingraham Glacier while the ice wall made cracking noises and came to the edge of a colossal crevasse. Standing in silence, we gazed down into the abyss in the darkness. The same ice wall that had avalanched six years earlier broke the silence with a loud "CRACK!" I swallowed hard and whispered in a shaky voice, "I don't like this, Rob, let's get the hell outta here!"

We moved quickly across the glacier and stopped when we lost the route. The cleaver loomed in front of us like a giant wall. I decided to let Rob lead. He wasn't sure which way to go, so he started climbing straight up the side, kicking his crampon-fitted boots into the soft pumice. He was going nowhere. I noticed some frozen footsteps on the other side of a small crevasse and realized that that was the route, but I didn't say anything to Rob because I wanted him to figure it out on his own. After about five minutes of futile attempts and frustration, he noticed the footsteps and, without saying a word, we proceeded over the ramp to the Cleaver. We reached Emmons Glacier in about forty-five minutes. The sun was just beginning to show a soft red glow in the east. We sat and ate a snack and watched the sunrise. Orange-colored crevassed glaciers surrounded us, and beyond them was a sea of orange and gold clouds. Off in the distance, the horizon held a blazing golden sun. That was contrasted with the dark silhouette of Little Tahoma. It was a spiritual experience that I will never forget. I finally felt secure as I realized we were going to make it to the summit.

We started out again. Climbing was getting more difficult each step at the high altitude. We were becoming physically exhausted. At about 14,000 feet, I started to get my second wind. When we reached the crater rim, I felt really good and Rob and Brian could hardly move. They both lay there moaning while I acted like a kid, running around taking pictures.

The wind practically blew me over at the top of the rim. Then I started getting a bad headache and feeling the effects of the altitude. My first reaction was to throw up. I sat down next to the guys and kept myself perfectly still so I wouldn't get any sicker. As I lay there in agony, they got up and said, "Well, let's head for the summit."

The summit was just on the other side of the crater about a quarter of a mile away. I looked at Rob and said, "I can't make it over there. I'm too sick."

Rob encouraged me "You can do it, Tim."

But I had convinced myself that that was as far as I could go and no one was going to change my mind. I watched the two of them walk slowly across the crater and head up toward Columbia Crest, the true summit. I kept thinking I should be with them. *I've got to get up and go after them. Rob and Brian are going to Register Rock and put their names in the summit register and I won't be in there. I'm the climb leader, I have to be in there.* Sick as I felt, I got up and began the trek across the crater. With the freezing wind blowing in my face, it was one of the most physically taxing things I have ever done. I had to keep my head down and look at my boots. I stopped at one point and looked up, I could see the two of them in the distance walking up to Columbia Crest. I slowly walked off the snow and onto the crushed pumice rock; I'd made it. The sound of my crampons on the pumice made a grinding noise each step I took. I was feeling sick again. I was trying to keep from vomiting. I crawled up on my hands and knees to the register box. The big metal box, with two giant wing nuts holding the door shut, had a green hardbound book inside with "Mt Rainier Register" engraved on the cover.

Rob and Brian were on the summit taking pictures. Then Brian took off his pack and started unraveling his items. He gently took out his grandparents' ashes as if they were super delicate and might break if he dropped them. The remains of each grandparent was in its own small but heavy box, each weighing over ten pounds. He began slowly walking south until he was about twenty feet away from the summit. He set down one box on the snow and opened the other. As he opened it, he stood straight up. After releasing the contents he said "Happy Birthday" in Finnish, his grandparents' native tongue. The wind was blowing so hard that it looked like a giant cloud of white smoke rising up into the air, never touching the snow. The ashes were carried off until they were gone. He set down the empty box and picked up the other. This time he said "Happy New Year" in Finnish. After setting down the box next to the first, he stood up and just stared off into the distance with his back to us for about five minutes while the ashes dispersed and his grandparents were gone. He wiped his eyes, grabbed his composure and the empty boxes, and slowly walked toward us. He had carried them both, side by side up to the summit of Mount Rainier; he had accomplished his task.

It was very emotional for me—I felt as though I had done a very good thing by taking him up there. I'm sure it's illegal and he would have been cited if he'd been caught, but it was their final request and it was all worth it. As I braced myself in the bitter cold wind, I realized that I was standing on the top of Mount Rainier at Columbia Crest and I felt good. I had finally made it.

As we stepped in the slushy snow in the bright sunlight, the sweat running down my face, the bliss of the experience began to wear off. We were about to head down and I thought about crossing the Ingraham Glacier graveyard again. I could hear echoes of the climbers crying out as they were engulfed by the giant slab avalanche. My heart hurt at the thought of the family and friends who lost their loved ones. *Is this the way I would want to die?*

We made it down to Disappointment Cleaver in about two hours. Then we hiked down the Cleaver to Ingraham Glacier. I took a deep breath as we walked out onto it. I was leading with Brian in the middle and Rob on the end. I was going fast because I felt so uneasy. Brian yelled out, "Slow down!"

I turned around and shouted back, "I want to get out of here! I have to pee!"

He shouted back, "Pee when we get to Cathedral Gap!"

I ignored him and began going faster. He wasn't happy with me.

When we reached Camp Muir, I made two promises to Rob: One, that we would never take this route again, and two, that we would climb this mountain every year for the rest of our lives.

After coming off Panorama Point heading down, we took the wrong trail and got totally lost. We kept hiking around one trail and ended up at a dead end in a ravine with nowhere to go. We could see all the sightseers and tourists walking around in shorts while we were in full gear. We finally had to ask a tourist and his wife, "Which way to the parking lot?"

"Ach, you don't know vere unt parking lot ist?" They were German or Swiss. We felt pretty dumb. They told us, "First you head down to da right, den you see da concrete trail, den follow it to zee parking lot."

At that point I began laughing, maybe out of frustration. I told them my name was Louie Whittaker and introduced Rob as my brother Jim. They got excited and wanted to have their picture taken with us. Brian took the picture with their camera and it was all we could do to get away from them. "Vee are so excited to meet you, vee have heard so much about you in our country." Obviously, they had never seen the Whittakers before.

You could have rung the sweat out of my long underwear after three days of nonstop wear. I must have smelled pretty ripe when I had my arm around Hans getting our picture taken. I went into the lodge to call Debbie. Every person who passed me while I was on the phone either grimaced from the aroma or said something like, "P.U.! What's that smell?!" It was me, Louie Whittaker II.

Brian's family had quite a celebration for us in the parking lot, with food, desserts, champagne, and diet pop. We were so dehydrated, it didn't matter what it was as long as it was wet.

The following winter, Brian and his wife moved to Omaha and I haven't seen him since.

Chapter 14

Harbinger, Sage, or Fool

"On the north face there lives a man and he stands alone in the wind,
There are people who gather there and they believe he is the friend.
Does anyone know where he comes from?
Does anyone know where he's going?
'Cause we're going there, too."

— Dan Seals

THE BUILDINGS AT CAMP MUIR HAVEN'T CHANGED MUCH. What's changed are the glaciers. Global warming caused many of the glaciers to recede. It was hard to believe it could ever be that warm up here as a chilly October wind began blowing so hard that I had to brace myself. *Why am I up here all alone? Why have I always felt alone? I have married and my wives have had no interest in what I love to do. Why?*

Gibraltar Rock, the once-standard route to the summit, was gleaming with ice. There used to be a ledge that wrapped around the left side of the giant rock, making it easier to get to Ingraham Glacier. The ledge avalanched away and the standard route moved to Disappointment Cleaver.

I had attempted the summit on Rainier twenty-two times. Rob and I were going to climb every known route but we only did three of the many routes, three times each.

• • •

The summer of '86 holds fond memories for me. It was the summer Morgan got out of the Navy. I put a new roof on my house and received a huge promotion at work. I bought my old motorcycle back and finished restoring Debbie's MGB. It was also the summer I climbed many mountains.

Debbie was contracting work from a couple of guys named Mark and Rick. Mark's dream was to climb Mount Rainier and they both begged Debbie to talk me into taking them to the summit. Rick's brother Doug wanted to go too. I made them my priority since they were Debbie's co-workers and friends. I taught them the fundamentals and proper use of an ice axe on the slopes of Mount Pilchuck. I took my students to the slopes below the summit and we would practice self-arrest and team arrest for hours. If they wanted to climb, they would have to learn the fundamentals first.

One of my favorite basic training instructors, Ken, had taught me the proper ways to self-arrest using both hands equally well. "I've never seen two people pick up the technique as fast as you and your brother," he told me. "I'd love to climb with you both someday. I'd feel safe knowing that you could stop me from a fall." I really liked Ken.

After the lessons, Mark, Rick and Doug successfully summited a couple of smaller mountains, Del Campo Peak and Vesper Peak.

Then came Mount Baker. Mount Baker is a perfect mountain to acclimate to before Rainier, and that was my only reason for climbing it.

Mark, a wiry, eccentric art designer, was a bit of a comedian. Rick (who we called "Buttons, I'm not sure why he got that nickname"), a big guy—well over six feet—had just graduated from the University of Oregon with an art degree and was serving an internship at the company where Debbie was doing freelance artwork. His brother, Doug, average size with bleach-blond hair, a Michigan grad, worked as a top engineer at Boeing. I loved razzing him about the Huskies beating his beloved Wolverines in the fall of '84. The brothers' dad gave me explicit instructions to not put the two of them on the same rope team. I guess if anything happened, he didn't want to risk losing both of them. Rob had to work so he couldn't join us on this climb.

We took off toward Mount Baker early on a beautiful summer day in July in Doug's old beat-up Jeep Wagoneer. We arrived at the town of Glacier at around ten in the morning and, after a quick stop, headed up to the trailhead of the Heliotrope Ridge Trail. Feeling responsible for their safety, I chose the easiest route up Baker for a first-time climb.

We started out on the trail that leads up to the ridge, keeping a real fast pace. I told them, "There are about fifteen switchbacks on this trail." They secretly kept count. I was feeling a bit stressed since it was the first time I'd taken informally trained people up a mountain higher than 10,000 feet. This was their chance to show me what they had learned, and for me to see how good an instructor I was.

As we marched up the trail, they mumbled among themselves and looked at me and snickered like they knew something I didn't. I stayed pretty quiet. After two hours of nonstop hiking, we reached the foot of Coleman Glacier. With sweat dripping off my nose, I barked out, "We'll stop here and rope up!"

Mark walked up to me and blurted out, "Twenty-one!"

Puzzled by his outburst, I just stared at him for a couple of seconds and then managed to say, "What are you talking about?"

He quickly retorted, "There were twenty-one switchbacks, we counted 'em."

Then they started laughing. I just sort of smiled to myself. *I think I'm in trouble here with these guys, I'm taking three nerds up Baker.*

After roping up and burning my hand making foot prusiks, we began to ascend the lower part of Coleman Glacier with Doug on my rope and Mark and Buttons on the other. We hadn't gone more than seventy-five yards when Buttons stepped into a small, hidden crevasse. He fell down about fifteen feet and hit hard on the wall of the crevasse. I ran up and then cautiously looked over the edge down at him. I was a little concerned, but somehow I knew he was fine. He was actually trying to put his right foot into his foot prusik. I yelled down. "Just hang on, Rick, we'll pull you out!" I carefully hiked around the crevasse where Mark was in an arrest position. I threw in an anchor and tied it off with a prusik. Mark was able to get up. I took out my rescue rope and threw it down to Buttons to tie into. Then the three of us were able to get a good grip on the rope. He is a big guy and it took all we had but we all worked together as a team, just like I had taught them, and Buttons came out unscathed. In bit of shock, his hands began to shake a little . But I kept calm by talking like it was no big deal, soon he calmed down, and the incident was quickly forgotten. We headed up to our base camp at the top of Heliotrope Ridge, which divides Thunder Glacier from Coleman Glacier. From the top of the ridge, you can see Bellingham, the San Juan Islands, and Vancouver Island in the distance. The view is fantastic.

One of the most disgusting things that mountain climbers do during meals, that most people would find unacceptable, is flatulence. There is nothing more harmful to the sinuses than mountain gas. When you combine trail mix, Gatorade, freeze-dried fruit, and other unknowns, the body produces what most climbers call "mountain gas." It causes other climbers to go into a rage of coughing, wheezing, shortness of breath and finally, an uncontrollable gagging fit. I myself, have never developed this unusual mountain gas phenomenon, although some of my climbing buddies would disagree. After dinner, we watched the sun set to the background chorus of farting. I swear, if those guys could have farted the Star Spangled Banner, they would have. It sounded like they were trying to.

I got the guys up at 3:30 a.m. and told them we could leave by 4:30, but it didn't turn out that way. Buttons and Doug were almost ready. Mark was slow getting ready and it was pissing me off. It took him an hour just to make his breakfast, and he ate it like we had all day. I finally I asked him in a sarcastic tone, "What's next, Mark? You gotta put on your makeup?"

He looked at me sternly, got up and started throwing things around, then blurted out, "If I had known that we were joining the Marines when I asked you to take us up Rainier, I never would have asked!"

It was stone quiet after that. I looked at Buttons, he looked at me and smirked but didn't laugh. Doug was trying desperately not to laugh too. As Mark was in the midst of his mini tantrum, I began to think about what was said and I realized that I was being a total jerk. I then made an attempt to apologize to him. He looked like a little kid with this sad expression. Then he sat on a rock with his back to us. Then he got up and reluctantly accepted my apology. He was acting like a little kid that had to have his time out and then was okay with me.

We finally got on the glacier at 5:15 and didn't stop until we reached the saddle between Demming Glacier and Coleman Glacier. From there is the steep Roman Wall. We had to wait because there were other parties climbing up. While waiting, another party started talking to us casually, which is normal, but these guys were strange. They were roped together with industrial wire, yes, wire, and, the person I assumed to be the leader of the party walked over to me, held up his ice axe quietly and asked me, "Which end of this ice axe do I use if I fall?"

To an outsider, these guys would have appeared to be experienced climbers… I didn't say anything at first, and just looked at this guy with my mouth open in amazement. I had to think of something to say. So I told them, "If you don't know which end of an ice axe to use, you shouldn't be up here!" That climbing party were an accident just waiting to happen.

He didn't like my answer. They walked away grumbling.

The Roman Wall toward the summit is a very steep final ascent, but we made good time and reached the dome at nine. We didn't stop until we reached Grant Peak, the highest point of Mount Baker. Buttons let out a big "Yahoo!" as we walked onto the top, then we all shook hands.

Most of mountain climbing can be truly boring. Most of the time you're just plodding along, but… anything can happen when you least expect it. We sat down on the dirt area around the summit and ate a bite. Doug and Mark took some pictures and then at around ten I was ready to leave.

With me in the lead, we headed down. I was in a hurry. I could tell it was going to be a warm day, and I didn't like the idea of heading down through the giant icefall at Black Buttes along the north side of Colfax Peak. *If we can just get by the Buttes before it gets too warm…* I began to quicken my pace even more.

When we reached the top of the Roman Wall, the snow was still crusty-frozen, but I didn't even stop to catch my breath. I plunged my crampon fitted boot heel into the hard crust going downhill practically at a jog. I didn't take any time to socialize with passing climbers, still climbing up. I would just nod and say, "Hi." If any of them asked a question about the summit, I would just say, "Yep."

Doug was doing really well considering I had the rope pulled tight between us. We were almost to the bottom of the wall when I heard someone yell, "FALLING!"

I turned around to see a climber tumbling over and over. *He's going too fast to get control, I hope he's roped up!* Then I saw the guy he was roped to get pulled right off his feet and both of them were tumbling down. *I'm sure glad they're not in my party!* Then I recognized one of the climbers. It was Mark.

I could only watch with a knotted stomach. Buttons finally got control and stopped Mark. They both just lay there in the snow. Doug and I climbed down to them. When we reached them, they were both getting up, half dazed. They brushed the snow off themselves.

"You guys okay?" I asked.

Mark's ankles were sliced up from his crampons but, fortunately, not too bad. His gaiters—or, I should say, my gaiters that he'd borrowed—were ruined. I didn't care as long as he was okay. All Mark could say was, "Sssorry 'bout the gggators man…"

Buttons was okay, but Mark was in a state of shock. I had to treat him by getting him warmed up and taking a long rest. I checked his eyes and head for any signs of concussion; thank goodness he was okay. Mark said he'd stepped into a frozen footstep and lost his balance.

After reviewing the experience over and over, we began our descent at a slightly slower speed. It is so easy to get overconfident and put your party in jeopardy when you don't stay focused. I realized I hadn't taught them that you can't use your feet to self-arrest when you're wearing crampons. The toe points on crampons cause you to flip over backward head-first, especially on frozen snow. You must bend your knees, with your feet up in the self-arrest position, and use your knees and ice axe to stop you. I felt really bad, but they forgave me.

After passing Black Buttes quite quickly with my uneasy feeling, we reached base camp about noon and began to tear down. All and all, we agreed it was a good climb; we had accomplished what we'd set out to do and learned a few things on the way. Mountaineers always take a piece of the mountain with us when we leave, but the mountain always takes a bigger piece of us.

The weeks following the climb found me running, working out at the gym, and putting a new roof on my house. But before the roof was finished, I had to fulfill my next commitment: Mount Rainier. It was a couple of days before the climb, and I was up on the roof in the blazing sun, frantically tacking down shingles, listening to my little radio, when the phone rang. I heard Debbie talking to someone and she sounded unhappy.

Then she told them, "He's on the roof, I'll let you tell him." She handed up the portable phone to me with a shocked look on her face. It was my brother. He had some distressing news.

A fellow mountaineer had been killed on a mountain in the Canadian Rockies. It was Ken, my favorite instructor. Ken was a mentor, the one who taught me patience, how to use my ice axe properly. He taught me the true art of climbing. He told me once that to be a good guide you must first be patient. His death hit me really hard. All I could say to John was, "I can't believe it. I was just talking to him last week when I checked out a couple of climbing ropes at his house. He was really excited, telling me about this climb…"

As I switched off the portable phone, anxiety washed over me. The last words Ken had said to me were, "We've got to go climbing together soon. Okay?"

I didn't want to dwell on death too much, but this time I couldn't look away. Of all the times I'd gone into the mountains and climbed, outran avalanches, managed to stop myself from falling over cliffs, outlasted snow storms, and stepped clear of crevasses and giant ice boulders, this was the first time I felt mortal. It could happen to me. There on the roof, I broke down. *Do I really want to die in the mountains? Is that where I want to end up, frozen, entombed in a glacier for hundreds of years?*

In mid-August, Rob, Mark, Buttons, Doug, and I set out for Mount Rainier. It was nearly dark when we reached Boulder Basin. Almost immediately, things began to unravel like a snagged-up rope. It started when I told Rob to go up to the spring and fill the water bottles. Rob knew where the small spring was, about two hundred yards up the trail, and had no problem with taking all the bottles up there and filling them. He casually grabbed the bottles and, with his muscles bulging out of his tight base-layer shirt, was off, headlamp lighting the way.

I was busy setting up the tent, and the boys were also too busy to notice that it was taking Rob a long time to get back with the water.

Where the hell is he? About forty-five minutes had gone by and I was starting to get worried. My worries disappeared when I heard him tromping down the trail with the bottles, but I was not expecting them to be empty. He didn't say anything, just threw the bottles down at the entrance of the tent, took off his boots, and crawled into his sleeping bag. The rest of us were perplexed at Rob's strange behavior. I crawled into the tent. "Rob, where the hell is the water?"

He answered with an evasive tone, "Oh, I'm not really hungry tonight. I'd just as soon go to bed. Goodnight."

What in the hell is his problem? I blurted out, "I guess I'll get the water!" as I gathered up the water bottles in a huff.

"Okay."

Buttons and Doug were busy as I rifled through my pack for my fleece jacket. I heard Rob whisper my name I crawled over to him. "What is it, buddy?"

"The reason I didn't get the water is because…" He hesitated and I could see the whites of his eyes in the dark like he had just seen a ghost. He swallowed hard, then continued, "There… there were these two eyes staring at me when I was walking down the trail."

"TWO EYES?!" I shouted back.

"Shhhhh!" Rob said quickly, like he was afraid of anyone hearing. Then he continued with his story. "I started to walk over to where the eyes were and they blinked at me. I got freaked out and walked quickly back to where I thought the trail was, but I got lost. I turned to see where the eyes were, but they were gone. I wandered around looking for the trail, but it's so dark I couldn't see anything." He swallowed again, hard, and continued. "Then those eyes lit up again right in front of me about thirty or forty feet away. I took off running and finally saw the light of our campsite in the distance. I don't want to go over there again. Let's just go to bed and get water in the morning."

I was amazed. I had to think about what to do. How was I going to tell the other members of the party that we didn't have any water to cook dinner? I wanted to, as a team, investigate the weird phenomenon that this tough guy was so afraid of. When I came out of the tent, Mark immediately hounded me about the water. Then the other two started up. "Yeah!" "We're hungry!" "Come on!" "What's going on?!"

I just said in a quiet, calm voice, "I think we should all get the water as a team."

They didn't like that answer at all, so I told them what happened to Rob. No sooner had I finished telling them, they were ready to go, with ice axes in hand, to kill and skin this creature like a bunch of primal hunters off to kill a mastodon. I'm not sure I felt more secure with a bunch of armed and hungry mountaineers pumped up for a kill.

We all headed off, water bottles and ice axes in hand, in the direction of the man-eating eyes. Rob came with us, rather than stay alone in his tent. We were walking pretty fast when, all of a sudden, everyone stopped as if they'd run into a rock wall. I ran into the back of Buttons. Doug whispered, "What is it?"

Mark said, "I don't know."

I recognized it immediately. "Hey, you guys, that's just a couple of luminous stickers on a 'no camping' sign. I remember seeing it last year."

They weren't convinced. Rob said, "Tim, they blinked at me!"

"No, Rob. You blinked and it gave you the illusion that they blinked. Come on, I'll show you," I said with confidence. *I have this scenario all figured out.*

I walked over to the eyes. The boys followed cautiously behind, at a safe distance. Mark said, in a quivering voice, "I don't know, Tim, those look like eyes to me."

"You guys are a bunch of wieners." I blurted out.

We didn't have our headlamps on, or flashlights, but it didn't matter. I knew what it was. Besides, we had our ice axes and water bottles. We were safe. Now, there was one colossal fact that I didn't remember in the midst of my over confidence. They didn't know that I am slightly near-sighted and I didn't have my contacts in. I was blindly leading them.

When we got within twenty yards, the eyes blinked. My heart stopped along with my body. They really were eyes. *Shit!* I began walking backward into Mark, and he backed into Rob, who backed into Doug, and Buttons was practically holding all four of us up. I think I had my mouth open but no words would come out. Then the thing, whatever it was, made a loud grunting noise and stood up. It started coming toward us. The ground was quaking from the weight of it; it was huge! I could feel my hair standing on end and kept pushing back on Mark, but he couldn't move back because the other guys were frozen stiff in their tracks. The thing came closer and all I managed to yell, "IT'S A BBBBBEAR! RUN!"

But we didn't run. First we tripped and fell all over each other, then we got up and ran, stumbled, fell, rolled in mud, tripped over logs, and ran some more. We made it back to the tents eventually, wet, mud-covered, and out of breath. We'd lost our water bottles, but we still had our ice axes. Rob had slashed open his leg and needed stitches. I put a butterfly bandage on it for the time being. We agreed to go to bed without dinner and get water in the morning. I was amazed at how the guys could still create mountain gas without eating. As I lay in my sleeping bag trying to sleep, listening to the fart brothers next door, Rob whispered, "I told you…"

I snapped back, "Shut up! Go to sleep! We gotta get up early tomorrow."

It wasn't long before I heard him snoring. *I hope this episode was not an omen of what's to come on this climb.*

Everything seems more ominous in the dark. The light of morning revealed the identity of the two eyes. A bull elk was calmly lying in a misty field with three large cows—in the same spot we'd disturbed him from the night before. He was huge, so it was no wonder I had mistaken him for a giant, thirty-foot tall grizzly...

Arranged in a somewhat straight line were five water bottles lying between us and the elk. As we retrieved our bottles, the elk decided they'd had enough of us and took off. I don't know why they let us get so close the night before.

The boys were packed up by six, probably thinking I would get on their case if we weren't early enough, but, ironically, I was the last to be ready. We left at around 6:15 and reached the base of the Inter Glacier at 6:30. We proceeded to rope up. We managed to get on the glacier at 7:15.

The glacier was in really bad shape—crevasses and exposed rock. Rob led the way with Doug on his rope, and I was last on the other rope with Mark leading and Buttons in the middle. They were all confident, and I felt content knowing that I'd trained them well and they were now experienced enough to climb this mountain. We reached Camp Schurman shortly after noon. We were the first party up there so we got the best camp spots. I took a nap while the boys boiled snow and filled the two-gallon water jug. We ate dinner around five thirty and turned in so we could get up at eleven and attempt the summit at midnight. It's really hard to sleep that early when it's still hot and sunny, but I managed to snag a few hours.

It took a long time to get ready. The other parties heard us and started to get ready too. I felt like we were in a race to the summit. We left first, Rob leading. Buttons led on our rope with me comfortably in last place. There was a freeway of headlamps behind me and I felt like I was in the Rainier 500. Rob kept stopping, which in turn stopped everyone behind us. The guy behind me started to complain and it pissed me off, so I decided to lead the way. I told Mark and Buttons to wait while I passed Rob and Doug, pulling Mark and Buttons with me. It really wasn't a smart move on my part, but I was extremely competitive and was not going to be beat by anyone.

It was a strange... I wasn't tired. I just kept going and going like the Energizer bunny; I couldn't stop.

Then Mark pulled on the rope, out of breath, and yelled, "Let's take a break!"

I looked down at their headlamps shining at me in the dark like two lost boys. I yelled back, "In about five minutes!"

This happened about four times until Mark and Buttons finally just sat down. I felt the weight of them and couldn't go any farther. They'd had enough. I wasn't even breathing hard. Seeing the freeway of headlamps about a half mile below us made me feel really good; we were winning.

Then that feeling began to fade as my conscience kicked in. I'd left Rob and Doug behind, and part of a leader's role is to keep the party together. They could be heading back down or hurt and I would never know. So, to the discontent of my rope team members, I decided to wait for them, which was one of the best decisions I made on this climb.

We were at the 13,500 foot level and the sun was just starting to peek over the hills of eastern Washington. I was mesmerized by what I was watching; witnessing the sunrise from that height never bores me. For about an hour, while six other rope teams passed us, we waited for Rob and Doug to catch up. I began to think of a song by Dan Seals as we were standing on the north face of Rainier. I thought of the words, *We are the daysprings and we all fill the pool, there's the man on the northface, Harbinger, Sage or Fool.*

The weather was not too bad, a mild wind, clear sky, and temperature near freezing. I no longer cared about being the first to summit that day. After realizing what I had done leaving Rob and Doug, being first wasn't important; getting to the summit as a team was. I chuckled, remembering how silly Alan and I had been, holding hands, walking side by side the last ten feet to the summit of the mountain we had just climbed. It had been important to us that we reached the summit as a team. We'd worked hard together to get there; we'd had each other's back. I felt his spirit with me. I wasn't going to ask the guys to hold hands, but I did want all of us to walk up together at the same time.

Rob wasn't kick-stepping when he approached us; he was angling his feet sideways like he was walking upstairs on the insides of his feet. He was in pain.

"Rob, what's wrong with your feet!" I asked.

"My blisters are bleeding," he replied.

"Do you want to go back down?"

"NO WAY!" he yelled back. "I made it this far. Nothing is going to stop me now!"

He sounded almost as if he was angry with me for leaving him behind. We rested a bit longer, ate some food, and began to head up at a right angle toward the crater rim. Rob and Doug were in the lead, and on July 17, 1986, at approximately 8:15 a.m. we reached the summit register. That was one of the most exhilarating mountain moments for me.

After we all signed it, we headed together side by side to the summit. When we walked out on that snowy little hill, each of us reacted in a different way. Buttons and Doug both screamed out a big "YEAH!!" Rob, Mark and I gave each other high fives. As I watched them stand there on top of the world, talking to each other, pointing out in the distance, shaking hands, and taking pictures of each other, I started to feel the effects of the altitude… I had a big lump in my throat. I wasn't feeling sick; I was just emotional about being there. It's a good thing I had my sunglasses on because I couldn't control the tears rolling down my face. When you stand on the summit of Mount Rainier, or any mountain, and see the incredible world we live in from that vantage point, you realize that this world is one giant gift to all of us.

We left the summit behind at ten and made it back to Camp Schurman around noon. We didn't waste any time packing up; we wanted to hurry back and tell the world what we had just accomplished. We glissaded almost the whole way down Inter Glacier and made excellent time. Exhausted and hungry, we were happy to see a picnic waiting for us when we reached the White River campground. Debbie and the kids had laid out a fried chicken lunch like she knew exactly when we would be there. I was happy that she was so supportive of my climbing and I felt amazing. I grabbed the girls one at a time and threw them up in the air. It was a perfect ending to a perfect climb.

Debbie started working from home so I never saw her co-workers again after that climb. I thought it strange that, after all that we had been through together, they never even said "Thanks". But it was okay, I feel great about taking them to the summit.

I was pretty content the months after that climb. I felt I had satisfied my climbing obsession for a while and could put climbing off for a few years and be a husband and father. Later I could join the intermediate climbing class, with hope of becoming an even better climber. Ultimately, I wanted more than anything to go to Nepal and attempt Everest someday. Rob and I talked about that dream all the time: the two of us summiting Everest together. But, could I put climbing on hold? In the summer of 1987 Rob got heavily into bodybuilding and was planning to compete. He got so big that I don't think he could have attempted Rainier. Then he hurt his knee and couldn't compete. He was devastated. He began to just focus on climbing.

Rob and I climbed Mount Baker and Big Four Mountain later in the summer. I toned things down a bit and took Melissa and Amanda on a few hikes. I thought if I put my guiding on hold for a summer it would be good for my relationship, and it did.

Chapter 15

I Know She's Out There Somewhere

"I see the world, and I'm looking from a high place
Way above it all, standing on higher ground.
I breathe the air, while they're running in a rat race
Way above it all, standing on higher ground."

— Alan Parsons/Eric Woolfson

IN THE SPRING OF 1988, Dave, who I hadn't heard from since our failed Rainier attempt in 1983, called me out of the blue. "Hey, Tim! I wanna climb Saint Helens, Mount Adams, Rainier, Glacier Peak, and Baker this summer. What do ya think?"

What did I think? "Hi, Dave, how are you? What have you been up to for the last five years?"

"Great!" he blurted out. "So what do ya think?"

"Well, I'm not sure." He'd caught me off-guard but… it sounded like a challenge, and I was always up for a challenge. But I didn't want to just climb the big mountains anymore, I wanted to climb other mountains in the Cascades. I felt like I was missing out. We talked for a while and made plans to climb Pilchuck later that spring. I talked to Debbie about what Dave had said shortly after I hung up from our phone call. She wasn't very happy with me.

"I thought you were going to put your climbing on hold for a while. You know, focus on being a dad. What happened to that?"

"It's only this summer and that's it." Another empty promise. I was not good at communicating with her. Usually, I would just not say anything or simply assure her that everything was fine. I would do whatever it took to make it up a mountain but when it came to Debbie, I never followed through with anything. She was beginning to show serious signs of resentment.

A few days before the climb up Pilchuck, Dave called and asked if he could bring a guy he worked with—who supposedly had climbing experience. I agreed. Steve, seven years younger than me and a dead ringer for Charlie Sheen, was full of himself and seemed like he was always looking for a fight. But I liked him.

I was skeptical about Steve's climbing experience. He was more of a rock climber than he was an alpinist. He had climbed Mount Shuksan in the North Cascades, which was no easy feat, but...

We climbed Pilchuck together and worked on self-arrest techniques so I could see what he knew. He had it down. We made plans to climb Mount Baker, then Rainier after that.

Then Steve asked me if I would mind taking his brother-in-law, Greg, up Rainier too.

I was irritated at first and didn't say anything for about a minute because, once again, I would be responsible for people I didn't know and would have to trust their ability to handle a potentially deadly experience. I didn't like it. I told Dave and Steve that I couldn't risk taking Greg up Rainier.

In the first two weeks of June 1988, Rob and I climbed Del Campo Peak, Big Four Mountain and Columbia Peak. The third week of June, we climbed Mount Baker. The team consisted of Rob, his soon-to-be wife Shelly, Morgan, and me. Steve couldn't make it. Rob had trained Shelly personally; she was a natural climber. Gorgeous, with long dark hair, he'd met her at a small diner while having breakfast with his ex-girlfriend. He was awestruck. They'd kept making eye contact throughout breakfast and finally he told his ex that he need to go to the bathroom. When he walked by Shelly he mumbled to her, "Meet me by the back please."

Shelly thought he was crazy, but she went back there and asked him, "What's up?"

Rob told her that he thought she was the most beautiful woman he had ever seen and wanted to see her again. She was a little confused and asked, "Aren't you with someone else?"

Rob said, "I don't love her. I love you. This has never happened to me before, and I know it will never happen again."

Just like in the movies, the two of them were together in no time. It was great to have her on the climb with us. Dave just kept staring at her. "Knock it off, Dave!" I kept saying to him. "You don't want to piss off Rob!"

We left the trailhead parking lot on Saturday morning and headed up to Heliotrope Ridge via the Kulshan Cabin trail at around nine thirty. Taking it slow, we made it to the ridge around two. It was a beautiful day. Morgan made dinner—which included a small flask of Yukon Jack and two cigars. We sat up there sipping our Yukon Jack and puffing on our cigars, looking out at the most amazing sunset ever.

We got up at three that morning and were on the summit by six thirty. It was an excellent climb. It was windy and cold but incredibly clear. Everything went almost perfectly until Shelly began to head down the Roman wall off the summit dome. She was so scared that we had to help her. She backed down the Roman Wall. We made it out in great time and went to a "do it yourself" barbeque restaurant in Glacier.

The week after the Baker climb, Rob and Shelly were married on top of Mount Erie near Anacortes. I photographed the wedding. It was a match made in heaven—they truly loved each other. I was so happy for them.

The Rainier trip was coming up soon, so I called Steve to make sure he was going. He was psyched. It was as if I had found the perfect climbing group, the "world's greatest climbers" as we called ourselves. On the last Friday in July, Morgan, Rob, Steve, Dave, and I set out to climb Mount Rainier.

Things seemed to be going well at home. Debbie seemed happy with me and my obsession… at least I thought she was.

• • •

The bitter wind gusted again—hard and then harder still. *Shit. I hope it stops soon.* I braced myself, then started walking to the shelter. I went in and shut the door behind me. I could hear it outside. *I swear that mountain knows my thoughts. Every time I think about Debbie, she starts howling.*

I thought about what happened on Rainier during that climb in 1987. Morgan and Dave had wanted to climb Rainier so bad. Steve didn't seem to care.

I didn't want to go via Disappointment Cleaver this time. We decided to do the Emmons-Winthrop Route.

• • •

The weather was perfect: hot, low humidity, blue sky, light wind from the north. It would be clear sailing to the summit if the weather held, but the weather can change fast in the mountains. I was the climb leader, the person making all the decisions, the person with all the answers. Rob had left earlier that day in hope of reserving a campsite for us at Glacier Basin. Dave and Steve were coming up later. Morgan and I left just after noon in my 1981 Subaru, listening to Alan Parsons' "Higher Ground." We were full of optimism about the climb.

When Morgan and I reached the trailhead to Glacier Basin at the White River campground, I realized I had forgotten my climbing logbook. It upset me at first, because it was always with me on my climbs; it made me feel safe. I began to get an uneasy feeling. There was a small store at the campground that had a small plastic three-ring binder. I bought it, along with a pen, but still had no paper.

We reached the trailhead at five and we set out immediately, making it to Glacier Basin in two hours and twenty minutes, which is practically a jogging pace. Steve and Dave showed up shortly after Morgan and me. Rob had found us very good campsite and we quickly got ready for dinner. We took a hike down to the White River after dinner, since Steve could not sit still for two minutes. There we met the park ranger who was staying up in the basin. She was a Gorgeous Ranger Goddess. I had to keep the boys' minds on the climb at hand. Thank goodness she had some paper for my makeshift climbing logbook. I think she thought I was going to use it for toilet paper.

In the morning, we were packed and on our way by six o'clock, which was good time considering Steve didn't like to be pushed. We arrived at the foot of Inter Glacier at 7:15, and began to rope up into two rope teams: Rob leading Steve on the first, and me leading the other two. We made short time of our ascent to the top of the glacier. On the way down from the top of Steamboat Prow to Emmons Glacier, I slipped and fell on my crampon. I managed to stab the top of my right thigh with the bottom of my left foot. A clean puncture, it wasn't too painful. I was more upset about the tear in my new Polypro underwear. Even wounded, we arrived at Camp Schurman in excellent time. There was virtually no wind so I didn't secure my new, expensive tent down. I had forgotten about the experience with my brother. I was forgetting the rules. Hey, it was a beautiful day, no wind, no signs of any foul weather, the middle of summer, about 65 degrees. We were walking around in our shorts and tank tops. Nothing to worry about… forgetting that Mount Rainier takes no prisoners.

We planned to get up at eleven in order to leave by midnight. By midday we were surrounded by at least thirty climbers at Camp Schurman, most of whom appeared incompetent like the one I'd met on Mount Baker who was clueless about his axe. One of these jokers came up to me and asked, "Ah, excuse me, but do you know what time we leave for the summit tomorrow?"

I told him, "I'm not sure, sometime around four or five in the morning."
"That early?"
Then he wanted to know if I knew how to rope up!
"Didn't you rope up on Inter Glacier coming up here?" I asked.
"Was that a glacier we came up?"

I couldn't believe that the park service let these guys come up here. I just walked away toward my two good climbing friends, shaking my head. Rob and Morgan were too wrapped up in a fierce game of chess to care about my story. So I headed back to my tent to check on my other two climbing buds. Dave was lying on top of his sleeping bag with his eyes shut and a violent headache. Steve was talking to the ranger about everything from surviving in snow caves on Mount Pilchuck to someday climbing Mount Everest, solo. I knew he would be there for a long time. Steve could carry on a conversation for a very long time; smart, but too ADHD to sit long enough to ace an IQ test.

I finally crawled back into my tent with Dave and tried to sleep. As I lay there on my sleeping bag I was lulled by the gentle hum of conversation. Then Steve came in, fidgeting, and lay down.

"Could you please stop moving around?" Dave asked Steve in a mournful voice. His headache was getting worse.

It was hard to get comfortable in a three-man tent full of guys and gear. And it was way too early and hot to be going to bed, for normal people. With Steve's thrashing about and some really smelly gas… you have a virtual hell. I lay there with my scarf over my nose to muffle the smell and listened to all the noise the other climbers were making around us: hissing stoves, clanging pots, and stupid conversations. At one point, I yelled out at two guys arguing about whether or not to put garlic in their freeze-dried spaghetti. "Put the freakin' garlic in it and shut the hell up!" I yelled out.

"Who asked you, jerk?!" one of them yelled back.

I couldn't take it anymore, so I got up and left to see how Morgan and Rob were doing on the other side of the camp. When I unzipped the door of their tent, I found them both sleeping like babies. I rolled my eyes in disgust. *Not fair.* I had reached my summit of frustration. I felt compelled to shake the tent and wake them up so that they could suffer like me, but I didn't. *At least some of us will be rested for the climb.* I walked back to my tent and tried again to fall asleep. I began thinking about Deb and the girls. *Debbie has been so supportive to me in the last two years. She feels confident about my climbing abilities and, because of my training, knows that I won't take any risks. I sense apprehensiveness in her when I tell her about my climbing plans, but we always work it out. She loves Rob, Dave, and Morgan, but she's concerned about Steve. She thinks he's reckless. It angered me at first, but then I can understand why she feels that way. My daughters don't understand what I'm doing, they seem oblivious. Melissa is eight and I never spend any time with her in the mountains. She loves her friends and playing in her new playhouse that I built for her and her sister. At three, Amanda loves to climb on things. She is a natural and finds any way she can to get up on the counter or her dresser to look out the window. I remember just last week I caught her on the monkey bars halfway across hanging there with a three-foot drop below her. I sprinted out to catch her just before she let go.* I finally fell asleep.

I was awakened by my alarm watch, and quietly woke up Dave and Steve. It was eleven and we had a lot to do to get ready for our ascent. The words of the Bruce Hornsby song, "I know she's out there somewhere, on the western skyline" kept playing over and over in my head as I looked at the lights of the Seattle skyline in the distance.

While we were getting ready, more and more climbers started to stir. In no time, many were frantically getting ready. I always get the feeling that prep time turns into some kind of a competition. Everyone wants to be the first to hit the summit. I had to prompt Steve to hurry, we were waiting for him. With our headlamps brightly lighting the way, We were the first party to leave, resembling a group of race cars at the Indy 500. Fifteen other rope teams were breathing on Steve's back behind us. I was leading one rope team with Dave in the middle and Morgan on the end. Rob was leading the other with Steve on the end. After about twenty minutes I decided to let Rob and Steve go in front because Dave was not doing too well. There were plenty of frozen footsteps to step into, so the climbing was easy. The moon appeared from behind the other side of the mountain. It was a beautiful sight as it lit up the north side. Eventually, a group of climbers tried to pass us on the right. Lo and behold, it was the group of morons that had asked me what time to leave in the morning and how to rope up. There were five of them on one rope, no prusiks, no emergency equipment, and what looked like granny knots on their harnesses. I was not going to let them pass, so I increased our pace, which didn't help Dave. We all had to stop at a large crevasse and cross a small snow bridge one at a time. I'd gotten there first. The moron party had a difficult time crossing the bridge, and we were able to distance ourselves from them at a leisurely pace. They also slowed all the other parties down behind them. We kept on going at Rob's slow pace, and at around one thirty we stopped to rest and eat. Dave was very quiet.

I barked out, "Let's get going."

Rob started with Steve following. Steve was having problems with his crampons and his headlamp. He always seemed to have some kind of equipment malfunction. Every now and then I would find a battery or screw lying in the snow.

A cold wind began to pick up. In no time it turned into a howling, freezing wind; it got ugly fast. I yelled at Steve, who was five feet ahead of me, and told him we all needed to stop and put on our foul weather gear. He yanked on the rope to stop Rob, and Rob came back down to us. My fingers and toes were getting numb and I was sure everyone else's were too.

I yelled at Morgan over the wind, "You guys OK?"

He gave me the thumbs-up. Dave was bundled up, All I could see were his eyes. He just stood there like a zombie, shivering. I yelled at Rob to go on ahead, and I watched as his headlamp faded into the darkness. The rope finally ran out and Steve began following. I turned around to see that Morgan had his arm around Dave, both were squatting down. Morgan looked at me with a pained look on his face as he got up and walked over to me. His headlamp was in my eyes so I held my hand up to block it. "I think Dave has altitude sickness," he said. "He's not feeling very good."

I could feel myself getting more irritated. "What do you mean, altitude sickness?!" I yelled back, making sure Dave could hear me too.

I walked over to Dave, bracing myself against the wind. He just looked at me and said, "I think I have altitude sickness."

"What kind of symptoms are you—" Then I remembered something important. *Oh shit! Rob and Steve think we're right behind them!* Before I let Dave say anything, I took off after the other two, but they were gone. Only the darkness and the howling wind lay before me.

Just then, some climbers caught up to us and began taking off their packs to warm up. Morgan came over to me and yelled, "I think we're gonna have to take Dave back down!"

Now, I have been in this situation many times before, and it did not make me happy. I went over to Dave and asked him how he was feeling.

"I've got to go down, Tim, I'm sick!"

"You'll feel better when the sun comes up, Dave. We're almost there! Just another thousand feet—that's it! You can do it!"

I didn't want to quit, and I didn't want Dave to quit. I was being selfish and acting arrogant.

Morgan yelled, "Tim? He could die up here!"

That's when it hit me. We're on Mount Rainier at 13,500 feet. The temperature is about 25 degrees, with the wind chill making it around −10. Rob and Steve are probably halfway between us and the summit by now and I have a sick friend roped to me that might need hospital attention. He has a wife, two sons, and a daughter who are at home sleeping. They probably prayed that night to make sure their daddy would make it back safe.

Morgan and Dave were looking at me, waiting for me to make a decision. Was there a decision to be made? *I hate this shit!!* I looked at Dave's deer eyes begging me to take him down. I looked at Morgan's angry eyes punishing me for bringing Dave with us to begin with. I looked inside myself, standing silent, listening to the howling wind. *Is this what it's all about? You take people up a mountain. You are so close to summiting then you have to take them back down because they can't make it. What am I learning here? Why is this summit so unobtainable for me? So much time and preparation involved in leading these damn climbs—all for nothing!*

I looked at them, hesitated, took a deep breath and said, "Okay, let's go."

Dave just nodded and Morgan scowled at me. The wind was practically blowing us over. I had to brace myself and Dave fell over as we were leaving. I helped him up to his feet and said, "You'll be fine, buddy. We'll get you back safe, I promise."

When he looked at me, all I could see were his sad eyes. We passed a few climbing parties on our way down. They asked me how the summit was and I had to stop and explain to them what had happened. I thought to myself that it couldn't get much worse… but it did.

The sun was just breaking over the mountains as we approached Camp Schurman. The wind, lessening a bit, was still gusting hard. We noticed that some tents had blown over and were hanging down in a crevasse. *Shit! I never secured my tent!* I immediately unroped myself when we got to Schurman and ran over to where my tent once stood. *Oh well, it was just my new 250-dollar Jan Sport four-season tent with my 150-dollar Kelty sleeping bag, a new Themarest, and all of my food. Not to mention all of Dave's and Steve's gear. All gone, nowhere to be seen… No big deal…*

Immediately, without a thought, I made Dave rope up with me to hike down the glacier to see if we could locate my stuff in a crevasse somewhere.

Morgan said, "For all we know, Tim, it could be in Enumclaw by now."

I was not interested in Morgan's humor at that point. I took Dave with me because he was trained in crevasse rescue techniques. Morgan had no clue, he'd only been trained by me in the basics. I didn't feel comfortable with Morgan. Dave was sick and, once again, I wasn't thinking right. I made him follow me into an extremely dangerous area that had crevasses all around, thinking only that my tent must be around somewhere.

Then Dave said something that made sense, "Tim, I don't think your tent is worth risking our lives for."

I took a deep breath and closed my eyes in frustration. I realized he was right. I turned to see him lying in the snow trying not to throw up. I felt like an idiot. I didn't know what to say, so I just said, "Come on, let's go back up."

After we reached Camp Schurman, Dave's face was white and he was coughing. He looked terrible; I felt terrible. "Go crawl into Rob's and Morgan's tent and try to get some sleep, bud." I gave him some aspirin and off he went.

Morgan was unhappy about not making it to the summit and he was blaming Dave. And me. "If you knew he had physical problems, why did you bring him up here?" he drilled me.

Years before, Dave had contracted viral meningitis and he was never the same after he got out of the hospital. I was in no mood to be berated and have to defend my friend, and I told Morgan, "Dave has more qualifications than you'll ever have! He at least has formal training and knows how to rescue someone. What do you know? I'll tell you what, Morgan, next time you can pay the guide service to take you up here! Okay?"

Morgan didn't say anything. We were both spent, and I was not really thinking about what I was saying. Morgan went over to the spot where my tent had been. He laid down in a fetal position and used my collapsible five-gallon water jug as a pillow. He looked like a baby and in no time was sleeping.

I was not in the mood for sleep. I was irritated and wanted to find my fucking tent. I looked off in the direction my tent had probably gone and noticed that about ten feet below me, a group of climbers were sleeping. At least they appeared to be sleeping. One of them, who looked like one of the nerds in the movie *Revenge of the Nerds*, looked up at me, so I asked him if he had seen a tent go by. He answered in a condescending tone, "A tent? No, not really."

He didn't sound convincing. I turned around and looked at Morgan lying there, snoring, and wondered when Rob and Steve would be getting back. There was nowhere to lie down, nowhere to sit, and I was at the peak of frustration. I kept looking down at the climbers that were all lying in a row in their warm sleeping bags. Then one of them looked up at me and I said, "Why didn't you guys go for the summit?"

He answered back with, "It was too cold!"

Really?! I couldn't believe what I was hearing. *These guys are climbers? Pussies.* "Are you sure you didn't see a tent fly down around you?" I was desperate.

"Well, now that you mentioned it, there was this green tent-like thing that landed on us earlier. We pushed it off. I think it went that way." He said, pointing to the east.

My heart rate was already above normal from the altitude, but now I was boiling. I can't remember exactly what I said, but it was something like, "You stupid assholes. You knew I've been trying to find my fucking tent and none of you fucking idiots would tell me that you saw it?"

I'd awoken all five of them and they weren't happy either. I didn't give a shit, but I thought I better try to smooth things over. After all, we were sharing the same mountain and you never know when you might need a friend out there. Besides, I didn't have Rob to cover my back. So I went down and explained to them what I had just been through and they were somewhat understanding.

Rob and Steve finally made it back. They had been the only ones to summit because of the violent weather. They both rambled on and on about how Rob saved Steve by keeping him warm in an emergency shelter that he'd built. Then Rob literally pulled Steve up to the summit. I said, "That's no surprise, Steve, he does that all the time."

It was an incredible story to those who were interested, but I was only interested in getting my tent back. After they finished, I began telling them my woes. Rob looked at me and said, "It's no big deal, Tim. We'll get your tent, no problem. Don't worry!" I love Rob, he is so confident. Like it would just happen and I had nothing to worry about. I began to feel better.

The three of us roped up and hiked down the glacier about a hundred feet. We hiked right over to a huge crevasse that might contain my tent We had to climb around it and put in protection devices. I approached the lower part of the crevasse cautiously and looked over the edge. There, wedged in the dirty ice about twenty feet down, was my tent. We quickly set up another anchor and lowered Steve down to it. He grabbed it and we pulled him up with it. It was simple.

I was happy until I began beat myself up for being such a jerk. It was my own fault that the tent blew away because of my negligence. Yet I was taking it out on everyone, including those other climbers.

Dave began to feel better, so we packed up and left Camp Schurman. As we descended, I turned around and took a long, wistful look back. When we reached the campground, Debbie, the kids, and Dave's wife and his kids were waiting for us with lunch. I felt bad for Dave. I knew his obsession to climb that mountain was controlling his emotions, but he tried to keep it hidden. I could see it in his eyes as he listened to Rob and Steve relate their incredible story to everyone around. I didn't mention anything about my tent. We never did climb the rest of the volcanoes in Washington. We all went off in different directions, to the other realities of our lives.

Chapter 16

Falling into Recklessness

"I think I mainly climb mountains because I get a great deal of enjoyment out of it. I never attempt to analyze these things too thoroughly, but I think that all mountaineers do get a great deal of satisfaction out of overcoming some challenge which they think is very difficult for them, or which perhaps may be a little dangerous."

— Edmund Hillary

IN EARLY AUGUST 1988, Rob and I made plans to climb Rainier together—just the two of us. But it turned out he had some friends who also wanted to summit. So once again, we didn't climb just for us. Taking people to the summit was beginning to irritate me. *Why are we doing this and not getting paid?*

They were a group of inexperienced climbers, hikers really, and they treated us like we were their servants. We did the Emmons-Winthrop Route. It was a successful climb, even though I pissed them off by ragging on them about the importance of being ready when I said so. "Conditions can change extremely fast, and if you don't get a jump on leaving before the other climbers, you can be waiting for parties and risking symptoms of exposure!" I really didn't care whether I ever saw those people again or not.

It was a fast descent after minimal time on the summit. I was in a hurry to get back to Debbie, since she was not happy when I left. I was spending less time with her and the girls and I could tell it was beginning to upset her. After this climb I felt maybe it would be good to take time for my family.

In the fall of 1988 things were not going well for me at work or at home. I was having difficulty with communicating with Debbie and I couldn't figure out how to fix it. My job was not going well and things were beginning to change with the hierarchy of my employer. They were making cuts and I was under a lot of stress. Then, that September, my mom asked us if we wanted to move into my grandmother's house and take care of it until they could sell it. It was a beautiful old house on Serene Lake in Lynnwood. Debbie didn't want to do it but I did. After a while, she conceded.

• • •

I sat down again next to my pack and lay back, looked up at the sky, and recollected the events of 1988 and 1989.

We were renting out our house in Marysville and living rent-free at my grandmother's house. I thought it was a perfect time for me to go back to school and learn digital electronics. I was tired of the printing business and felt I needed to learn something that would benefit my future. Debbie resisted. I told her I would find a part-time job to help pay the bills while I went to school. When Garry learned that I needed a job, he asked me to come work for him and his construction business. "You can start whenever you want" he told me. It was a full-time job with night school—it would be hard, but I could do it. I told him it would be in the fall of 1989. He was okay with that.

• • •

In the spring of 1989, I was mostly focused on getting registered at Edmonds College so climbing was not a priority, for a change. But that all changed when Rob called one night in early May to invite me to join him and Steve to climb Mount Baker in a day. "Mount Baker in a day? Are you guys crazy?"

At first I really didn't want to go. I declined and left them without a leader. It weighed heavily on my mind, though, to think that Rob and Steve were going to climb a mountain without me. I couldn't take it. Late that Friday night before their climb, I decided to go.

When I told Debbie, it was the first time in our relationship she displayed resentment with words of anger. She forbade me to go and threatened to leave me. I was torn inside. I thought about it and said I wouldn't go. Then I thought about Rob and Steve, and this uneasy feeling came over me. *Something is going to happen to them if I don't go.* I made a final decision and found her standing in the kitchen. The girls were in bed, asleep, and the house was quiet. I told her that I had to go. She got quiet for a moment and looked out the window at the lake. Off in the distance, you could hear some ducks. I could see her chin quivering and her eyes watering. She looked back at me and said. "Go, if it means that much to you, just go."

I didn't know what to say. I was happy, but not. My head was spinning and I wasn't feeling at ease with what was going on between us. I put my pack together and was ready to go by ten that night. I was still not sure if I was making the right decision. *Am I petting the sow again?* I ended up sleeping downstairs in the guest room.

I jumped out of bed the second the alarm went off and was out the door fifteen minutes later. When I got to Steve's, he wasn't ready. He came out and said, "I don't know man, I'm not feeling up for this." I just looked at him and said, "Get in the fucking car!"

We picked up Rob and made it to the trailhead in only two and a half hours. We put on our packs and off we went, running up the trail. At five in the morning, we were the only ones around. We were like obsessed machines stomping up toward the summit with nothing on our minds but getting it over with. What were we trying to prove? I wasn't sure.

Rob was first, with Steve in the middle and me last. The sun was just starting to shine on us about halfway up the trail, and all we could hear was heavy breathing and boots stomping. We arrived at the lower part of Coleman Glacier by six thirty, roped up, and were on our way in ten minutes. The whole thing was like a dream; we hardly said anything to each other; we just knew what to do and did it. We didn't put on our crampons, we used the frozen footsteps that were all laid out for us on a direct route to the summit. We passed many climbers who asked us what time we had left and were amazed to find out we had left the parking lot at five. Rob finally stopped at the bottom of the pumice ridge just before heading up the Roman Wall. The wall where Mark had tumbled down three years earlier. I told Steve that this is "Mark's wall" and explained what had happened, hoping it wouldn't happen again. As we began our final ascent to the summit, I ran out of steam. It didn't stop Rob, though. He began pulling me up, literally dragging me about fifty feet. I couldn't believe it and neither could Steve. We rested for a while and then walked the rest of the way side by side onto the summit dome of Mount Baker. It was nine o'clock.

I don't think I could ever repeat that feat again, even if I wanted to. We hiked over to the center of the dome and I lay down and fell asleep. Rob woke me abruptly to tell me that I was snoring too loud—loud enough to make other people take notice. I didn't care. Rob and Steve were laughing. It was ten o'clock and they wanted to head back down, so off we went.

First we ran, then it turned into a sitting glissade. We made it down the glacier so fast that we acted like we were in a marathon or something. I couldn't stop. After we unroped, I started to run down ahead of them and then it became a race to the trailhead. I came upon a family at a small creek that had just removed their shoes to wade through, and I came crashing through in my climbing boots and gear, spraying water all over them. I must have seemed like a real ass!

We ran out from the trail onto the road at five minutes to one. Four hours up, three hours down, seven hours total. Incredible, huh? I don't think there are a lot of people who could do that now, although I wouldn't recommend trying it. The three of us were pumped for a while after that climb and, two weeks later, we decided to tackle Glacier Peak—marathon-style.

Chapter 17

The World's Greatest Climbers

"Yes we are the world's greatest climbers,
We leave all the others behind us,
We'll climb all the mountains before the day's through,
We run down and drink all the brew"

I HEARD A NOISE THAT STARTLED ME for a moment. I looked up quickly. It sounded like it came from somewhere around the top of Cadaver Gap. I squinted as I scanned the area. It sounded almost like something metal that echoed. Then I noticed something I hadn't before. There were tracks leading up there. Someone had climbed through the gap recently. I thought about Steve again. Debbie was right, he was reckless and inexperienced. I liked him, though, and thought that if Rob and I took him up Glacier Peak it would increase his skills and make him a better climber. Also, we needed a third guy. Rob and I wanted to start a guide service. We were confident and excited about the idea. Although Rob had reservations about Steve.

• • •

Steve and I were averaging sixty miles an hour up roads that were designed for thirty-five, tops. My Subaru was worthy of the task. We left Steve's apartment in Lynnwood at 5 am and I was obsessed with getting there as fast as possible.

"Why are you driving so fast, Tim? I'm getting sick."

"I want to get to Kennedy Hot Springs before Rob gets out of his tent. I want to surprise him. I told him we wouldn't get there before noon." Rob had left the previous day.

We were arguing about who the greatest guitar player of all time was. As we rounded a corner at fifty, rocks and dust flying behind us, a bear cub ran out onto the road in front of us. I swerved and barely missed him. "I hope his mother isn't around, she might be a bit pissed at you, Tim."

I just pretended like it hadn't fazed me at all, but my hand were shaking slightly. We skidded to a stop going sideways and into a parking spot at the trail head at 6:35 a.m. "I always like to make a dramatic entrance," I told Steve as I jumped out of the car.

We threw on our packs and were hiking by 6:45, practically running up there. I felt great, and with Steve leading the way with his long legs, we were making good time. We were still arguing about musicians. I thought piano players made better songwriters than guitar players. Steve was in complete disagreement, but it made the hiking time go by fast. When we reached Kennedy Hot Springs, Rob had just started his breakfast. He was shocked to see us. "Hey, you guys, what time did you leave? Two a.m.?"

"Nah, we left Lynnwood at seven…"

Rob just laughed and shook his head in disbelief. He knew I was kidding. He knew me well.

He was all packed up by nine and off we went to our destination: the summit of Glacier Peak. We were actually thinking of just going straight for the summit that day rather than trying it in the morning. We were crazy. We called ourselves the World's Greatest Climbers. We even made up a dumb, Swiss-style theme song. It wasn't quite as good as Alan's and my song, mainly because it wasn't pot-induced. *We are the world's greatest climbers, we leave all the others behind us, we climb all the mountains before the days through, we run down and drink all the brew!*

Shortly after we hit the trail, we ran into a guy who had a huge malamute husky with him. He'd walked all the way from Madison, Wisconsin, with his dog and the clothes on his back. What he was doing up there, we couldn't quite figure out.

We began climbing the back-breaking, blister-burning switchbacks, which I nicknamed the "Brother John Switchbacks" in honor of my brother who had, years before lost his climbing virginity on them. It was ten when we reached the top of the ridge and we hit snow. There was no trail anywhere. No frozen footsteps, nothing. That's when I did something that I had never done before in all my years of climbing: We created our own frozen footsteps.

I navigated the three miles using my map and compass, and found the route to Boulder Basin, with Rob's help of course. It was about twelve thirty when we reached the cutoff to the basin. Steve was impressed. He gave me what he called the "Old Groaner" award of the day, which didn't amount to anything but a pat on the back.

We were running out of time to make the summit that day. "We lost a lot of time trying to find our way, so I suggest we try to make time."

They just looked at me with sweat dripping off their heads, breathing hard, and said, "Okay, Sir!"

It took us quite a while to get up there. It's very steep. I hadn't been up there for nine years and it was a lot different in sunny weather. A couple hours later, we walked out of the trees into the open area of Boulder Basin. There was no way we would try for the summit that day. We hiked up to the foot of the glacier and made camp. It was about the same place that Gary, Morgan, John, and I had camped years before.

Steve kept trying to call his brother on his ham radio while Rob and I looked at the map to figure out a plan of attack. We were the only ones up there.

We watched the beautiful sunset and the lights of Seattle appear. We fixed dinner and, as we ate, Steve and I continued our discussion about piano players versus guitar players. "What about Elton John?" "What about Chet Atkins?" and on and on into the night it went. Rob just quietly sat by and gazed off at the mountains.

After a restless night, with Rob talking in his sleep and Steve rolling all over us, we were up at three in the morning. We ate breakfast and began to climb at four. Rob led, with Steve in the middle of the rope, and yours truly on the end. We had to keep backtracking because we couldn't find a route. We had to keep stopping and pulling out the map, compass, and altimeter to figure out where we were. The snow was frozen so hard that our crampons could hardly dig in. As Rob climbed on ahead, the ice particles that came off his crampons rushed down beside me, making a tinkling sound like wind chimes. It reminded me of the beginning of "Shine On You Crazy Diamond" by Pink Floyd. As I sat there waiting for the both of them to get far enough ahead for me to start going up, that song played over and over in my head.

Glacier is not an easy mountain to climb, and all the memories of 1980 were coming back to me. When we reached Sitkum Ridge, Rob was beat and Steve had blisters. So much for the world's greatest climbers. Steve was trying to call his brother on his ham radio again while Rob and I decided on the best route to follow.

It's weird how you can't see the summit because it's so steep. We headed off to the right of the ridge and came to a small gully that went straight up to what we thought was the summit. Steve was ready to turn back, but Rob talked him out of it. Rob kept pounding his way up the gully, trying to kick steps out of the ice but it was tough going. When we reached the top of the gully, there was yet another steep hill in front of us. "It's the never-ending mountain!" Steve shouted out. "What's the elevation of this mountain, Tim? Fifteen thousand feet? Are you sure we're on Glacier Peak and not on Rainier?"

The questions wouldn't stop. Rob just looked at me like, "Please shut this guy up."

We were almost to the top of the hill when we realized this was it: the summit. We were here! It was a great relief. We practically fell on our knees. What an incredible view! We could see into Canada and eastern Washington. Years after summiting in a blinding storm in 1980, I finally got to see what the world looks like from the top of Glacier Peak.

It took us six hours to reach the summit from the base camp, which really wasn't that bad considering we had to create our own route. We headed back down via an easier, and faster, route. We were back at base camp by one o'clock, and decided to break camp as fast as we could. We left at two. On our way down, though, we ran into some problems. Our footsteps from the day before had melted and vanished. Once again we got lost. All the ridges look the same up there, and with snow, it's hard to tell where you are. So we had to take out the map, compass, and altimeter.

I thought we had gone too far south, so I sent Steve north on a scouting mission to see if he could pick up our footprints from the day before. As he walked away from me, I began thinking about the possibility of him getting lost, so I followed behind him after telling Rob to wait for us to come back. He didn't realize I was behind him. I started to climb over a large log on my belly and Steve yelled out, "Oh, shit!"

I said, "What?"

"A fucking bear!"

I stopped halfway across the log, then yelled back, "Where!"

"Right there! In front of me!"

I slid off the log and landed on the ground as gracefully as a smelly, sweaty guy with a sixty-pound pack on his back could. Then Steve yelled, "RUN!"

I got up and ran over to an old dead tree with no bark on it and frantically started to climb it. Then Steve said, "Wait a minute, what are you doing over here, Tim?"

I looked down at him from about ten feet up and asked, "What do ya mean, what am I doing over here? I was following you."

"Why were you following me?"

"Because I didn't want you to get lost." I began to slide down off the tree.

"Aren't we already lost? How could I get lost if we're already lost?"

"Well, I didn't want you to get even lost-er. Where's your bear?"

By then, Rob had meandered over to see what was going on. He figured it out the minute I said, "Steve saw a bear."

We deduced that the bear was the black tent bag that was tied to the top of my pack. As I was climbing over the log, all Steve could see was a black thing moving in the trees. I began to laugh hysterically, but Rob didn't find it all that funny.

Steve tried to shift the blame on me by saying, "Well, if you hadn't been following me or if you'd told me you were behind me, I wouldn't have freaked."

Rob just wanted to get going so we looked for a way down, but to no avail. We were drenched, shivering, and exhausted. With no food left between us, we knew we had to find the route back before we ran out of daylight. The snow was deep, and hard to negotiate with heavy packs on. Everything looks the same when you're lost: the trees, the rocks, the snow. We trudged on as if in a trance. It wasn't until we felt broken and defeated, bereft of hope, that we came upon a set of frozen footsteps. Our hearts were gladdened; our spirits began to soar—for we recognized them as the same footsteps we had created on the way up. They would lead us back home safely.

Chapter 18

Dancing on the Summit

"Rising and falling lighter than air, Silently calling, no one is there,
Oh, bird that is flying so high and so free, Closer to heaven than you and me"

— Alan Parsons/Eric Woolfson

WE'D BARELY RECOVERED FROM GLACIER when we began to make plans to climb Rainier. This time we were going to climb it via the Kautz Route. I tried to talk Dave into going, but he didn't feel comfortable about it. Steve asked me again if we could take his brother-in-law Greg. Greg was an avid rock climber and knew climbing well. So I gave in and said okay this time. The climbing party members was going to be Morgan, Steve, Greg, Rob, and me. We left Friday, July 7th 1989 and planned for two nights on the mountain. Morgan and Rob met me at my house at ten thirty. It was overcast with mild temperatures in the city. The forecast was for rain that weekend. I didn't care. I've had to turn around so many times off that mountain that one more time wouldn't matter. Morgan drove his '83 Subaru up to Paradise. I tortured Morgan by making him listen to Alan Parsons' "Stereotomy" and "Gaudi." When we reached Paradise, it was extremely foggy. We could hardly see the lodge. We met Steve and Greg next to the information booth. We put together a plan of action. I was always regarded as the climb leader and took on that responsibility automatically. The others argued about routes

161

and other climbing-related things, but I always had the final say and they respected that.

We left the parking lot at 2:45 and started up the asphalt trail. It always seems so strange to me to begin a fourteen thousand foot expedition on an asphalt trail. I don't think there are any asphalt trails on Mount Everest… asixty-five pound pack and climbing boots are not the best attire for the hard surface of asphalt trails. It was much better when we finally reached the dirt trail and headed down onto Nisqually Glacier. It was so foggy that all we could see was the big black pumice rocks and dirt embedded in the ice of the glacier in front of us. We circumvented a couple of crevasses. There were plenty of frozen footsteps to follow while I led the way. Steve and Greg were on the other rope.

There was a steep cliff at the other side of the glacier and a small gully that led up to the lower part of Wilson Glacier. It was steep going up the gully but we finally made it and began our traverse over to Wilson Glacier, which leads up to the Turtle. The Turtle is a giant snowfield that is shaped, coincidentally, like a turtle. In every picture you see of Rainier from Paradise, the Turtle is an unmistakable landmark. It took us four hours to reach the upper part of Wilson Glacier, and when we got there, the fog was below us and we were basking in the evening sun. We decided to make camp there at 9,452 feet, almost as high as Camp Schurman. We were all feeling really good. Of course, Morgan had brought Yukon Jack and cigars for the after-dinner sunset.

We got up around six o'clock. We ate a leisurely breakfast and got ready to go up the Turtle. I was a lot more relaxed, so didn't bark commands like usual. I didn't know how Greg would take to my usual persuasiveness, so I tempered it. He knew a lot more about rock climbing than I did, so I found him intimidating. I didn't feel comfortable being his climb leader.

We left our first camp at 9:30 a.m. and headed straight up toward the Turtle. "Man! This is a lot farther than it looked!" Greg shouted when we were about halfway up the Turtle.

"Everything on Mount Rainier is bigger than it looks from a distance, Greg," I said back.

It was noon. We were standing on the whitest snow I have ever seen. The sky was the deepest blue you can imagine. About 5,000 feet below us, a sea of clouds covered everything for as far as we could see, with the exception of Mount Adams, Mount Saint Helens, and Mount Hood. Looking west, a sea of clouds stretched out across Puget Sound to the Olympics. There was just a vast sea of clouds to the east. The heat was unbearable.

We stopped twice on the way up, and I estimated our arrival at Camp Hazard would be around one thirty. Camp Hazard is located right below the Kautz Ice Cliff. Its elevation is 11,500 feet. The ice drapes down on either side of Camp Hazard. It's protected because of its unique shape, like a triangular wedge. It can accommodate about ten to twelve climbers.

We reached Hazard at exactly 1:15 p.m., and I must say, my party was quite impressed with my ability to estimate climbing time. Not like when I would totally under estimate things and it would get me in trouble. I had become a bit wiser. After finding a good spot for tents, we set up camp. It was very warm and there was water melting off the ice cliff above us. So Steve and I hiked up with everyone's water bottles so we wouldn't have to melt snow. Not long after we left, Greg began to get altitude sickness. It's strange how it affects some people and not others. Steve and I crawled around getting water under a giant slab of ice. I was jumping from rock to rock like a little kid, not thinking about the fact that we were 11,500 feet above sea level and the air was a lot thinner. As I was gathering water, I looked down the steep large ice field I was standing on. It led down to rocks. One slip would have meant instant death but it didn't even faze me. As I walked off the ice with as many water bottles as I could carry, I began to feel sick, and in no time at all the effects of altitude were setting in. I staggered back to camp. Steve came down about ten minutes later, complaining of nausea. Rob and Morgan were smart. They had rested when we arrived and acclimatized themselves. So while I lay there sucking on Rolaids with Greg, they set up the tents and got everything ready for the climb in the morning. Once all the work was done, I began to feel better.

Later, Greg climbed out of Steve's tent feeling alive again. He wasn't sure if he could make it up to the summit in the morning, but we talked him into trying. I wanted to get up just after midnight and leave by one thirty. I didn't really know how long it would take to get to the summit on this route, or what the conditions were like, so I wanted to play it safe by leaving extra early. It was six when we turned in. It was still hot and muggy, and there was no wind—bizarre weather for the mountain.

Rip Van Winkle couldn't have slept in that tent, between Morgan's gas and Rob's sneezing. I was about ready to crawl into Steve's and Greg's tent, but then they started in with the farting. *If you can't beat them, join them.* We attempted the "Blue Danube Waltz" with four fart tubas. Greg would occasionally add a long belch for emphasis.

My watch alarm went off, but it didn't wake me up. I wasn't asleep. I had lain there all night listening to Rob and Morgan roll around, farting and sneezing. I was feeling apprehensive about the climb. I had never climbed this route. The what-ifs had stressed me out. But I didn't want my climbing party to know how I felt, except Rob. Rob was my strength.

Whenever I felt this way about a climb, Rob would reassure me that things would be fine. There was a lot to be responsible for, and for the first time I didn't feel so immortal. This wasn't fun anymore; it was like a job to get four guys up a mountain and safely get them down. I realized I wasn't climbing the mountain for me. *I was taking a group of guys, mainly Morgan because of what had happened the previous year, to experience the summit of Mount Rainier. In fact, I don't think I ever summited Mount Rainier just for me.*

It was almost one o'clock when I finally got up and began to get ready. Rob and Morgan followed suit. Steve and Greg heard us and got ready too. A half hour later, Rob, Morgan, and I were roped up, ice axes in hand, packs on, food in our bellies, crampons on, watching Steve and Greg try to fix Steve's MSR stove.

"Steve," Rob said, his voice tinged with anger. "You can use my stove."

"I don't want to use your stove! If I wanted to use your stove, I'd have asked for your stove! Okay?" Steve was not in a good mood.

"Well, if we don't leave by two, we might as well forget it," I added, not hiding the fact that I was pissed off.

164

Morgan interjected. "I didn't come all this way to have to turn around and go back because of a stove! Why don't we just leave them here and go without them?"

Steve didn't like that remark and said something back, and then it got ugly. I'm not sure how or why, but—still roped together—Rob, Morgan, and I crawled back into the tent and waited for them to figure it out. Deep down I really didn't want to go anyway, and was looking for any excuse to get out of it.

Steve finally fixed his stove and cooked his food, and while he was out there cussing and throwing things around, Rob was sneezing in Morgan's face. Not to be outdone, Morgan stuck his butt in Rob's face and let out one of his most potent chili-farts of the night. "That's it. I'm outta here!" I crawled out of the tent and sat on a rock looking at the stars while Steve and Greg finished their meal and got roped up. While pondering my life and where it was going, a bright shooting star went by. For the first time that night, I felt okay about everything.

We were finally ready to go at three. It took fifteen minutes to climb down the ice shoot to Kautz Glacier. I let Rob lead the way with me in the middle so I could tell him which way to go, and also to keep an eye on everyone else. Steve and Greg were behind us.

For the first thousand feet, the route was almost vertical. It's one of the steepest grades I've ever climbed. The ice was breaking off and falling from Rob kicking steps and it would hit pretty hard. Not all of us were wearing hard hats and Greg got beaned a couple of times. Then Steve's crampon broke. He climbed up to me so I could try to fix it, but to no avail. The thing was shot. So Steve climbed the rest of the way with no crampons.

The glacier began to level off a bit as we headed toward the upper Nisqually Glacier. It only took us an hour to get there, then another hour to reach the bottom of the crater rim. We were making great time, but I had to keep stopping to rest. Rob and Morgan were anxious to keep going, but I was exhausted. I hadn't slept since Friday night. Mix that with the altitude and it's a wonder I could stand up.

Rob kept yelling down to me, "Come on, Tim, we're almost there!"

The sun was coming up over the mountains. We climbed up a little farther and I fell down on my knees again. Rob was about ten feet from the crater rim, so he just pulled me up like he was pulling up an anchor. After he pulled me up to him, he hiked up to the top of the rim. Then he just kept pulling me up toward him. I didn't care, I let him pull me up the rest of the way. Morgan couldn't believe what he was seeing. The three of us sat and waited for Steve and Greg to join us. I just lay there, falling in and out of sleep.

I managed to look at my watch when I heard Greg fall down next to me. It was 6:43 a.m. and he was sick. Rob, Morgan and Steve all unroped and walked over to Columbia Crest while Greg and I just lay there. "Hey Greg, you gonna make it okay?"

"I think so. Just tell me when we can leave."

"We gotta get up and walk over to the summit, man. If I can do it, so can you."

He didn't say anything to me.

"I'm going to get up now, Greg, and I'm going to walk over there. You can do it too, okay?"

He didn't say anything. It was about another three hundred yards to the summit, but it seemed like three miles. I kept lying there saying, "Okay, here I go."

Then I watched Rob and Steve dance around on the summit. That did it for me; I finally got up enough energy. I stood and said, "Well, here goes one of the world's greatest climbers," and began walking over to the summit.

Greg got up and walked behind me. By the time I got there, I was beginning to feel better. Morgan came over and yelled, "We made it!" and gave me a big high five. He was a very happy man.

The sun was up over all the clouds below us and the tops of the mountains were poking through. There was no wind and it was a balmy forty-five degrees. I walked up to Rob and Steve, who were standing on the summit with great big smiles on their faces. We shook hands and Rob handed me an open can of Rainier beer. I took a big gulp. "This is great! It doesn't get any better than this!"

Rob and Steve just laughed. Greg lay at our feet, moaning. We talked him into taking a gulp of beer, but he didn't believe it would make him feel better. He was wrong. Five minutes later he stood up, feeling better. Beer—the magic elixir, the remedy for mountain sickness. How it works, I'll never know, but it does work. It's a good thing to take up with you.

We took some great pictures, signed the summit register, and, after our shared ordeal, we all became great friends again as we shared our victory. This is why we climb mountains: it gives you a high like no high you could ever get from drugs—a spiritual high, like you are closer to God.

We left at eight forty-five and made it back to Hazard in an hour and a half. Incredible time. We walked over to our tents, took off our boots and harnesses, threw down our ice axes, and crashed for about an hour. Debbie was to meet us at Paradise at four o'clock, so we had plenty of time before we needed to leave. After a solid one-hour nap, I felt really good. We quickly broke camp and got ready to go.

We slid straight down the Turtle on our butts with one thing on our minds: icy cold beer at the lodge. When we got to Nisqually Glacier, the fog was like pea soup. We made it across okay, but then… that dreaded asphalt trail. I hate the stinking asphalt trails; we got lost again. It was worse than a maze in the fog. It took us forty-five minutes of backtracking and going in all directions until I finally asked someone which way the lodge was. Man did I feel dumb. One of the world's greatest climbers once again had to ask for assistance from some greenhorn from Kansas who had never seen a mountain in his life before that day. We eventually made it to the car and then into the lodge for that icy cold pitcher of beer. We made it back to our wives and families—to the "real" world. I will always remember the challenge, the pain, and the triumph of that weekend.

Chapter 19

A Toast to the Climbing Rope That Was Used Too Late

"Within each of us there is a delicate part that can be broken.
It is called the human spirit. It heals but is never the same."

I LOOKED AT MY WATCH: 8:55. *I've been up here almost an hour.* I took a long draw from my CamelBak. It tasted better than usual, like the water from the dispenser at my old job. *When was that?* I left there in 1989. So much has happened since then. My heart ached for that time as I thought about how much I loved my little girls, how important they were to me, and how much I loved my wife and all she did for me. I was young, naïve, and so unhappy with my job. It affected my relationship. Deb would always say to me, "I just want you to be happy. All you have is now, Tim. Make the best of it."

I worked hard to make the best of now. *Now is eternal.* I grabbed some pumice and began tossing the tiny stones as I counted. *All the years that I dreamed about the future and dwelled in the past, never thinking about how important the now is. It's all that exists.*

• • •

169

I finally quit my job in September. I had reached a summit in my life, and was about to embark on a new mountain. This mountain, unbeknownst to me, was deadly.

It all started innocently. I went back to school to learn digital electronics. I felt it would help me find a better career. Then I went to work for Garry's construction company during the day. He was my best friend, always there to help me no matter what. I think he wanted me to learn the business and eventually become a partner. The partner part I could handle; learning the business was the problem. It was a very physical business and I had spent the last seven years basically sitting down on the job.

Things went well at first, but by mid-October, everything started to unravel. Living in my grandmother's house and renting out our house in Marysville was getting to be too much for Debbie. We decided to sell our house, buy property, and have Garry build us a house. Our house sold in two days, but trying to find property was virtually impossible. We finally found five acres near Snohomish. We tried to secure financing. Between my working full-time and going to school full-time, the burden was left on Debbie. When my grandmother's house sold, we had to move in with Debbie's parents. It was okay at first, but when things didn't work out with our property, we became somewhat of a burden on them. Then, one week before Christmas, a co-worker and I were erecting a sixteen-foot wall at a jobsite and the bottom of the wall broke loose, crashing down on me. It didn't break my back, thank God, but it was a bad sprain. I couldn't work for a while. I also couldn't go to class.

I slowly improved through weeks of physical therapy and by summer I was back in shape, but I didn't want to return to construction. I found a job working for another printing company. Things were getting better. We had our property, I had a job again, we were still living with the in-laws. All was well. Then Debbie had something to tell me: "I'm pregnant, Tim." Melissa and Amanda were ecstatic to get a baby sister or brother, but thatdidn't matter to me. I was focused mostly on starting the guide service business. So I was happy with everything. I also wanted to climb Rainier again.

Rob and I planned another Rainier summit trip in the spring of 1991. It had been almost two years since we last climbed. Rob and Steve were chomping at the bit to go, and for me to be their leader. They acted like they couldn't go without me. May didn't work out, so we aimed for June to climb Glacier Peak in preparation for Rainier. Debbie was upset. In fact, once again she forbade it. "Why do you want to do this? You've climbed it before, please don't go!"

I thought she was freaking out because she was pregnant or because of what had happened to my back, so I didn't take it too seriously. We discussed it further and I explained to her that it had been two long years since I had done anything, and I really needed this. She begrudgingly gave in… again.

A week before the climb, Steve called and told me that his brother had lost his hand in an accident at work, and that he didn't think he should go. He was really shook up about it. We decided to postpone the climb. Then on Wednesday, he called back and said he'd changed his mind. "Make up your mind, Steve. Do you want to go or not?" He wanted to go. He asked if Greg could go too. I told him absolutely.

I picked up Steve and Greg on Friday afternoon. Greg had always wanted to climb Glacier Peak, so I was happy to bring him. Rob joined us and we all climbed into my new Subaru. We headed to the Kennedy Hot Springs trailhead while listening to the Allmann Brothers. Steve and I played air guitar. It was hard to drive and play air guitar at the same time. Rob and Greg sat in the back, talking about previous climbs. It was overcast when we got to the parking lot and started heading down the trail.

After we had arrived at Kennedy Hot Springs, we didn't waste any time setting up camp by the river and eating our dinner. It was raining and we didn't want to go into the smelly hot springs, so we just turned in for the night.

Not optimistic about climbing in lousy weather, we didn't push ourselves to get up early the next morning. After breakfast, we took a vote on whether to continue or not. Rob didn't really want to go any farther because he'd just had a vasectomy and wasn't feeling comfortable. Steve and I, on the other hand, wanted to go up because we both thought the clouds were low enough that we could get above them at Boulder Basin. Greg wasn't sure one way or another, so to break the tie, he voted with Steve and me to go on. In the face of Rob's discomfort, we went up the trail.

"Just think of the good shape you'll be in after we get back, Rob!" I spouted off as we rounded the first switchback.

There was a miserable, cold, misty rain. When we finally reached the top of the ridge where the trail flattens out, it was getting foggy and the rain was diminishing. We rested at Boulder Basin for some time, so Rob could regain his strength. Nobody seemed real keen about continuing. There was quite a bit of snow all around and we knew that it was going to be a difficult climb. I finally broke the silence with, "Well, we had better get going if we want to do this."

Nobody answered. So I got up and began hiking up the trail. Steve followed. Rob and Greg just looked at each other with disgust, and then got up and joined us. It seemed like it took us forever to get up there this time. We kept stopping every five minutes, mostly because it was hard to find the trail in the fog. I really thought that we could get above the clouds if we kept going up past Boulder Basin and camped up on the lower part of Sitkum Glacier. So after reaching the basin we kept going up, and up, and up, and up.

"How long are we going to go up, Tim?" Rob yelled up to me.

"I don't know, I guess we can stop when we find a flat area to camp at!" I yelled back.

It was getting so foggy that we could hardly see ten yards in front of us. My lightweight trail boots were soaked; I hadn't wanted to take the time to put on my big climbing boots. Instead, I was lugging them in my pack. We finally found a flat area below the lower part of Sitkum Glacier. After setting up camp, we got into our tents and tried to dry off. Rob set up his stove and we hung our boots up over the flames. It smelled like cooked boot in our tent.

Steve yelled out at us, "Hey, what are you guys cooking over there, smells good!"

I yelled back, "It is good, come on over and have a hunk!"

All the while, Greg was belching so loud we needed earplugs. After dinner, I made some raspberry tea. The smell drew Greg and Steve to our tent to join us in a cup. So there we were, four of us crowded into a three-person tent full of equipment having a tea party

Steve and Greg fought to see who could get out the door first when I let go with one of my famous mountain gas farts. Rob wanted to go with them, and, frankly, so did I.

Three o'clock came really fast, and it wasn't easy trying to motivate the guys to get ready. Rob and I climbed out of the tent with our headlamps on. It was so foggy that the light of our headlamps reflected off the fog back into our faces like car headlights. We couldn't even see five feet in front of us. So we turned them off and couldn't see anything at all. I turned my headlamp back on and looked at Rob. "There's absolutely no way we can climb this mountain."

"I think you're right, Tim."

"I think we should just go back to bed, get up in a few hours, pack up and go get breakfast in Darrington." We often frequented a little café in the small logging town nestled in the mountains about twenty minutes away.

"That sounds like a good idea to me."

He was probably thinking about their Logger Special. It was so big, Paul Bunyan and Babe together couldn't eat it all. So we went back to the tent, woke Steve and Greg to tell them to forget about the climb and go back to sleep. Relieved, I got back into my bag, closed my eyes, and drifted off into a deep sleep.

I was awakened abruptly by the weight of Rob's knee in the back of my leg as climbed over me to look outside. "What the hell's going on, Rob?" I was pissed because I'd been sound asleep, warm and comfortable.

"The sun's out, Tim!" Rob said in an excited tone.

I crawled out of my bag and looked out the door of the tent with him. All the clouds had dropped below us and the summit of Glacier Peak was sticking out up above, pristine and beautiful. "Hey Steve, Greg, you guys should see this, it's incredible!"

They got up and crawled out into the sunshine, squinting and staggering around like old men. The sun was just coming up, but the temperature had dropped considerably since three o'clock.

I was putting on my wool sweater and wind pants when Steve said, "Look, there's some guys climbing up there on the glacier!"

I squinted to see a party of four roped together, heading up the glacier about half a mile away.

"They aren't going very fast, are they?" Greg said. He and Rob were already getting their stuff packed to go back down and have breakfast.

Steve broke the silence by yelling, "Let's climb it!"

The three of us looked at each other and said in unison, "What?"

"Let's climb it, we can do it. We can run up and then run down. It won't take that long! Come on!" He was so excited.

Greg and Rob were not as excited, but... I looked up, scratched my two-day whiskers, and thought, *We can could do this!* I wanted to do it. Steve's enthusiasm was getting me pumped to climb it. "Let's go for it!" I shouted.

Steve said, "Yeah!"

Greg and Rob were not convinced; they were thinking about the Logger Special in Darrington.

"You guys don't have to go," Steve assured them. "Tim and I will climb it and you guys can wait for us."

"Okay, Rob and I will go down and have breakfast, you two can climb your mountain, and we'll pick you up at the parking lot when we get back from Darrington." It sounded like a good plan.

So much for my level-headed thinking... a "real" climb leader would never do what we were about to do. I was too caught up in the excitement. The adrenaline and testosterone were pumping through my body like an out-of-control freight train. Steve and I decided that we'd pack the tents down later so Rob and Greg could get going. While they packed up the rest of their stuff, Steve and I got our climbing gear on. I grabbed the rope and started to unravel it.

"Tim?" I looked up at Steve with the rope in my hands. "Let's hold off on roping up."

I didn't say anything for a moment.

"We can make better time if we don't rope up now. Let's wait until we get higher on the glacier."

I was still thinking. Everything he said was kind of making sense, but it went against everything I'd been taught. I watched the four climbers on the glacier for a couple of seconds and then looked at Steve. "We'll rope up higher on the glacier. As soon as we get up to where those climbers are now, okay?"

Steve smiled and nodded a little. He said, "Yeah, that'll work."

I coiled up the rope and threw it over my shoulder. We said goodbye to Rob and Greg and told them that we'd probably catch up to them before they got to the car.

"I don't think so, Tim," were Greg's last words as they took off running.

Steve and I looked at each other and smiled like, "You wanna bet, Greg…?" Then we started to climb like we were being chased by a bear. Steve was practically running and kicking steps at the same time. I was gasping for air right behind him. We just kept going and going. Steve was starting to get ahead of me, I couldn't keep up.

On the way up I noticed something black lying in the snow. It looked like a sleeping bag or a pack that someone had lost, but we didn't stop to check it out; we had a mission. We wanted to eat a Logger Special, too!

It only took us twenty-five minutes to reach the top of the steep grade of the lower Sitkum Glacier. When we reached the frozen footsteps of the other climbers we'd seen, we went even faster. It took us another fifteen minutes to reach them. They'd seen us coming, so they waited for us.

"Hey, you guys know the correct route to the summit?" they asked when we reached them.

"Yeah," I said back, then I explained the upper Sitkum Glacier route to Sitkum Ridge. I got my map, altimeter, and compass to pinpoint our exact location. We had put everything we thought we would need into Steve's pack and I carried rope. After looking at the map and altimeter, I realized that we were a lot higher than I'd thought. We talked to the climbers for about ten minutes and resumed our climb. Two of the climbers in their party didn't look real enthusiastic about climbing. The temperature had dropped even more and the snow was crusty, making it harder to kick steps into. Before I could mention to Steve about the possibility of roping up, he was on his way. I thought about the climbing code, the words burned into me: "Rope up on all exposed places and for all glacier travel. All glacier travel!" I was breaking the third rule of the code—a rule that I had sworn I would never break. But there didn't appear to be any danger. The snow was deep, the crevasses were covered. I had convinced myself that we were doing the right thing. Besides, we were in a hurry. My competitiveness, and the challenge of succeeding at our plan, had destroyed my better judgment.

Steve and I left the four climbers literally eating our snow dust. He was obsessed with this summit, driven like no other climber I'd ever seen. He led the way at least fifty yards in front of me, and was widening the gap. I was too exhausted to yell at him to slow down. By the time I had reached the top of the ridge, he was already heading up the last steep snowfield to the summit. This was the snowfield that, eleven years ago, had seen a very young climbing team, poorly equipped, struggle up in fog and snow, and summit for the first time. A young man, in his early twenties, had fulfilled his dream of climbing Glacier Peak like his best friend had, years before him. That young man had been me. And, here I was again. As I watched Steve ascend the steep snowfield that separated me from the summit, I had no idea that would be the last mountain he'd ever climb.

I tried to yell up to him but he was too far away, so I began to climb up that last steep hill to the summit. Using his footsteps made it easier to climb. By the time I was halfway up, Steve was already on the summit. I stopped twice on the way to catch my breath and then, with the sweat dripping off my face, walked up to Steve with a big proud smile. He had his ham radio in hand and was talking to someone in Vancouver, sharing his victory with someone other than me. I eavesdropped on their conversation. It was John, an ex-climber. I looked at my watch, it was 9:20. It only took us two and a half hours to summit. Amazing. I realized I was starving. Steve finally finished talking to John and we had our celebratory high-five.

"Two and a half hours, Steve! Can you believe it?"

Steve was shocked. We each ate a Milky Way and drank some Gatorade, and I took some pictures with Rob's camera because I hadn't wanted to bring my bulky Nikon. It was incredibly clear above the clouds, with many mountain tops sticking through. It looked as if it was clearing off on the east side. We wanted to get back down quickly, so we left the summit at a jogging pace. Steve was ahead of me stomping down in the frozen snow. It didn't take him long to get a big lead on me. When I got to the top of the ridge, I stopped and looked up to see where Steve was. He was already down on the glacier, glissading like a kid on a water slide. I thought, *Oh what the hell*, jumped down on my butt and took off. He waited for me in the middle of the glacier, but he didn't say anything when I got there. He smiled and took off again. As I was trying to catch my breath, I watched him disappear from my sight. *He's just going to have to wait for me at camp anyway, why is he going so fast? He's out of control.* After he'd left me on the upper part of the glacier, he kept gaining speed. He tried to slow down with the shaft of his ice axe, but the snow was frozen solid. It was like cement.

He was picking up speed and literally catching air, completely out of control. He reached the steep hill at the lower part of the glacier, trying desperately to remain calm, hoping to slow down when he got to the bottom of the hill. As he tried to roll over to self-arrest, the heel of his right boot caught a frozen footstep. It was like hitting a cement curb on a street. His leg immediately snapped at the point of impact. Then he began to tumble head over heels. He had to grab his leg and move it out from under his chest. As he tumbled out of control, some divine hand brought him to an instant stop. His arm almost ripped out of the socket when the shaft of his ice axe pierced the ice and stopped him like an anchor. Thank God he still had his wrist strap on.

Steve would have gone over the cliff if his ice axe hadn't stopped him. It was a miracle.

I began glissading down in the crusty snow, following the trough he had made. I picked up speed. When I reached the top of the steep incline of the lower Sitkum Glacier, I was out of control. I had to self-arrest immediately. The snow was so frozen I couldn't slow down with just the pick of my ice axe. I pressed the pick harder into the ice and finally began to slow down. After I finally stopped, it was all I could do to slowly stand up: the snow was now a frozen sheet of ice. I surveyed the hill to see if I could find a trace of Steve. Nothing. I looked down the glacier and could make out three figures toward

177

the bottom. At first I thought they were looking at the article of equipment that we had seen earlier on our way up. So I sat back down and attempted to glissade down to them. I hadn't gone more than a hundred feet when I realized it was too icy to be glissading. I was completely out of control; I immediately went into a self-arrest again. I had to press with all my weight to get the pick into the frozen crust. Like before, I kept slowing down more and more until I finally came to a stop. I got up, brushed the snow off, and walked down to the group.

Steve was lying on his back, with two climbers on either side of him.

Steve had his head tilted back, looking at me upside-down. His arm was stretched up behind him, his hand was still in the wrist strap and the shaft of his ice axe was buried all the way to the pick. "Tim… I broke my leg."

"What do you mean, you broke your leg? You're kidding, right?"

One of the climbers said, "He broke his leg, man. He's not kidding."

"Rats," was all I could say, but inside I was in disbelief. "Which bone did he break?" I asked the climber as I looked down at Steve. I hoped it was a fractured ankle or simply a bad sprain.

"His femur," the other climber said.

Shit! A rush of adrenaline immediately poured through me;

• • •

I'll never forget that moment. It changed my life. I sat back down on the rock that I now call my "Muir Thinking Rock." *One small event can turn into a nightmare.* I remember exactly how I felt then. Even decades later, my heart still races just thinking about it. *How did I let that happen? This single event changed me more than anything I had ever experienced before. I became mortal and subdued and lost all my confidence after this happened.*

• • •

I didn't want to scare Steve any more than he already was. I looked down at his leg and saw that it had swollen to the size of two legs. I swallowed hard. *No, God, not here… Not now…* I tried to remember all the things I'd learned in Mountaineers first aid. My mind was blank. *First act like it's no big deal.* "How ya feeling, bud?" I asked nonchalantly.

"I can't feel anything, Tim. My leg is numb."

I started to shake, thinking there was nerve damage and he could lose his leg, but I didn't say anything. I looked at the two other climbers. "Do either of you know first aid?"

The bigger of the two guys said, "Well, yeah, I'm an EMT and a fireman for the Issaquah Fire Department, and so is he." He pointed to his partner.

I just stared in silence for a second, absorbing this news and realizing they knew way more about what to do than I did. "Well," I said, "Steve is in good hands."

"He's in really good hands," said the big climber. "The two other guys that are with us are doctors. One is a neurosurgeon at Harborview Hospital."

I couldn't believe it. I was so lucky. "The first thing we gotta do is get his pack off and pull out his radio," I said in an authoritative tone.

"A radio?" the big climber shouted.

"Yeah, I've got a handheld radio," Steve answered. "It's in my pack."

"Wow! you guys have a radio, that's incredible," said the other climber.

The bigger guy introduced himself as Ben, the other was Nick. We worked to get the radio out and I handed it to Steve. He set the frequency and began calling for help. "Mayday! Mayday! Is anyone out there?"

There was nothing but static. He handed the radio to me because he was starting to feel some intense pain. "You're… gonna… have… to get up higher, Tim." He was grimacing, then he began to scream in agony.

Ben held him down. I grabbed the radio out of his hand. "We've got to get him warm," I said.

"We have sleeping bags with us," Ben offered. "We'll get them out and cover him. Why don't you go call for help?"

"Okay."

Steve was calming down, showing signs of shock. I hesitated as the guys covered him.

"You'd better get going!" Ben said impatiently. "He'll be fine."

I hiked up about thirty feet above them, then turned on the radio. "Mayday! Mayday! Is there anyone there?" I asked into the radio. I could hear some men talking.

"Hey, did you hear someone say 'mayday'?"

"Yeah," said the other.

I pressed the talk button frantically and started to talk again. "I have an emergency! I'm up on Glacier Peak and I have a victim with a broken femur who needs medical assistance immediately! Please help me!" I let go of the talk button and got static.

I heard one of them say, "What'd he say? He got a broken leg?"

The other guy said, "Yeah, ya know, that kind of reminds me of when Blossom broke her leg and you had to call on your radio for help—"

I interrupted him and shouted this time, "I HAVE A MEDICAL EMERGENCY, PLEASE HELP ME!" I let go of the talk button. Static.

Then one of them said, to the other person, "Hey, let's find another channel with less interference so we can talk."

I couldn't believe what I was hearing. They didn't care about what was going on. I was completely distraught. I went back down and handed the radio back to Ben and said, "I can't find anyone to help us." He tried diligently. Then, a voice. Finally! It was John, the radio operator from Victoria that Steve was talking to on the summit. After hearing what had happened, he immediately called another ham radio operator in Everett. Another radio operator in Matthews Beach, Seattle was listening in and he telephoned the Snohomish County dispatch center, who got in contact with the Snohomish County Sheriff's Department. Everything happened so fast and started to fall into place.

Steve was showing signs of severe shock. We needed to get him warmer.

"I've got a Thermarest pad," Ben said.

We were able to slide the pads under Steve and keep him covered with down sleeping bags. My job was to keep him warm and keep him from going into shock, so I stayed as close to him as I could. Ben conversed with the rescue team. Steve was white.

"How did it happen, Steve?" I tried to keep his mind off the pain by keeping him talking.

He told me the story and I began to feel sick as I listened to each gruesome detail of the accident. I began to feel responsible, and started to apologize.

"Hey, it's not your fault, Tim. I was the one who didn't want to rope up. Remember?"

I was holding back the tears as I said, "We're gonna get you out of here, I promise." I could hear Ben talking to the head of Snohomish County search and rescue. They had already dispatched their helicopter with an EMT and a first-aid specialist.

While we were waiting, we saw the other two climbers and yelled out to them. The two doctors saw us and came over. We had things pretty well in hand, so they didn't have to do much right then. But things soon got worse.

The pilot of the helicopter radioed that he wasn't sure he could land in the swirling wind conditions. We needed to get Steve stabilized so they could drop a litter down and raise him to the helicopter. The two doctors put their heads together and came up with a plan to make a splint out of Steve's ice axe and my climbing rope. It was the rope we should have used to rope up with, and now we wereusing it for a splint. It was used too late. It was cut it into several short pieces and tied around Steve's leg. Sean, the neurosurgeon, crammed the head of the axe into Steve's crotch and pulled on his leg. Never in my life have I heard a man scream in so much pain. All the training in the world couldn't have prepared me to witness that level of suffering.

After a few futile attempts to place the ice axe, they decided it was too painful. They ended up using his other leg as a splint and tying them together. It was the most intense moment of the whole procedure. I had to hold Steve down, reassuring him that he was going be fine, not knowing whether he was bleeding internally. He was in imminent danger of losing his leg if it took much longer to get him out of there. I kept trying to keep his mind off the pain. He was slipping in and out of consciousness, so I mostly focused on keeping him warm. I kept praying that things would work out okay.

After two hours of listening to discussions between Ben and everyone else involved, over the radio came, "Ben? Ben, do you copy?"

"Yeah. Over."

"You should have a visual on the helicopter, over."

We looked up. Off in the distance above the clouds, I could make out a tiny orange dot flying toward us.

"Copy that. I see it!" Ben said.

It was two and a half hours since Steve broke his leg. I could feel myself wanting to cry from relief but I held it back. I was so happy to see that damn helicopter. I swallowed the huge lump in my throat and said, "There it is, Steve, you're gonna fucking make it!" I grabbed his hand and held it.

He was almost comatose.

• • •

The tears began flowing out of my eyes as I remembered that day. *I was so happy to see that damn helicopter.*

• • •

The helicopter circled around us, then disappeared. We kept waiting for it to come back around. I saw some smoke above the snowfield and began to fear the worse. "Where did they go?" I asked.

Then Sean shouted, "There they are!"

I looked up to where he was pointing. Three people were hiking down the glacier, carrying a litter. We practically cheered. It was Kathy, the EMT; her husband, Howard; and John, the head of the Snohomish County Search and Rescue Department. They had landed the helicopter up on a ridge about two hundred yards above us.

They wasted no time loading Steve onto the litter. He was screaming, out of his mind with agony. I held on to one corner of the litter to help carry him up toward the helicopter, but I was too weak and fell over, almost fainting. I was wasted. I hadn't eaten anything except a candy bar and some Gatorade. I was physically and mentally drained, nothing left.

Steve didn't want me to leave his sight. He needed the security of someone he knew, and in that moment we were best friends. I was elated that we were getting him to a hospital, somewhat euphoric in my mixture of relief and low blood sugar.

The helicopter glistened in the sunlight. It was strapped down because of the wind, and the pilot was holding the rotor blade with another strap. It looked unnatural to see a helicopter resting precariously on that narrow ridge. As we loaded Steve into it, a strap around his legs that had fallen through the bottom of the litter caught one of the bolts on the floor, pulling down on his leg. He screamed out of his mind. We had to pull him back out and get the strap off the bolt. After he quieted down, he told Kathy he wanted me to go with him, but there would have been too much weight with me in there. Howard had to stay behind too. Before they shut the door, I told Steve one more time, "You're gonna be okay, man. Right? I'll see ya tomorrow at the hospital, okay?"

He barely looked at me, still in a state of shock. They closed the door and he reached up to touch the glass. I put my hand on the glass too. I waved goodbye and walked over to join the other climbers. The engine started and the rotors began to turn slowly against the wind. The rotors kept going faster and faster, with the pitch as far forward as they could go. It was so loud that it was literally shaking the ground as it began to lift off. Then the tail started going back down and the nose lifted up like it was going to flip over. *Oh my God! They're not going to make it!*

The pilot shut down the engine a little to get the skids back on the surface so he could start over. It was intense. *This isn't over yet...* The helicopter tipped back again and nearly flipped over. We started to back away, thinking it was not going to make it. I started to pray again. At that moment, the wind died down enough to get enough forward thrust to pull the complex piece of machinery off the ground in the right direction, and finally they were off. The helicopter flew out and then down, disappeared, then came up again. I saw Howard give a sigh of relief. I watched as the helicopter disappeared out of sight.

I began to hike back down toward our camp. Howard said he would help me bring out Steve's equipment. It was all like a long, bad dream. The fire that burned in my heart to climb mountains had been doused with cold water, and a numbness came over me like I had never experienced before in my life. I'd had a motorcycle accident, experienced babies coming into this world, but this was the most traumatic event I'd ever witnessed. I didn't say anything as Howard and I gathered up our stuff and packed it into packs. I put my pack on and Howard put on Steve's. He grunted when he felt the full weight of it on his back. I said, "Well, I think you know the way."

He didn't say anything. I quickly learned as we hiked down together, he was not a conversationalist. So I quit trying to talk to him. I just kept going faster and faster until he was well behind me. I felt angry and empty. *What are going to be the repercussions of all this? What is Debbie going to say?* Maybe no one will find out. Many things raced through my mind.

After reaching Kennedy Hot Springs, I started running the five miles to the parking lot. It was hot and humid, and sweat was running off my head. I was about a mile from the parking lot when I was greeted by Rob and Greg. They had heard the news from the search and rescue volunteers at the trailhead and ran in to find me. Rob carried my pack the rest of the way. My knees were killing me; I could hardly walk. We waited for about an hour for Howard to show up with Steve's pack. We loaded it in and took off. My knees had swollen so much that I could barely move my legs, so Rob drove. I turned on the radio. So much for nobody finding out; it was all over the news. When I got home, Debbie embraced me without a word, just tears rolling down her cheeks. I looked at her and said, "I don't think I'll be climbing anymore."

The media had a heyday with the accident. It was on the radio, on TV, in all the local papers, and they even did a segment on *Evening Magazine*. The show's producer called me to ask if I would be willing to do an interview. I agreed.

All the climbers involved with the rescue met at Steve's house, and I led the convoy to Stevens Pass. The plan was to film a short clip, re-creating the event. The interviewer asked me questions like, "Why didn't you and Steve rope up? You were the climb leader, right?" I couldn't come up with a professional answer. I kept scratching my head and adjusting my sunglasses and said something stupid. When I lowered my hand, my finger caught the string of my sunglasses and they came flying off my head and hung off my nose, askew. I must have looked like an idiot.

I visited Steve every day at the hospital for a week, until he got sick of seeing me there. Actually, he was so drugged up he probably never remembered me being there. Over time, his leg healed well, considering the extensive damage that the bone fragments made to the surrounding muscle and tissue. I had a very difficult time with what had happened; I always felt somewhat responsible. After the accident, our friendship faded.

The following January, my third daughter, Michaela Sibley, was born. I had lost the desire to climb. I had lost my confidence. It wasn't in me anymore to risk my life and others' lives to stand on the summit. I thought I would never lead a climb again. I focused on my wife, my children, and my job.

Dave and I at Camp Muir
Summer 2001

Terry in his almost super excited
mode. Summer 2006

From left to right: John, Randy,
Little Bob (Rob), Me and the
Lowenbrau's. Three Fingers 1982

Steve on the summit of Mt Baker
after summiting from the road in
5 hrs. May 1989

Jeff setting his GPS device
Summer of 2003

Brian after giving up his
Grandparents ashes to the sky.
September 1984

Garry and me in our early hiking
days. Late August of 1973

John climbing up Steamboat Prow.
Rob just below him. Winthrop
Glacier below. June 1983

Ron and I at Camp Muir early
June 2003

Me, Jeffs dad David and Jeff
on Pilchuck after climbing the
Iodine Gultch route.

Mt Baker summit June 1987.
Neeling down from the left: Dave,
Morgan, Me Shelly and Rob.

Me and terry at the top of
Dissapoingment Cleaver
September 2001

Alan and me on one of our climbs.
Sometime around 1976

Rob getting his mountain face on.
July 1996

Summit of Rainier 1989: Rob, Steve
Me, Greg and kneeling, Morgan.

Hanging out with the Wittikers.
Jim, me and Lou.

Rob and me at the summit register.
September 1994. I was really sick

Summit of Rainier 2003: Terry,
Paul, Ron, Me and Jeff.

Rob relaxing on route to the
Summit 1988

Doug, Me, Buttons and Mark on the
Mt Baker Summit Summer 1986

Garry left and Morgan heading up
toward Sikum Ridge on Glacier
Peak 1980

Ron, relaxing for a minute before
we headed up to Ingraham Flats
on Mt Rainier 2002.

Morgan resting on our way up
Liberty Peak.

Mark taking it all in on Mt Baker. 1986

Morgan and John on the summit
of Glacier Peak 1980.

Rob, Me and Brian on the crater
rim of Mt Rainier moments before
I got sick.

The infamous Three Finger
Ladders.

Ed Viesturs Left and Me Right. One
of my best days ever to drink a beer
and talk climbing with Ed. 2017

Brian and Rob getting ready to start
up Mt Rainier September of 1984

Me left and Terry below down
climbing the Kautz Glacier. Thankful
that there were fixed anchors. 2003.

Chapter 20

Something Spiritual

"You have to grow from the inside out. None can teach you, none can make you spiritual.

There is no other teacher but your own soul."

— Swami Vivekananda

I LOOKED ABOVE TO CADAVER GAP, Cathedral Rocks, and back to Cadaver Gap—so-called because in 1929 a climbing party was caught in a storm and two of the guides fell into a crevasse. After the storm, other guides went up to retrieve their bodies. With great difficulty, they brought the bodies back down through the gap. *What if we'd have had to bring Steve's body down from Glacier Peak? If I could have gone back to 1929 and told that climbing party not to go, would they have listened to me? If your best friend came to you in a dream and told you not to jump, would you listen to him?* The wind was beginning to pick up as I walked back over to the climbers' hut. "Home away from home," we used to call it.

•   •   •

Debbie and I finally sold our property and bought a nice house. I focused on remodeling it and making myself a man cave. With all my climbing pictures on the walls, I was inspired to compile the climbing stories from my logbooks. I started obsessing about mountains again. I had a great job, a wonderful family, a beautiful house, and my relationship with Debbie was improving. I thought I had it all. Still, something inside me was not right.

I had a dream that I was walking through a raked rock garden. I was very high in the mountains, and there was a trail in front of me. Something in my dream told me I was in the Himalayas. There was a large monastery made out of reddish colored stones. It looked as though it had just been built. There were large steps leading up to a large wooden door that had metal plates and beautiful designs carved in the wood. I walked up to the doors and found the one on the left slightly open. I walked into a cavernous room with a stone floor and giant doors on the right and left. There were statues of Buddha and other amazing objects that I did not understand. Ahead of me was a large stone staircase leading up to another room. The stairs had a stone handrail on both sides that were at least two feet wide. The top of the handrail was made with flat stones. I could feel their rough, sandpaper-like texture as I glided my right hand along the handrail and walked up the stairs. When I reached the top, there was a short hall that led to a large window with no glass. Standing in front of the window was a short man with his back to me. He had a shaved head and was wearing a brilliant red robe. I walked up to his left side and looked out the window. There were mountaintops as far as I could see. I looked over at him and he looked at me. He was an Asian man with piercing black eyes. He gazed deeply into my eyes and he smiled, but didn't say anything. He raised his arm and pointed out the window. I looked back out, and it was all cloudy. Then I woke up.

It gave me a good feeling that I didn't truly understand. I felt that life is beautiful and I knew everything was going to be okay. I also felt confused about it—almost as if I had actually been there physically. But how could I?

I called Rob the following day. "What do you think about climbing Rainier again? One more time. Just for us."

He was quiet at first, but then got excited about the idea. We made plans to do the Kautz Route. I sat down with Debbie and told her that this would be the last time. I told her I needed this expedition to end my book and find closure on my obsession with Mount Rainier. She gave me her blessing. She said, "You and Rob have always gone up there for someone else. It's time you went for yourselves as best friends."

Rob and I left Friday after work on the last weekend in May 1996. He drove his Volkswagen Rabbit like a madman all the way to Longmire. We were fortunate to get registered before the park ranger station closed. We arrived at Paradise at around nine o'clock, threw on our packs and were off by nine thirty. We managed to get up on Wilson Glacier by ten, and it was still light enough to see. I was tired from the long work week. The moon was so bright on the upper Wilson that we didn't need our headlamps, so we just kept climbing in silence. We found a flat spot right below the foot of the Turtle for our first camp. I was so tired that I didn't want to set up the tent, so we just dug out a hole in the snow, laid the tent in, and put the rainfly over our sleeping bags. We didn't even eat dinner.

We got up early the next morning and began the next leg of the climb—the biggest snowfield on Rainier. The trip up the Turtle was slow and arduous, but we managed to make it up in about four hours. The weather was hot, and when we got to Camp Hazard I was dehydrated, hungry, and beat. We set up the tent and Rob decided he needed a nap, so I told him I'd get the water. Water was melting off the ice cliffs so I cautiously climbed over to it. With water bottles in hand, I began crossing a very steep ice field, not realizing what I was getting myself into. With no crampons, no ice axe, and just a couple of water bottles, I found myself in the middle of the ice field on my hands and knees slowly filling the first water bottle with a little trickle of melting glacier water. I didn't look down until my bottles were full. Then I realized if I were to slip, I would probably not stop until I hit the rocks far below Camp Hazard. Fear gripped my mind and I literally froze.

Isn't it funny how we think we're invincible and then, in our most unsuspecting moments, we find out we're not. We find ourselves either praying, crying, or both. I stayed motionless for a minute, getting mad at myself. *Damn it! I should have kept my crampons on! What the hell was I thinking! I wasn't.* I moved my feet just a bit and tried to stand up. *Shit!* My foot slipped and I started to slide. I looked way down the ice shoot at the rocks. *Hmmm… I am really stuck!* I wasn't mad anymore. I decided to do the unthinkable: Yell for help from my climbing companion. He was asleep. It did no good. No one could hear me. I stood there with my knees slightly bent, full water bottles in hand, not wanting to move, for a good ten minutes. It seemed like an hour. *Damn! Where the hell is Rob when I need him? He could just throw me the rope and life would be so good!* My legs were beginning to burn and cramp. Especially since I just got through climbing a really steep snowfield with a sixty-pound pack on. *Maybe this is where I start to pray. It can't hurt.* I looked down on the ice and saw a small hole made by someone who had gotten water earlier—someone smart enough to bring an ice axe. The hole was just big enough to put my finger in and hold on long enough to take some of the pressure off my legs. Good thing I wasn't wearing gloves. I could have let go of the water bottles and watch them fly down the ice field and use both hands to crawl my way out of this mess, but I couldn't do that. We needed the water.

Just as I began sliding my boot over to get in a better position, I heard, "What in the hell are you doing?" It was Rob.

"Rob?"

He was laughing at my predicament. He walked over to me on the ice, with no crampons, and grabbed the water bottles from me. "Come on! Quit fucking around! We've got to get dinner going!" He walked back like he was just strolling down the beach.

How is he doing that? I was still crouched there, looking down at the ice field that went down for about five hundred yards into the rocks. I began crawling on my knees and sticking my fingers into the tiny holes left by the smart climber with the ice axe. I managed to get myself out of the mess. I had not climbed a mountain since Steve broke his leg on Glacier Peak. The experience had left me feeling my mortality in a way I never had before. I was not the same. Yet I still loved climbing.

We got up just after midnight. It was as surreal as always—and we didn't get any real sleep, as usual. We ate a power bar, roped up, and—since we had no one to wait for—we headed toward the ramp to Kautz Glacier in about thirty minutes.

It was not a routine climb. They hardly ever are. I was feeling uneasy and frightened the whole way up. Even though the weather was perfect and the moon was bright, I kept coming up with excuses why we should turn back.

Rob said, "We're almost there. Why would we turn around?" He was such a strong climber. I was glad he was there.

We stopped just below the crater at around four o'clock. I was feeling really sick and lay down on my back. So, once again—and for the last time ever—Rob started pulling me up there. He was smaller than me, but he was built like a mini Arnie.

At the top of the crater rim, Rob and I just lay there for about forty-five minutes. I had no desire to sign the summit register or even walk out to Columbia Crest.

Rob rolled to his side and said, "What do you want to do, old man?"

I lay there looking up at the blue and gold sky listening to the wind whistling through my sunglasses strap and my stomach growling. "Let's go down and get breakfast, a power bar wasn't enough for me".

We headed down and made it back to base camp in a little over two hours. We packed up and glissaded all the way down the Turtle. I was feeling better and better. We stopped at the Log Cabin Cafe at around 12:45 p.m. for breakfast. After we ordered, we sat back and sipped our coffee with triumphant expressions. All of a sudden, Rob's eyes got really big.

"What's wrong, Rob?"

"It's LLLou ..."

I turned around, and sure enough, there in the flesh was Lou Whittaker walking toward us, smiling. Rob stood up and held out his hand saying, "Hey Lou, how's it going?"

He came over and shook Rob's hand and said, in his raspy voice, "Pretty good. You guys just come off the mountain?"

I couldn't say anything because I was in shock; my mouth was open, but words would not come out.

Rob said, "Yeah, it was great, wasn't it Lou?"

"Yeah," he said back. "Wasn't the moon great, shining down? We didn't even need our headlamps. Did you guys use headlamps?"

Rob answered back, "Nah, we didn't need ours either."

I was still trying to get words to come out of my mouth but all I could muster was, "Uh huh." That was it! That was all I could say to the guy I had admired for years, the guy I always wanted to meet. I didn't even shake his hand or get his autograph. I just watched him get into his car with three other people and drive away.

"Why didn't you say something, Tim?" Rob asked.

"I don't know. I guess I just couldn't believe it."

"You blew it," Rob finished, laughing at me.

Yeah, I blew it. But, oh well… maybe I'll meet him again. Who knows?

The following year I gave up climbing, once again, Debbie was happy. I sold all my equipment to Dave. I didn't see Rob for a long time.

• • •

Years later, I regretted selling my climbing equipment. *What was I thinking?* I guess I really wasn't thinking at the time. *Time…* I looked at my watch again. *I need to head back down soon…* Instead, I lay down on my back on the pumice rocks and looked up at the sky. The sun felt warm and I felt secure. I tried to recall what happened after that.

Chapter 21

Think About What You're Doing Before You Jump

"Life isn't about finding yourself. Life is about creating yourself."

— George Bernard Shaw

IN MARCH OF 1998 I sent a copy of my manuscript to a publisher. Two weeks later I received a rejection letter. I was sad when my oldest daughter Melissa had just come home from school. We were having tea and cookies together and I told her what happened. She said, "Don't give up, Dad. Maybe it's not done yet." I was consumed with self-pity and couldn't even consider how prophetic her words might be.

•   •   •

In September of 1999, Melissa went off to school in Ireland. Then in early 2000, the King Dome was taken down to make room for the new stadium. I was in my living room on a Saturday afternoon when all of a sudden our pet cockatiel began going nuts. Out of the corner of my eye, I saw something big fly by. When I ran outside and looked up, I saw a giant owl sitting at the peak of the roof. He was staring down at me. When I moved closer to the house, he looked down and screeched loudly without moving.

I ran in to get Debbie because no one would believe this. *Where is she?* I called her and she answered from the back bedroom. She slowly came down the hall, then down the stairs, and finally outside . The owl was gone and Deb looked at me like I was crazy.

The next day I told the story about the owl to my co-workers. One of them, named Cyndi, who was Wiccan, told me that it was an omen. I really didn't believe her but my curiosity was heightened, so I went on line and looked it up. The internet took me to a native American website. According to legend, the owl is a messenger. At night he brings good news, but in the daytime... it's bad, because they are only seen at night.

I really didn't take it to heart, in fact I forgot about it until the following Sunday when I got a phone call. It was Garry's mom. Garry had fallen off of a four-story apartment roof in Juneau, and was being airlifted to Harborview Hospital. He was supposed to leave Juneau to return to Seattle that day. He'd gone up on the roof to give some last-minute instructions to his work crew when he slipped and slid off. Normally, he would have grabbed his hammer and used it like an ice axe to stop himself. Not this time; he wasn't wearing his tool belt. He landed on his feet, snapped his femur and ruptured his spleen. The complications of a ruptured spleen are devastating.

I visited him every day at Harborview Hospital, but I'm not sure if he knew I was there. I would hold his hand and he would squeeze lightly. I would talk about growing up together and that he was "It" so he needed to get better to tag me back. He died one month later from a blood clot at the age of forty-six. Garry wasn't supposed to die... not like that. I was lost.

One night, about six months later, I had a vivid dream. I was at a family reunion, only I didn't know anyone there. While watching people mill about, talking and eating, I felt someone behind me.

"Tim!"

I turned around; it was Garry. It was so real. He was younger, like when we were in our twenties or early thirties. He was very serious, looking me directly in the eye.

"I need to tell you something," he said. There was a lot of commotion from the reunion and it was really hard to keep my attention on him. He disappeared and I couldn't find him. I woke up and looked at my clock. It was 2:20 a.m. I fell asleep again, only to continue the dream. Sure enough, I felt someone touch my shoulder. I turned around and there he was again, all serious. "I came back because I need to tell you something. Look at me! You need to know something."

The commotion from the party was getting out of hand. People were running in between us and I couldn't keep my focus on him. He walked over to me very sternly and said, "Think about what you're doing before you jump!" Then he was gone.

I woke up and started crying. I really felt him there. Debbie tried to comfort me but to no avail; I felt so broken. *What the hell did he mean?* The dream hadn't offered any clarity; I was just getting more confused about everything in my life.

• • •

I had lost touch with Rob in the spring and summer of 2000. He had started a business and was so absorbed that he didn't have time for anyone or anything. He was working almost twenty-four hours a day. His wife Shelly was going out at night. In September I got a phone call from Shelly.

"Tim, Rob is in the hospital. He tried to commit suicide."

I was in a state of panic as I took off to the hospital. When I rushed into his room, he was in the hospital bed smiling with his gown on and his muscles making the gown look like it was too small.

I looked at him with a mad expression (because he was smiling) and said, "What the hell, Rob?!"

He kept smiling at me and said, "Yep, I tried to kill myself. I would have been successful but Shelly found me too quick."

"So she found you right away?"

"No, I was clinically dead when the paramedics got there. They revived me."

"Holy shit, Rob! Why?"

He took a bite of jello and said as he chewed, "I guess I just didn't want to live anymore." like it was no big deal. I wanted him to be more serious, but he was detached from the seriousness of it all.

We talked for a while about Shelly and how immersed he'd been in his business. The nurse came and told me it was time to leave, that Rob needed to rest. I left the hospital more confused than ever. *Why would he do that*? He always had everything to live for. He was so strong and confident. Why Rob?

After he was released, Rob asked me if I wanted to climb Mount Index. I had never climbed it. I thought it would be good for him, and I wanted to support him in doing something that he had once loved. And, he was asking—so that seemed like a positive sign. "It's an easy mountain if we do the south peak," he said.

I picked him up at his house and we drove up to the parking area to hike up to Lake Serene. We had absolutely no climbing gear with us—just our lunches and some extra clothes. It was a great time of year to climb. All the leaves were turning autumn gold; the mornings were crisp and clear, and the sun came up over the mountains at a reasonable hour. We got up to Lake Serene in about an hour. Rob assured me that he was fine and that he had no more desire to take his life. I was relieved and happy that he hadn't succeeded, but I wasn't very comfortable about it all. Then it came out.

"Tim," he started. "Shelly's been having an affair. I just couldn't deal with it."

"Are you sure?" I replied.

"Yes. It's been going on for a while."

I wasn't sure what to say after that, except "What are you going to do?"

"I don't know."

When we arrived at the lake, he started heading toward the north peak. "Where are you going, Rob?"

"I just want to check out the north face route."

"Why? We don't have any equipment with us to climb this route."

"Let's just see what it's like, and if it gets too hard we'll just turn around and do the south peak."

I tried to figure what was going on here. *Let's see, he wants to try to climb the north peak of Index. We have nothing with us except lunch and some extra clothes. Hmmm…* I finally broke the silence with, "I'm not sure we can do this, Rob."

He kept on going, crashing through the underbrush, bushwhacking his way with me close behind. We kept going up, getting closer to the rocks that led up to the approach to the summit. I stayed quiet. Then we started scrambling up on the rocks. It was only a class 3 scramble, but I still wasn't comfortable with his decision. This is a well-known technical route on Mount Index. It's not an easy scramble up some class 4 rocks. It's mostly 5 to 5.5 rock climbing pitches.

As we got up higher, we began to notice nylon webbing slings that had been left by previous climbers who had rappelled down. "Hey Rob, maybe we could slip-knot all these slings together and create one giant tied-together sling that would work as sort of a rope. What do ya think?" I was becoming desperate to come up with any idea that would make this sidetracked climb safer. His energy was not right, and I was not feeling comfortable about anything.

"Yeah, we could do that I guess."

I grabbed as many slings as I could find. It's not something I would recommend to just anyone. In fact, it's a good example of "petting the sow." I really didn't know why this was happening, why he was so adamant about climbing this part of the mountain. He wouldn't listen to me at all. He just kept climbing up into class 4 and some class 5. I was just going along with it, and when I made a suggestion about which way we should go, he would go the opposite way. It was like he was pissed off about something.

"Rob, are you mad at me?"

"No," was all he said, without even looking at me.

By the time we got to the lower part of the north peak, I had combined about twenty feet of slings. I tied one end around my waist and said, "Here ya go, Rob."

He tied the other end around his waist. The rest of the way up was all class 5 or more, so I told him maybe we could do a running belay by wedging the slings into cracks and under rocks. "If one of us slips, we'll be okay. Right?" Like I was trying to convince someone… maybe myself. It was a stretch, and I wasn't even fifty percent sure it would work, and the slings were old. When you make a sling out of webbing, you date it with a permanent marker so you can throw it away after a couple of years. Some of these slings dated back to the seventies. Not good.

Rob began to rock-climb, looking for handholds and rock climbing about ten feet up on a large slab. He stuffed the sling rope into a crack, turned to look at me, and smiled.

"Tim, I want you to know that you are, and always will be, my best friend. Thank you for teaching me to climb and for everything you've showed me." Then he turned around and started to climb again.

That doesn't sound good… Is he going to try to take his life again? With me attached?

I had just lost Garry. Rob was now my best friend. *What the hell is he doing?* He was leading me up a six thousand foot mountain on a very technical route with questionable nylon slings as a rope. *He's crazy!*

We inched our way higher and higher. I didn't know how to tell him that I didn't want to do this, and I had no idea how we were going to get back down. Usually you rappel, but you can't do that with slings. We would have to down-climb.

We were about sixty feet from the summit when Rob got himself into a situation. He was stuck. He looked down at me and said, "Do you see a way to get past this area from where you are?"

I finally came out with it. "Rob? I think we should stop. Now! Look at where we are. Look at what we're doing. This is so unsafe. This is not something that we learned in the Mountaineers. We have kids, families that love us. We don't have to prove anything. We already have. You and I have climbed so many mountains together. We have stood side by side on the summit of Mount Rainier. So many times we have witnessed and experienced things that the average person has never seen or ever will see. We have saved other people's lives. Let's not attempt to kill ourselves now. You've already tried that and it wasn't worth it. Let's just turn around now and head back so that search and rescue doesn't have to drag our dead bodies off this mountain tomorrow with the same helicopter that rescued Steve off Glacier Peak. Okay?"

He looked at me like he was about to go into beast mode. Then his expression fell and he turned his head away. *Is he crying? I've never seen him cry. I've seen him mad, I've seen him frightened, but I've never seen him break down.*

After a couple of minutes or so, he wiped his eyes and looked back at me and said in a quieter voice, "Help me back down, okay?"

"I've got you on belay, brother!

After the climb, we stopped and had a beer together. He smiled and said, "Thanks for bringing me to my senses." A month later he filed for divorce.

We never climbed together again. My climbing drive was dead. So I thought.

Chapter 22

The Climber, Resurrected

"High standing before him is the challenge he must face today,
High stands a mountain can he climb it? He will find a way.
The mountain has seen the climber, and he'll ever go higher and higher.
On belay, on his way, climb away to your destiny,
On belay, climb away, on your way to your glory ."

"THIS HAS BEEN AN EMOTIONAL EXPERIENCE for me today," I said out loud. Then I thought to myself, *Life is unpredictable.* You think your team is going to lose, so you shut off the TV and then they kick the winning field goal. You're in a hurry to get in and out of the grocery store, but you run into someone you haven't seen in twenty years. You never know what's going to happen…

It was 8:20 a.m. I looked down the Muir Snowfield again at the sun reflecting off the ice. *I really don't think I'm going to find what I'm looking for up here. This is dumb. I need to go back down.* I was cold and tired. *If I could only go back. I would sell my soul to go back in time and make everything right.*

• • •

The years that followed that last climb with Rob into the new millennium were difficult. My health was going downhill. I was gaining weight and feeling like I needed to make a change. I bought a mountain bike and began to ride it home from work. I would take my bike with me the day before, leave it at work, get a ride to work in the morning, and ride my bike home fourteen miles. It became a routine that I really enjoyed, and I was getting in great shape. I had started fly-fishing and was enjoying that but when I would drive up to a river or lake to fish I would become obsessed with wanting to climb again. We went on family camping trips but Debbie didn't like to go so it was usually me and the girls. Melissa eventually moved out after she got back from Ireland so I didn't see that much of her anymore. Amanda had started high school. She was popular and all of her friends were either juniors or seniors. They all drove so she never needed a ride.

In the spring, Amanda's friend Jeri-Lynn asked me if I could mentor her for her senior project. I had no idea what a mentorship for a senior project was. Melissa hadn't had a senior project. Evidently, seniors were required to find someone who had a specific talent, shadow them, and learn from them. Then the student was to write an essay about what they'd learned. Jeri-Lynn asked me to teach her how to rock climb. I considered saying no, but I didn't.

Neither Debbie nor I were really comfortable with Jeri-Lynn. I don't know what Amanda saw in her. But there was something about her that I admired. She was obnoxious and she aggravated me—but impressed me at the same time. She exuded confidence, was outspoken and fearless. She loved to play jokes, a real trickster. She had no respect for me or anyone of her parents' age, but she needed to ace this assignment in order to graduate and I guess she thought rock climbing would be interesting and easy. She was all about easy.

I had to buy a new climbing rope and harness. I took Jeri-Lynn to the climbing rock at the University of Washington, and Amanda tagged along with us. Spoiled child that she was, Jeri-Lynn had a top-of-the line climbing harness and new climbing shoes. Her parents spared no expense. I had gone to a climbing store and picked up some old, worn-out rental climbing shoes that were on special for twenty dollars and were too big for me. I didn't know.

I hadn't actually rock-climbed that much. I didn't really know how to belay properly, because things had changed so much since I'd graduated from the Mountaineers over twenty years earlier. So much had changed.

I still did the hip-belay. Other climbers looked at me like, "What the hell is he doing?" I tried to teach Jeri-Lynn some basic bouldering moves on the climbing rock, but that rock had about forty years' worth of human oil on it from so many hands that it was slippery. It was nothing like it was back in the seventies when it was new and Alan and I were young. I couldn't even climb up two feet, my hands and feet kept slipping. It was embarrassing.

The following week, I took the girls to the climbing wall at Marymoor Park in Redmond. That was even worse. There were climbers there who showed Jeri-Lynn things that I knew nothing about. They showed her how to use the new belay devices and how to tie into a rope. I was learning and so was Amanda. When I started to climb up the wall, Jeri-Lynn started whipping me hard with the end of the rope and laughing. I was extremely pissed. It was my fatherly instinct to turn her over my knee. I knew I couldn't do that but I wanted to whip her back with the rope. I jumped down and sprinted after her. She started yelling "Rape!" at the top of her lungs, causing everyone to stare at us. I was exasperated. I wanted to kill her!

"I'm not sure I'm going to do this, Jeri-Lynn," I said to her after we were done and had loaded up her car to leave. She said, "I'm sorry, I won't ever do that again. I promise." She was so convincing when she acted nice. Like she really meant it. She got in with Amanda and, before I could get into the back seat, she took off and left me standing there. She stopped about twenty feet away, rolled down her window and said, "Sorry, get in."

The minute I reached for the door, she took off again. I yelled at her, "That's it! I've had enough, Jeri-Lynn! You can get someone else!"

She was very apologetic and let me in. It was like she was testing me to see how much she could get away with, but then she would turn on the charm and be so sweet.

One of the climbers at Marymoor told me about a climbing gym called Cascade Crags in the city of Everett. I thought it would be good to see if I could get some help with this mentorship, so we went. We met Lance, an employee there. He was not only a good climber but looked like he'd just stepped out of GQ magazine. The girls were instantly enamored. He was so helpful, obviously interested in the girls too. He invited us to Leavenworth to learn the basics of rock climbing the following Saturday.

Lance took us to several rock walls, and I learned all the awesome places to climb in the Icicle Creek area. They have names like "Barney's Rubble" and "Roto Wall." They have been bolted with anchors to make climbing easy. Lance considered me an old-school climber. He wanted to learn more about me and listen to all my alpine climbing stories. To him, I was a legend. Teaching Jeri-Lynn was easier with his help, and in no time at all she was good. The best part of it was, Amanda and I were getting free climbing lessons.

By the end of May, I was spending more and more time at the gym. I was riding my bike both ways—twenty-eight miles a day. Jeri-Lynn went from a 5.0 to a 5.11+ climber. She learned how to place protection devices. I've never seen anyone become so accomplished so fast. The girls were both in love with Lance. So the fight was on. Lance was playing them both. He would take one of them rock climbing on one day, then the other the next. Then out to dinner. He was dating my daughter and her friend at the same time. That didn't sit well with me and I told him so. He was very respectful, and so quit seeing either. They both cried when he told them he was moving to Colorado. He said that his friend, Jeff, would take over the training and he would do a good job of it.

Jeff was the all-American good guy—they just don't make them like that anymore. We became instant friends. He knew everything about rock climbing and was keen on helping me, partly because he was sweet on Amanda. I liked and trusted him so had no problem with him dating my daughter—he even asked me if he could. Amanda was crazy about him.

I became what the gym called a "belay person" at Cascade Crags. They would call me in to belay people for an hour, and in return I would get an hour of free climbing. I would go any chance I could to get a free climbing stamp on my belay card. Whenever I showed up with Amanda and Jeff was working, I would get to climb for free without losing any stamps. I had over twenty stamps by the end of June. Michaela was learning to climb too.

Even though I was getting closer to my daughters, my relationship with Debbie was falling apart. She was not at all happy with the time I was spending at the gym. I was becoming more confident and was feeling that Debbie and I had nothing in common anymore, we just existed in the same house. When I was at home, we were continually arguing, . I was happy with the new life unfolding in front of me, I was obsessed with becoming a 5.11 climber. Just two years before I thought I'd never climb again, Now, I was a climber that had been resurrected, but things were not going good with my marriage? We just couldn't communicate. I could tell that Debbie was not happy with this new-found love that she thought I had let go of. Not one to initiate difficult conversations, I hoped that things would get better.

After Jeri Lynn graduated I no longer had any reason to be a part of her life, but a new life was unfolding. Jeff, Amanda, and I climbed almost every weekend. On one of our climbs, Jeff and I talked about attempting Mount Rainier.

I had a co-worker named Terry who was recovering from a painful divorce by engaging in retail therapy. He bought thousands of dollars' worth of climbing gear. Terry was full of energy. He had moved his wife and daughter to Seattle from Texas, hoping his wife would stop her screwing around if she was in a new, more wholesome place. It didn't help. She picked up right where she left off. So they divorced, and he was looking to get into the outdoorsy Northwest lifestyle. We became friends and began a great relationship of hiking, climbing, and mountain biking.

He had studied mountaineering, so I felt he would be a good candidate to take up Rainier. He really wanted to go with me and Jeff. At first was a bit reluctant to have him come. That weekend, in late April, I took him up Cowboy peak at Stevens Pass and taught him how to use his ice axe. He was a natural. I taught him how to tie into a rope and how prusik's worked. He quickly learned how to prusik up a climbing rope. He did well.

I set up the climb via Disappointment Cleaver—the route I'd sworn I'd never take again. But that was a long time ago, and it's a good route for new people. Those new people included Jeff's dad, David and Dave. Dave had stopped my Rainier climb back in 1988 when he contracted altitude sickness, but he was doing better and was in good shape. We had been fly fishing together that spring in May, and when I mentioned another summit attempt he wanted to try it one more time. I asked him, "are you sure you can do it"? He wanted to go. So he and I hiked up to Muir with a friend that was visiting from out of state. Dave did well and had no issues with altitude. I was excited to bring him with us. We planned to stay at Muir, taking as much time as possible to get acclimatized. I wasn't worried about Jeff or Terry, but David was not in the best shape. With all the bike riding I'd been doing, I was ready.

We arrived at the Paradise parking lot around eight on July 28th 2001. We put on our packs and took off up the paved trails. It didn't take long to reach Pebble Creek. We got water and geared up for the long trek up the Muir Snowfield. Terry and I took off at a quick pace and made it up to Camp Muir in record time: two and a half hours. A new record for me. This was my thirty-fifth trek to Muir; it was starting to feel like my second home.

After Terry and I got our packs off and set up in the climbers' hut, Jeff arrived at the hut with some distressing news. "Hey, Tim, Dave is not doing well."

"What's going on?"

"He's about a thousand feet down there on the snowfield and he's really sick. We may need to get the ranger."

I immediately took off to see what the hell was going on. I ran back down the snowfield, passing tons of climbers on their way up. It was already three o'clock and the day was slipping by.

It looked like Dave was having a yard sale. Everything from his pack was strewn all over the place. He was just lying there on his Thermarest with a blue and white scarf over his face. There were people milling around him like it was a sideshow.

"Are you okay, Dave?"

"Tim!" He pulled his scarf away just a bit to look out at me, then covered his face with it again. "I'm not feeling too good."

"What the hell, Dave! What's going on?"

He just peeked back out at me and looked a bit annoyed, like, can't you see what's going on? I'm sick.

Someone next to me asked, "Shouldn't we get him down? I think he needs to go to the hospital."

Then Dave slowly got up, rolled up his Themarest and said, "I'll be okay. Just a bit of altitude sickness."

"Why is everything out of your pack, Dave?" I asked.

He looked around, a bit dazed. "I don't know, I guess I was looking for something."

"Are you going to be okay or should we go back down?"

"I'll be fine. I'm starting to feel better already."

I helped him pack up his stuff and I carried his pack up to Muir. He followed me and told me that he drank too much Citrimax. "It needed to settle a bit."

When we arrived at Muir, Dave immediately went into the shelter and went to sleep. The rest of us made plans for our ascent in the morning. I wasn't counting on Dave to be well enough for the attempt. My plan was to leave at midnight. I would put David on my rope and have Jeff lead Terry on the other. It was a good plan, and we were all in agreement.

Dave slept until eleven that night as the rest of us were getting ready. "How are you feeling, Dave?" I asked.

"I'm feeling really good now. I'm not good enough to go for the summit, though."

"It's all good, Dave."

That was Dave's last attempt to climb Rainier. I think he finally realized, he just wasn't ready to climb it but, maybe someday. When I walked out to the hut, Terry and Jeff were all ready. David wasn't.

"I don't think I'm going to go, Tim. I'm really not feeling that good and my knee is sore. I would just slow you down."

When I first met David, I knew where Jeff got his goodness from. His father was such a great guy. Jeff was upset that he didn't want to go with us. I put Jeff on the front end of the rope and Terry in the middle. Being on the end of the rope put me in the position to supervise everything and assess anything that we might encounter.

We left Camp Muir at 12:45 a.m. We headed down Cowlitz Glacier and then up to Cathedral Gap. We had to coil up the rope and hold on to it after leaving the glacier. It's ground pumice and small volcanic rock all the way up. Sometimes, one of the crampon spikes gets bent slightly from the rock, but no one ever takes the time to take off their crampons when they head up to the gap. And that's how crampons get so beat up.

We reached Ingraham Glacier after an hour and the wind was picking up speed. Hard, cold gusts almost blew us over. We crossed the Ingraham after winding around some crevasses big enough to swallow a large house. I feel strangely sad when I'm at the "Graveyard" on Ingraham. When we arrived at the bottom of Disappointment Cleaver, the wind was blowing so hard that we had to brace ourselves. Ground pumice was getting in our eyes. We coiled up the rope again. Only our headlamps were lighting the way, with the sounds of metal crampons crunching and ice axes banging against the rocks.

There was a small snowfield on the top of the Cleaver and when we were crossing it, a gust of wind came out of nowhere and blew Terry off his feet. He landed in self-arrest position but slid about fifteen feet because the snow was soft. I started to feel uncomfortable about the conditions. We exited the Cleaver and headed out to where the Emmons and Ingraham glaciers meet. From there, it's straight up to the summit.

We were the only ones up there but you could see the headlamps of the guided parties heading up the Cleaver. It was a stream of small lights in a perfect row, moving very slowly. They weren't that far behind us. We sat for a while, drank some water, ate a power bar, and got ready to leave. Jeff was feeling sick but said he could keep going. The new day was beginning to light up a little and reveal the weather conditions. The clouds were moving up higher and it felt like the high pressure was deteriorating. The wind was gusting even harder. I didn't feel that continuing would be a good decision, so I stopped the climb. We huddled together and discussed our options. I said, "Let's turn around now and climb this another day, guys. Okay?"

They didn't have a choice. We turned around and headed back.

After we got down to Muir, the weather was falling apart. By the time we packed up, it was snowing hard. The other parties were coming down, unsuccessful. I talked to the guide service leader and we both agreed that it was a good decision to quit. When we reached Paradise Lodge it was raining hard. We enjoyed a few beers and headed back to the reality of having to tell everyone that we didn't make it. That was the hardest thing of all.

When Monday morning came, there were patient co-workers waiting for me with bated breath.

"Did you make it?" "What happened?"

It was so good to have Terry there because he was more eloquent, animated, and much more captivating with his excitability than I was. I just let him tell the whole story. It made me feel good the way he talked about me making the right decisions, taking care of Dave, turning around at the right time. I still think we could have made it, but it would have been risky.

Chapter 23

I'll Tell You What I Saw But Will You Believe It?

"Broke all the rules, Played all the fools
Yeah, yeah, they, they, they blew our minds,
And I was shaking at the knees
Could I come again please, Yeah, them ladies were too kind

You've been….Thunderstruck"

— AC/DC

As I looked back up at the summit, the wind blew hard at my back. *That's funny… It was blowing from the north, now it's out of the east.* The events of the summer of 2002 would finally send me in a direction that would ultimately destroy everything. I thought I had given up climbing altogether after Rob slipped away. I was never going to climb again, and Debbie was so happy about that. Then Jeri-Lynn, and because of her senior project and my willingness to teach her, my daughters both caught the love of climbing. Now, my obsession was in full flower again. Climbing had, once again, become the focus of my life. I thought about when I met Ron.

I loved him just the same as he loved me, we were like brothers from different mothers. I have never had such a close friend that I felt so connected to, but at times wish we had never met.

•   •   •

After listening numerous times to Terry's rendition of our failed summit attempt, our top salesman, Sam, asked me if he could climb Mount Rainier with us. And he wanted to bring a friend. I said, "Yes, if you learn how to climb." A few days later, Sam said, "Hey, Tim, this is Ron. I was hoping he could go with us up Rainier. If that's okay."

We shook hands and I had the strange feeling, as I looked into his eyes, that we'd known each other from somewhere before.

"Ron has climbed Rainier many times and I thought it would be good to bring along another experienced climber."

Normally I wasn't keen about taking someone that I had never met, but this time I felt different about it. Ron looked like a rock climber, tall and slender, with rugged features and bleached hair. He was married with two kids. We'd done the Mountaineers course at the same time, but at different branches. He'd only been twelve at the time—the youngest ever to graduate from the course. We made plans for the entire climbing party to hike up to Muir. We wanted to get Sam acclimatized and teach him the fundamentals. We planned it for two weeks before our summit attempt. Debbie didn't have much to say about my plans. She was sad, she was quiet, and becoming ever more distant.

I was spending time with Amanda and Michaela. Jeff had become my close friend. I felt that I was doing the right thing. I was a father first, and my daughters were happy. It was as though I was living a single parent life. Debbie didn't get home from work until late. I would make dinner for Amanda and Michaela and we'd all head to the climbing gym. I rarely saw Debbie.

Since Ron was the stronger leader, and my confidence was not where it should be, we decided that he would lead. We became the Hansen Party of Five.

On Saturday morning June 8th, 2002 Ron, Jeff, and I met at Sam's house in Maple Valley at five o'clock. Ron was boisterously talking in his deep, commanding and self-confident voice about the conditions and what we should bring. He looked silly wearing his expensive one-piece long underwear. We quickly took a tour of Sam's estate and his big boy toys, then Jeff and I quietly got into the back seat of Sam's new white Ford Sport Trac.

We arrived at the Paradise parking lot at around seven to find Terry busy packing and repacking his pack. Parliament Funkadelic blared out of the stereo in his green Jeep Cherokee.

"Howdy!" he yelled as we got out and stretched our legs.

"Hey Terry, what's up? What time did you get here?" I asked.

"Oh, I've been up here for at least an hour," he said in his excited Texan drawl. "Just fixin' my pack and gettin' ready."

The weather was perfect. We put on our packs and began our conditioning hike up the paved trails toward our goal. Ron's new red plastic climbing boots contrasted with my twenty-year-old leather climbing boots. I wanted to learn a bit about Ron. He told me that he was an amateur videographer and that he loved to edit video on his computer at home. His dream was to film a trip up Rainier and make it into a DVD that would capture the heart and soul of climbing and summiting.

We reached Camp Muir in about three and a half hours. It was your typical hike up the Muir Snowfield. The classic lunch, looking out at the mountain tops, with the spectacular view of Mount Adams, Mount Saint Helens, and, farther in the distance, Mount Hood. After eating we spent some time getting Sam and Terry acquainted with tying into the ropes. Jeff was adamant about using a bowline instead of a rewoven figure eight, which is the standard knot in mountaineering. Jeff felt the bowline was a safer knot.

Around five thirty, we got back to Paradise Lodge where we enjoyed a few beers. As we sat in the lodge talking about the upcoming climb, I noticed an older man and woman staring at us discontentedly. She would not stop looking at us and it was making us all very uncomfortable. Her husband finally sat down and asked her to sit down too but she declined. She looked extremely mad, like we'd done something to offend her. When we all stopped talking, looking at her, she slowly walked over to us and said, "What is up with you guys? Who in the hell are you? The Chip and Dale climbers? What in the hell are you doing here?"

We thought she'd lost it! All five of us sat there with our mouths open in disbelief. Ron finally said, "What are you talking about?"

"Seriously, you guys just walk in here and demand all this attention on yourselves talking loudly, and you all look like male strippers."

We looked at each other and started to chuckle. Ron said, "Well, thank you… I think."

We all started laughing. Then, oddly enough, she started laughing too. It was a very strange exchange, but it inspired a new set of nicknames. After that, Ron was Chip and Sam became Dale. Jeff was Mr. Bowline, Terry was T-Funk, and, for some reason, I became Camp Ho. I hope it was because I was always making sure everyone was happy and not some other reason…

On Saturday morning the week before the Rainier trip, I was down in the garage going through my pack and checking my gear when I heard the door to the garage open. It was Debbie. I smiled and said, "Hi, honey. What's up?" She stood there looking at me, not saying anything. "What's going on?" I asked her in an impatient tone.

She finally said, "I thought you were giving up climbing. Why are you doing this?"

I immediately got defensive. "I'm doing this for Sam and Terry. They want to summit Rainier. Why do you always ask these questions when I'm already committed to doing something that I can't stop from happening? You have done this so many times, why can't you tell me how you feel when I first tell you what's going on? Instead you wait until the last minute!" I was pissed. I turned my back to her. I was done. I needed to focus on my climb.

She turned around sadly and walked back into the house. We didn't talk to each other the rest of the week.

It was Saturday, June 22, 2002.

Jeff stayed at our house the night before we left. We got up at four on the summer solstice. I always liked to climb around the longest day of the year. The weather was perfect. We went through all our gear, then loaded it into his Subaru. I went in to say goodbye to Debbie. She was asleep, but I woke her up. "'Bye, Debbie. I'll call you when I get down, okay?" I gave her an awkward hug.

Ron began filming the expedition while we loaded our stuff into Sam's truck. I was getting annoyed with the way Ron and Sam were dominating the conversation. I just stared out the window and thought about my relationship with Debbie. *Where are we going?* I felt conflicted. When I was around her, she drove me crazy and I couldn't wait to get away from her. When I was away from her, I missed her. I had to push those thoughts away.

I thought about my dream of the Buddhist monk. *What did it mean? It was so real.* The conversation in the front seat lagged so I decided to get the guys' interpretation of my dream. They thought it was strange but had no real ideas about what it meant. They didn't seem very interested. Ron changed the subject by asking us what music we would like in the video. I said Alan Parsons. Sam blurted out, "AC/DC!"

"I could do AC/DC," Ron said as he pulled out his camera and began to film Sam driving.

I sat back and thought, *AC/DC? Seriously?"*

It was around six thirty when we arrived at Paradise. Terry was already there, packing his pack, only this time the music of James Brown was playing. Once again, he yelled out at us, "Howdy!" only this time it was louder and with more excitement. His energy bubbled bigger than his 5'7" frame, like nothing in this world could get him down right now. He was practically in a state of euphoria. He got us excited.

After we discussed what time we were shooting for to get up to Muir and who was going to carry which rope, we registered with Mike, the head national park ranger. After exchanging a few climbing stories, he told us that he had recently snowboarded down from the summit through the Nisqually ice shoot. That is a feat in itself. Jeff, an avid snowboarder, was green with envy.

I was always envious upon meeting a guy like Mike who seemed to have no life outside of his passion. He could put everything into it without having to clear it with his wife. *I wish I had a life like that.*

We got back to the car and put on our packs. The parking lot was full of people from all over the U.S. and the world: climbers, hikers, and sightseers. Some asked really dumb questions like, "I see you have a pick axe on your pack. Is that for climbing the mountain?"

Ron was really patient. "Yes, it's used to stop yourself in case you slip on the ice." Then he took off his pack, pulled off his ice axe and showed them all the parts and how to hold it—like he was teaching a class. I was getting impatient and wanted to go.

Once we got hiking up the trail, we kept stopping. I reverted back to the days when I was always in a hurry. I missed barking out commands and making my party bend to my will, but I wasn't the leader of this expedition. I had to let it go. When you hike up to Muir your mind wanders. You think of things like, *I hope everything goes okay and we make it to the summit.* I thought about Debbie and how things were not going well between us. I knew inside we were both unhappy and knew we needed help. But what could I do? I was not sure I could continue the relationship the way it was going. There was no communication between us. I felt like when I was with her I was alone in a small room with one door that would not open. Then I thought about my friends at work and how they were so excited about our expedition up Rainier. Cyndi wanted me to bring her back a rock from the summit. She was a good friend to me. She was into rocks and energy and had quite a collection of rocks that she believed had different powers. I remembered that I was carrying the company flag with me to hold it on the summit with Sam and Terry. Our owner wanted us to have a picture taken to hang on his office wall.

It was early afternoon when we arrived at Camp Muir. We had stopped at least twenty times to rest or shoot video. When we walked into the climbers' hut, I began boiling water and getting ready for our summit attempt. Ron was shooting video. Jeff was getting bearings of the route with his altimeter and compass. Terry was packing and repacking his stuff in his summit pack, and Sam was eating. Sam liked to eat the majority of the time. His pack was heavy with an assortment of snack food.

After boiling snow and making water for all of us, I needed a break. I headed outside to see what Jeff and Terry were up to. Jeff was out sitting on a rock talking to Terry about how he was going to take the Mountaineers course in 2003. I noticed a wood driver leaning against the stone hut. Someone must have brought it up and left it. I grabbed it and teed up a rock. I looked around to see if anyone was watching. All clear. It was a perfect swing and hit. The rock went flying completely out of sight.

"Hey, Tim! Smile!" Ron had filmed my moment. *Damn! I can't get away from this guy and his camera.* I smiled and said, "Hi, Mom!"

It was getting late so we settled down, had dinner, and tried to get some sleep. It's tough to sleep in a small hut with about fifteen guys talking, stoves hissing, and doors slamming. Also, it's the longest day of the year so the sun is still shining. You just lie there and rest.

I managed to get a bit of sleep and was awoken abruptly by my alarm watch at midnight. When I am on a mission, the mission is first priority. I don't even think of sleep. I become immersed in the task at hand. *We have a mountain to climb, it's time to go!* It didn't take long to get everything together and get out on the glacier. I was on the end of the second rope and Terry was roped to me in front. Ron was leading on the first rope with Sam in the middle and Jeff on the end. The strategy was that if anything happened to anyone in between us, Ron and I could work together better if we were on separate ropes. I carried the rescue rope and anchors. Ron had all the first-aid equipment and some anchors.

As we were finalizing everything, I looked back and noticed two rope teams of three coming up the Muir Snowfield. Most of the other climbers were just beginning to get ready

Terry had forgotten something. "Wait a minute, I've just gotta get something," he said as he started pulling things out of his pack.

While we were waiting, the first person of the two rope teams I'd noticed came walking by. He didn't say anything, he didn't even look at me. The rope dragged by me, then the next climber passed by. Same expression. Then the third. It was kind of weird. Terry finally finished messing around with his pack and was ready, but Ron said, "Let's wait for the next rope team to go by, okay?"

We agreed. We sat and watched the next team walk slowly by, and as the last climber came up to me I said, "Hey, how's it going?" He didn't even look at me. He didn't even acknowledge my presence. Just kept staring off ahead. "Hey! What's up?" I asked again. It was as if I weren't there. Or he wasn't. Ghosts.

We let them get ahead of us and proceeded onto Cowlitz Glacier. It was around 1:20 a.m. when we reached the bottom of Cathedral Gap, and it took another hour to get up to Ingraham Glacier. The climbers who had passed us were the only party that we could see ahead. Everyone else was behind us. The two rope teams that had passed us made a line of twinkling headlamps up Disappointment Cleaver. They were making good time and were well ahead of us.

We had to keep stopping because Sam was getting tired, plus there were a few crevasses in our path. *I hate this glacier!* I thought as I stood there waiting for Ron to get around another large crevasse. The wind was blowing, but it was warm and humid. The snow was soft. It was perfect avalanche conditions. "Come on!" I said under my breath. "Let's get the fuck out of here!" I was starting to get that uneasy feeling in my gut. I reached into my Helly Hansen parka and made sure my knife was easily reachable just in case I had to cut myself from the rope and run. *This wouldn't be the first time I'd had to outrun an avalanche. I'm not going to die on this graveyard!* Finally the rope started to move and we headed toward the ramp to the Cleaver. I was relieved.

As we followed the path of crushed pumice, a low rumble shook the ground. At first I thought it was an avalanche off in the distance. Ron looked behind us and pointed out, "Thunder!" in his overpowering voice.

The sky was full of stars, but off in the distance there was a thunder storm. Lightning was stabbing through the dark. "Probably over Yakima," I said to Terry, as I tried not to step on the coiled-up rope in my hand.

About three-quarters of the way up the Cleaver, there is a snowfield that banks off to the left. It drops down about fifty feet and then another two hundred vertical feet. If one person slipped, usually you could just team-arrest and all would be good. Not today. The snow was so soft that you would never get enough brake from the pick on your axe. The conditions were extremely dangerous. Fortunately, there was a fixed rope anchored in that ran up the snowfield. Ron clipped into it first and went up. Crampons were of no use in the loose snow. One by one my partners went up the snowfield, and then it was my turn. I got about halfway up and stepped into a hole that gave way to my weight. I slipped and fell about ten feet before the fixed rope stopped me. If that rope had not been there, I would have pulled Terry off his feet and we would never have stopped until we joined the other lost souls down on Ingraham Glacier. I slowly got up and hiked up to Terry. He was the only one who knew that I had fallen; the others had already headed up to the top of the Cleaver. Terry and I eventually joined them.

The darkness was dimming and we could barely make out the outlines of the electrically charged clouds. In the distance, the flickering headlamps of the two parties that had passed us weren't moving. There was a row of three lights about a thousand feet above us, and another three lights fifty yards behind them. We were finally moving up the glacier and I could see a rope team coming up behind me about a hundred yards back. The thunder clouds were over eastern Washington. It was getting louder in the distance.

Then, when all I heard was the faint sound of the wind blowing through my headlamp strap, Ron yelled, "FALLING CLIMBERS!"

I looked up quickly to see the headlamps of the first party tumbling down. They were coming right at us. Ron yelled, "Look out! Self-arrest!"

I ran to the right toward the wall that divides Ingraham Glacier from the Emmons and Winthrop Glaciers. I looked up. Terry was down in self-arrest position. I saw the headlamps tumbling down toward us, then they disappeared into a crevasse. The party behind them started tumbling down. They were out of control, falling fast. They slid onto the Emmons/Winthrop Glacier and disappeared into another crevasse. They were gone.

Ron was incredulous, as we all were. "Holy shit! What the hell just happened?!"

The party behind us reached us quickly and the lead climber asked me, "Did you see that? Did they just fall?"

I was in shock. I could only mutter, "I think so."

He pulled out his cell phone and called 911.

"Are you believing this?" Ron asked me.

I wasn't quite sure what to believe, or what I saw. Jeff and Terry were stunned. Sam was scared shitless. He finally said in a shaky voice, "They could have taken us out with them!"

When the sun broke over the horizon it hit the clouds and the sky turned blood-red. I swear to God, blood-red. We stopped all the climbers from proceeding up past the point where we were. News was traveling fast.

It didn't take long for the national park rangers to get to us. Between the rangers, the RMI climb leaders, Ron, and me, we had a long discussion about what we had seen. The RMI guides didn't want to stop paying customers from proceeding. Finally, the rangers decided to close the mountain. Everyone was called back.

Ron and I were asked to proceed up to the crevasse that we saw the climbers fall into. Our climbing party didn't want us to leave them. Ron and I looked at each other, thinking we shouldn't leave them. We declined the offer. I really wasn't keen on pulling dead climbers out of a crevasse.

"No one could have survived a fall like that," I said to Ron quietly as we headed toward Sam, Terry, and Jeff.

One of the Camp Muir rangers came over and asked us if we could take some other climbers down to Muir.

"What?" Ron shouted out.

The ranger continued, "They don't have a rope and their leader left them." He was angry. "I need to find out who their leader was and why he left them stranded up here."

Ron and I inquired where these stranded climbers were.

"They're right over there." He pointed to three men over in a rocky area. One of them had a sleeping bag pulled over him, head first—looking almost phallic. The other two were eating something.

We walked over. "What's going on?" Ron asked.

"We were left here by our leader," the older of the two men answered. He looked to be in his late 50s. He had what looked like a small canvas bag in his hand and extended it out to us, "would you like some dried cranberries?" I looked at Ron and thought, *does this guy even know what's going on?*

Ron took me aside and we started assessing the situation. "Okay, here we go. We just witnessed one of the most horrible climbing accidents ever. There are about sixty people standing around talking about what happened. The mountain has been shut down and they are bringing in a helicopter because of the fallen climbers, who are most likely dead. Now we've been asked to take down some stranded climbers with no rope and no idea what they are doing. What do you think?"

Meanwhile, one of the climbers held up his ice axe, "What exactly is this device for?"

Could this get any weirder? It was like some kind of bad dream, yet… it was really happening. I began to feel sorry for them.

The younger of the three, climbing out of his sleeping-bag cocoon, was almost crying. "Please help us," he begged.

So Ron and I decided to send down Jeff, Sam, and Terry on one rope ahead of us. We would follow with Ron leading, the older guy behind Ron, the guy that didn't know what an ice axe was after him, me, then the crybaby. Five on a rope. Not climbing code, but we had to do something.

The sun returned to its natural color as it came up over the clouds, but the storm was still raging in the east. Constant lighting strikes. One of the climbers asked me how to tie into a rope. I looked at Ron again like this is too weird. It took us twenty minutes to begin climbing down the Cleaver. We were the last ones to leave. It was slow going. The guy behind me kept stopping and the rope would pull tight on my harness. It was extremely annoying.

We finally reached the snowfield where the fixed rope was. Ron clipped into it and began going down. It was steeper than I remembered. *No wonder I fell so fast on this thing.* Ron, moving cautiously, had a strained look on his face. He was not happy with this situation. He kept sliding sideways toward the cliff that was looming to the right of us. When he reached the bottom, the older guy looked at me and asked if I had a carabiner. "You don't have one?" I asked. I gave him one of mine and clipped him into the fixed rope. He then started down the rope. He did okay, of course he wasn't carrying as much weight as Ron and me. Then the guy in front of me got down on his hands and knees and rolled over on his back. He started inching his way under the fixed rope. I lost it.

"What the fuck are you doing? Get. Up. Off. The snow. Now!"

He got up looking like a little kid who has just gotten reprimanded by his dad.

Who are these guys? I mean, seriously... how in the hell did they even get up here?

Ron looked up at us from below. I know he could hear what was going on even though the wind was blowing pretty good. I looked at Ron like, Please help me! I patiently showed him how to clip into a fixed rope using another one of my carabiners. He inched his way down safely.

I showed the guy behind me how to clip into the fixed rope. It was a good thing I had five extra carabiners with me. None of them had any idea of what a carabiner was or how to use it. I went down fast, mainly because I wanted to get out of there. The last guy finally made it down. They asked us if we could take a break. I didn't say anything. Ron just nodded, and they all took off their packs and started pulling stuff out.

The older guy pulled out his little canvas sack and offered me some cranberries again. I asked him, "How did you guys get up here without carabiners?" He said, "Oh, we didn't come up through here." "How did you get up here then?" I asked. The three of them looked at each other, then the older guy said, "Our leader left us there." I looked at Ron and he at me. He had a look of panic on his face and said, "Tim, I think we should unrope now. I think we should leave these guys here, and you and I go! This is not safe. We're not responsible for them. I don't want to risk my life for them. We don't even know them." He said it loud enough that they could hear every word.

After he was done talking, all you could hear was the wind blowing between the rocks. I said in a quieter tone, "Ron, I know this is dangerous. I agree with you, I don't want to take them down either, but we have to do this. We can't just leave them here.Look at them, this is the weirdest climbing party I have ever encountered. hey could die if we leave them here."

226

Ron looked over at them. Then looked at me hard. Then he looked away for a moment and took a deep breath. He looked back at me. "Okay." He paused for a second, took a deep breath, and sighed. "Let's go."

I turned toward the group and barked, "Get your stuff in your packs. NOW!"

They scurried about, packing up. They knew I had probably just saved their lives and they would now do anything I asked of them. The five of us came down the Cleaver and made it to Ingraham fairly quickly. As we began to cross the glacier, a bolt of lightning hit the mountain by Gibralter Rock. The electricity shot through the snow, up through our ice axes, and shocked our hands. *Wow!* Never before have I wanted to get out of an area so fast. When Ron stopped for a minute to adjust his crampon, the old guy began to take off his pack. I yanked hard on the rope, signaling the guy behind me to come toward me. Then I got as close to the old guy as I could and yelled, "Get your fucking pack on now!" He immediately did what I said.

As we crossed Cowlitz Glacier, a Chinook helicopter flew over our heads en route to find the fallen climbers. I breathed a sigh of relief when we finally walked into Camp Muir. There were people everywhere. Terry and Jeff were talking to the ranger. Ron and I quickly unroped and I collected my carabiners from the other climbers. The three of them just stood there looking like they had nowhere to go. As I was coiling up the rope the older guy said, "Thank you." I looked at him and all three of them were just standing there staring at me. It was weird. I turned to see where Ron was. He was walking away so I franticly threw the rope on my pack, threw it on my back and quickly walked toward Ron. I got there just in time to hear Ron say in his loud commanding voice,

"Where's Sam?!"

"He left," Jeff answered back.

"Why?!"

"It was too much for him. He kind of freaked out."

Ron was pissed. "Damn it!" He yelled out. I saw Ranger Glen with a radio in his hand and asked, "Did you find the leader of the climbers we brought down"?.

He was stressed as he said, "I can't even find their names on the register." "Where are they, by the way?"

I turned around to look. They were gone, nowhere in sight. "We unroped right over there," I said, pointing to a green and yellow tent on the fringe of the glacier. There was no one there. I stood there looking out at the Cowlitz Glacier thinking, *How did they get by us? Where did they go?* My attention was immediately drawn away by the thundering sound of the Chinook helicopter flying over us about 200 feet high at 100 miles per hour. I almost ducked.

We heard the helicopter pilot reporting over Glen's radio. "Yeah, we're not seeing anything here. Over."

The head ranger, Mike, replied over the radio, "Copy that. Can you fly by one more time? Over."

"Yeah, we did see a helmet and what looked like a glove down in one of the crevasses, nothing else though. Over."

Ron and I looked at each other with troubled expressions. Ron looked at Glen. "Come on, they've got to find someone down there. We saw them fall!"

Mike's voice came over the radio. "Where are the climbers that witnessed the incident? Over."

Glen answered back, "They're standing right next to me. Over."

"Put one of them on the radio. The climb leader. Over." Glen handed the radio over to Ron.

"This is Ron. Over."

"Tell the pilot what you saw, Ron."

Ron talked to the pilot. The pilot asked him where we were and which crevasse we saw the climbers fall into. I pulled out my topographical map and figured approximately the location of the crevasse, but I was not exactly sure. We could hear the helicopter flying up and down the Ingraham and Emmons glaciers. It was bringing back memories of Steve and Glacier Peak. Then Ron said, "I'll let you talk to the co-leader, Tim. He has a map in front of him." He handed me the radio and I began telling the pilot where I thought the climbers were. After about fifteen minutes of this, and no sighting of climbers, Mike came back on the radio and requested our presence in his office when we returned to Paradise.

"Meet in his office? Do you think he's going to fire us, Ron?" I tried to break up the seriousness with some stupid humor. It didn't work.

I was starting to wonder what the hell was going on. *What does this all mean? Where are the three climbers we brought down? They just disappeared. It was like they never existed. Just like the climbers we watched fall to their deaths on the mountain. Did we really see them fall?*

Mike's office was decorated with amazing photographs that he'd taken himself. With his tall, gangly frame and his own poetry gracing the office walls, Mike didn't seem to fit the role of a head ranger.

He asked me first to give a statement. "I'll tell you what we saw, but will you believe it?" was the first thing I could think of. "We saw tumbling headlamps coming at us, then disappearing into what we thought was a crevasse. The other rope team went off to our right and down onto the Emmons/Winthrop. You tell us, Mike, what would you think?" I said, as we all sat in a circle around his large desk.

Mike looked directly into my eyes with a half-smile on his face. "Did you see anyone climbing out of the crevasse?"

Ron interjected. "They were hanging on the edge of the crevasse. Two of them disappeared into it and the other followed."

Mike scratched his chin and looked at Jeff. "What did you see, Jeff?"

Jeff told him his version, then it was Terry's turn, and then Sam. I was beginning to see that each one of us had a different perspective. Our stories were not that much alike.

"Right now, I really don't know what to say to the media. 'Climbers were reported falling on the Emmons Glacier, but no one was found missing. Everyone was accounted for? There were about forty paying clients through RMI who shelled out a thousand dollars to summit Rainier, and they were turned around because of what you guys reported you had seen. What do I tell the owners of RMI? What you guys did today cost RMI forty thousand dollars." Mike finished with, "You tell me…what should I tell them?"

We all looked at each other. *What did we see? Seriously?* "We saw what we saw! We all witnessed it!" Ron was getting angry. "I'll talk to the owners of RMI! I don't know what happened, but I know what we saw! Shit happens!

They lost forty thousand dollars, that's their fucking problem! Not mine! I never told anyone to turn back."

Mike smiled at Ron. "This is off the record. I believe you guys did see something. There are some strange things that happen up here. I have witnessed things that I can't explain and have never told anyone about. There are energies up here that exist and don't exist anywhere else. I'll take care of RMI, you guys go home and don't worry." We left Mike's office feeling somewhat empty.

Later, as Ron and I sat across the table from each other in the Paradise Lodge pub drinking Moose Drool, I said, "Let's climb it next weekend, Ron… just you and me."

Ron's eyes welled up. He answered back with a smile and a strong stern voice, "Yes! Let's do this!"

Something happened to me at that point. I was becoming numb. I not afraid of anything anymore.

Monday morning at work was not fun—recounting the story of the climbers falling: Terry's version, Sam's version. I just sat at the computer and listened with my jaw clenched tight, making a fist with my hand. I was so tired of not summiting. It was getting to me. Our co-workers listened intently to every word they said. I didn't want to talk about it anymore to anyone. I just wanted to go back up there.

I hadn't told Debbie of my plans yet. I knew what her reaction would be. Mostly her reaction was silence these days—and the silence was getting louder. When I would tell her what I was doing, she would just turn around and walk away.

Tuesday after work, I went and bought my first cell phone. I figured it was the responsible thing to do—and time to join the twenty-first century. They had a special on. *I'll never use one hundred minutes in a month.*

At four o'clock on Saturday morning, Ron and I left for Rainier. We arrived at Paradise around six thirty. When we went in to register for the climb, there was Mike. He smiled and got up to shake our hands. "So you're back at it? Couldn't get enough last week?"

Ron laughed. "Did you find any climbers up there?"

Mike said, "Oh, they're still up there. We'll find 'em someday."

After talking about the ordeal for a bit, we said our goodbyes and took off on our mission. We were going to go to Ingraham Flats for the night, get up and summit in the morning, then come down and check out the crevasses that we thought the climbers might be in. We brought rescue equipment: two ropes and tons of anchors. Yes, we were on a mission. We got to Muir in two and a half hours. We stopped long enough to put on our harnesses and rope up. Then we were gone.

We were up to Ingraham Flats by 10:30 a.m. We were kicking ass!

"Let's not stop, Ron, let's just go on up to the summit tonight," I said as we stopped to rest.

"I'm up for that."

We headed up to Ingraham Glacier and crossed it in less than thirty minutes. We began heading up Disappointment Cleaver and met some climbers coming down. One was a guide for RMI.

"You guys aren't thinking of going up to the summit now, are you?" he asked.

"Yeah, we're thinking about it," Ron answered.

"It's too late to go up there right now," he said. "The snow bridge just collapsed on a huge crevasse and we had to pull two guys out. You're going up there with full packs at the worst time of the day. Probably not a good choice."

Ron and I looked at each other, then at him. He could see we weren't deterred.

"I'm not stopping you guys. If you want to go, it's up to you, but I wouldn't." Then they left.

"Maybe we should wait until tomorrow, Ron. What do you think?"

"Yeah, let's get a good night's sleep, then get up and do this," he answered back.

We set up his tent and relaxed in the sun. It was mid-afternoon when we started boiling snow and getting ready for the climb. We talked about what had happened the week before, but really didn't have any answers. We talked about the dream I kept having and I asked if he had any thoughts about it. He told me that I may find out someday what it meant.

We ate around four o'clock and began to settle down a bit. We planned to get up at eleven and summit by three or four. We would spend a few hours at the summit, then go down and look into the crevasses. We climbed into the tent, reclined on our Thermarests and tried to relax. It was tough. So much was going through my head. I decided to check out my new phone and see if I had coverage up here at eleven thousand feet. That was a big mistake.

I turned my phone on and waited for a signal. Then, bang! Five messages showed up on my phone. All from Debbie. I listened to the first one. Since I'd left, she'd had time to think about all that was going on between us. The messages were all the same. What it all came down to was, I really needed to go home. Now. If I wanted to stay married. I was confused and panicking. *Why did I turn on this damn phone?! What's Ron going to think?!*

"Fuck!" I yelled.

"What's up?"

"It's not good. I don't know what to do. I think we may have to head back down."

"Now! What the hell just happened?"

"Yep! Now! Debbie..." Then I just lost it. I told him everything. He sat there and listened. It was like speaking to a therapist.

After I had finished ranting and almost crying for twenty minutes about how miserable I was, he just smiled and said, "Man, you need a beer. Let's pack up and go get one."

I looked at him in disbelief and thought, *Can you believe that? Let's go get a beer?* "Ron, thanks for understanding man."

Here we were, up on the Ingraham Glacier at 11,000 feet. We had been all psyched to climb a mountain. We were on a mission to summit together and find those dead climbers. We were prepared to boast to everyone about our accomplishments. And now, we were packing up and heading down to drink beer. All because my wife was angry with me. What the hell?!

When we reached Cathedral Gap, the sun was casting a shadow of Mount Rainier to the east that looked like a giant pyramid across a quarter of eastern Washington. Ron pulled out his video camera and filmed me. It was the first and last time I'd come down off Rainier in the dark. The worst thing about not carrying out our plan was having to face the peeps at work on Monday. It would be so hard to tell them why we turned around. I couldn't tell them the truth, that my wife had given me an ultimatum. "You can climb it, but don't expect to find me here when you get back," she'd said.

When they were all standing around my desk like a group of reporters waiting to get a statement Monday morning, all I said was, "We didn't go for the summit. Something happened that prevented us from going up on Sunday."

"Why can't you tell us? Did something terrible happen?" I thought to myself,

Yes, something terrible did happen. I bought a cell phone!

Chapter 24

The Mountaineer Corrupt

"Fun, fun, tell me was it a dream? I awake and your essence is still with me,
Fun, fun, I'll take you as you are, You will always be our star, you are fun.
You are fun."

"WHY DO I LOVE THIS PLACE SO MUCH?" Now I was talking out loud to no one in particular. "I don't want to go back down. If I am dead, then it would be okay to stay here alone. How can so many things happen in such a short time? Does this kind of shit happen to anyone else?"

I looked down the Muir Snowfield once again to see if anyone was on their way up. *Wow! It's a long way down there.* I wasn't sure if I could find my way back down. The snow was frozen and there were no wands or trails to follow. *It's easy to get up here. You just look at Anvil Rock and stay slightly to the left of it. But, going down?* Everything slopes to the right and if you venture too far right, you could fall down a cliff to the lower Nisqually Glacier. People have lost their lives getting too close to that cliff. Over ninety percent of all climbing accidents happen on the way down. I remembered that statistic from a book I had read years ago. And, ninety-nine percent of climbing accidents happen because of human error. *Well, I guess that's pretty much all of them then, isn't it? Was I in error for coming up here? Just another error? I have made so many in my life.* The biggest was leaving Debbie.

235

• • •

When the dust finally settled in the aftermath of the failed summit attempt, I began to become distant from everyone: my co-workers, my family, my friends. I bleached my hair and pierced both my ears. I didn't care what anyone thought of my actions, even though it didn't sit too well with the conservative views of the owner of the company that employed me. He raised an eyebrow the first time he saw me with white hair and diamonds in my ears. But since Ron was a customer, and Ron and I were friends, nothing was said about my appearance.

In early August, I was invited to Cyndi's birthday party. Debbie didn't want to go, so I decided to go by myself. Another co-worker, Christy, met me at a Starbucks with her two friends and we carpooled to the party.

I jumped into the back seat. "Hey, Christy."

"Hi, Tim. This is Tara," she said as she pointed to the attractive girl sitting next to me and we shook hands. "And this is Sheila."

I looked at the other attractive girl sitting in the front seat, and she at me. "Hi, Sheila," I said, but she turned her head back really fast and didn't say anything, like something was wrong with her. *Okay… that was strange…*

The party was fun. We played Cranium, and Sheila ended up being my partner. We started talking about our likes and dislikes, and discovered that we had much in common. We actually had the same birthday, we liked the same music, she was a flautist and I played guitar. So we decided to get together to jam at some later date. After that night, I realized how miserable I was. *What am I going to do about my relationship, I feel like it's falling apart.*

By fall, I was stepping into my mid-life crisis with both feet. I had just turned forty-seven. I continued to ride my bike to work and back almost every day and was in the best shape I had ever been in. I was climbing mountains, running down and skiing with Jeff. My competitiveness was over the top. I felt as though there was no one faster than me and my bike on the trail coming home. Aside from my unhappy marriage, I never felt so good about who I was. I was strong and I was confident.

I would still have the dream about the Buddhist monk once in a while. Each time, I felt as though I had more control and tried asking the monk what the dream was about. He didn't say anything. He just smiled at me, but he gave me a little nod and it was almost like I could read his mind. He was proud that I had progressed to questioning in my dream. He slowly turned his head, looked out the window and pointed. It was so real, I really felt like I was there—like I could feel the perfectly raked stones beneath my feet. But I could never understand what it meant. I was longing to go to Nepal to find out what was calling me.

How can so much happen so quickly to turn a person's life upside-down? On a Friday afternoon in late September, I was getting ready to leave work early. It was raining so I didn't ride my bike. I planned to go home, maybe go to the climbing gym and do some bouldering with Amanda and Jeff. Just as I was grabbing my stuff, the cute little voice of our company operator came on my speaker phone. "Tim? Ron is on line two."

"Okay, thank you." I picked up the phone. "What's up, Ron?"

"Dude! You want to meet for a beer on Capitol Hill?" he said in his excited voice.

I thought for a minute. *Hmmm… do I really want a beer? Well, we could talk about our climb next summer.* "Okay, Ron, but I can't stay long. I have something going on tomorrow morning." I had made plans with Jeff and Amanda to go on a short hike and do some rock climbing.

"No worries, I'll meet you at the Kincora. It's on Capitol Hill. See you at three."

I had never heard of the Kincora. I didn't really know the Capitol Hill area of Seattle. After asking directions at the only gas station on the hill, I was directed to the pub. When I walked in, I was overwhelmed by the activity. *So this is the Kincora… an Irish pub that's anything but Irish.* It was a dive. But it did serve Guinness on tap, so I guess that makes it Irish. Right next to the cobweb-covered Guinness tap was a worn-out PBR tap. There were only two people there: the bartender, who was a dead ringer for the bird lady in *Home Alone 2*, and Ron. He was sitting on a bar stool with his back to the bar, a beer in his hand, and a cigarette hanging out of his mouth.

"Dude! Nice hair!" he said with a half-grin on his face as smoke curled out of his mouth.

"You smoke?" I asked in a perplexed voice. The smell of mold in that place was overwhelming.

"Only when I drink beer."

"You didn't smoke when we had beer after we came down off Rainier. What's up with that?" I said in a joking way as I looked around at the weird items that were hanging from every square inch of wall space. The place looked like it had been decorated by Norman Bates.

"I didn't have any cigarettes." He offered me a Camel Light.

"I don't smoke, even when I drink beer," I said as the mean-looking bartender slid a PBR over to me. "I didn't order this," I said as I looked at the foamless beer in the semi-clean glass.

"It's all they have on tap right now," Ron said quickly.

"Oh... kay." At that time I was a beer snob and the thought of drinking a PBR was repulsive to me. *Oh well, it's just one, then I'm outta here.*

We sat back and reminisced about the falling climbers, climbing Rainier again in 2003, and rock climbing in general. Ron kept ordering beers. We drank three, and then four, then... five. I called home and told Amanda to tell her mom I was hanging out with Ron and I'd be home around eight or so. Then I went into the bathroom.

Wow! I had never seen anything like this in my life. It must have been the most vile, disgusting place on the planet. The smell of urinal cakes was so strong that you could shove one up your nose and it wouldn't be any stronger. The urinal was a trough with ice piled in it. There were about ten thousand tiny flies flying around it. "Ahhhh... my kind of place," I uttered sarcastically as I peed on the ice, trying to kill flies with my stream. The walls had been painted over so many times, with new graffiti painted on them, that you could barely see where the corners met. The toilet had no seat and the inside was permanently stained black. The floor was coated with some kind of sticky substance. I washed my hands and they still felt dirty. There were no paper towels. As I walked out, my shoes made a peeling sound.

I was somewhat buzzed after all that beer. I walked back over to Ron and said, "That bathroom is—"

Before I could finish, Ron said, "Not good." Then he started laughing.

Then I started laughing. *This place is cool in its own way.*

After one more beer, Ron asked, "Have you ever been to the Cha Cha?"

"Nope."

"Do you want to go and have couple more beers?"

Really? More beers? "Sure… what's one more beer? But then I really have to go home."

Besides, it was a different place and I was up for experiencing new things. So we got up, paid for our beers, and walked two doors down to the Cha Cha. We walked in and looked around. The place was packed. There were probably fifty people in there. The smoke was so thick that you could barely see across the room, and the music was deafening, The Petshop Boys blared at 500 decibels. We went down a walkway into the Tiki Lounge, which was part of the Cha Cha. It was decorated with bamboo-leaf roofs over the booths and really weird paintings of wrestlers on the walls. We sat at a booth, and Ron reached up underneath the bamboo leaves hanging over the booth and pulled out a cigarette.

"Hey, it's still here!" he exclaimed. "I hide cigarettes up here so when I come back—"

He was interrupted by some girls who walked up to the booth. "You dudes mind if we share the table?" Ron and I looked at each other with raised eyebrows, then in unison, "No, we don't care."

Within minutes, we were old friends. After a while of yelling back and forth because of the loud music, I looked up to see that it was standing-room-only in the Tiki Lounge. It kept getting later and later; we were having a great time.

Someone behind us yelled, "HEY!" Ron and I turned to see a beautiful goddess smiling back at us. Her eyes were jade green, her hair was golden with red tints, and she had the most amazing dimpled smile. The unique birthmark on her forehead was beautiful in its own way. My mom had told me that birthmarks were the result of being kissed by an angel. She had been kissed by the super-angel.

Naomi, friends with the girls we were sitting with, crammed herself between Ron and me. She was somewhat intoxicated. She then proceeded to dump her purse all over the table looking for her ID. Then she slurred, "I'm having a party tonight at my house and you guys are invited!"

Ron and I looked at each other again with excited expressions. "Okay!" Ron replied. I was too drunk to talk.

She rifled through all her stuff on the table and found a piece of crumpled-up paper and a golf pencil. She wrote down her address and gave it to me. "Be there!" Her eyes twinkled and her voice was intoxicating. Ron and I were in love.

I looked at my watch. *Holy shit! I am so screwed. I promised to be home at eight.* I got up and staggered into the bathroom. *I'm really drunk.* I looked at my red eyes and bleached hair in the mirror. Ron walked in, and we looked at each other and both started laughing. Slurring, I said, "I really got to go home, Ron."

He grabbed me and said in a drunken voice, "The girls are on their way to Naomi's. You wanna go?"

"Who's driving?"

"I'll drive."

"Have you done this before?"

"Nope. I'm just going with it."

"I am in so much trouble. Oh well, what the hell, we only live once. Right? Let's go."

Ron started laughing again. Then as he looked at me, grinning, he said, "I'm in trouble too."

We got into his BMW and headed over to West Seattle. Naomi's house was a huge old thirties-style Craftsman. We walked up to the front door and knocked. Silence. We looked at each other. "Maybe this isn't it?" I said, hoping we could just call it a night.

The only light in the house came from a window down on ground level. "Come on, let's check it out," Ron mumbled as he ran down the front steps.

The basement window was in a three-foot well. We jumped into the well, crouched down, and looked in. We could see a double bed with a patchwork quilt and a big fluffy pillow. There was a tall dresser and a messy desk. There was a couch and chair, and what looked like Ansel Adams black and white photos on the wall. We scanned the room to see if there was anything that could tell us we were at the right house. "What do ya think Ron? Do you think this is the place?"

He looked around again intently. "Look," he said pointing to the edge of the window frame. "The window's open." He slowly slid it open. "Let's do it," he whispered.

"Ron, I think this is illegal."

What in the hell are we doing? I think we had been "Naomied." We were so entranced that we were willing to do anything to see her again. We climbed down into the room and Ron opened the bedroom door to see if there was anyone there.

"Hey, let's rearrange her room," Ron whispered in an excited tone.

"That would be awesome!"

So we began to move her furniture around. We found some fold-out lounge chairs in another part of the basement and brought them into her room. "I hope this is her room," I whispered. *What the fuck am I doing?! I was just going to have a beer with Ron, now I'm in someone's house in West Seattle, rearranging the furniture. I'm forty-seven years old! She's like, maybe twenty-five. This is insanity!*

Then I heard something. "Ron, I heard a car door shut!" We heard the front door open and five or six squealing, drunk women came in, laughing and talking loud at each other. We looked at each other in terror, ran to the window and fought each other crawling out the window, laughing as we bumbled our way out into the side yard. Then we ran up to the front door and Ron knocked. We heard one of the girls say, "I hope it's them."

Naomi opened the door. "Hey, we didn't think you two were going to be here." I looked at Ron, he looked at me, both trying not to laugh. "Come on in." Naomi grabbed our hands and pulled us in. We were like a couple of teenage boys learning the facts of life all over again. My heart was beating hard, I was sweating profusely, mainly because we had just climbed out of a window like a couple of thieves. We hung out in the kitchen for a while and drank some more beer. *This is crazy. They love us!*

Eventually, Naomi said, "Come and check out the downstairs." When Naomi walked into her room, she was stunned. "What the hell? Who did this?" With her sweet voice she really didn't sound that mad.

Ron and I started laughing. "Do you guys know something about this?"

We looked at each other and I said, "I think it looks great! Very Feng Shui."

"You guys did this, didn't you?" She sounded really cute.

"Well… maybe…" Ron piped in, then added, "I think it kicks ass." To Ron, everything that's good "kicks ass." Anything that's bad "sucks."

Naomi totally forgave us for breaking into her bedroom. She thought it was "bold" and later she told us, "I like what you guys did with my room."

"Well, Ron's a designer. What do you expect?" I said.

The night just got more fun. We played Jenga. We played Cranium. We told climbing stories. Then more people showed up and we were all hanging out in Naomi's room. It was packed, like the Cha Cha. At one point, Ron and I had four girls on our laps and someone was taking pictures of us. I looked at my watch. It was 3:10. "I really gotta go!" I was so shitfaced.

"Not until you see Naomi's tattoo," Ron said.

I tried to find Naomi but the smoke was so thick and my eyes weren't working very well. I finally found her talking to some dude about the photos on her wall. I touched her arm. She smiled at me. I tried to get the words out. "I heard you have a… taaaattoooo."

She sat me down on giant beanbag chair in the hall, unbuttoned her pants and pulled them down, underwear and all. I swallowed hard and tried to focus on her tattoo. It was the word FUN with a small arrow pointing to the most amazing thing. All I could say was, "Wow!"

"What do you think?" she asked.

I looked at her, all bleary-eyed and said again, "Wow!" I couldn't stand up after that.

She pulled me to my feet, gave me a tight hug, and we walked back into her room. It took me a while, in my drunken state, but I managed to say,

"Your tattoo is awesome… but I really need to go. Is there someone who can take me to my truck on Capitol Hill?"

"Yes, Jo will take you."

Jo was a beautiful part-Latino girl who had been sitting on my lap earlier. I told Ron he didn't have to take me back to my car, that I had a ride. He was relieved. As the party was breaking up, Jo walked me to her car. "I don't want you to fall down," she said as she squeezed my hand.

I got in her car and we headed back to Capitol Hill. "Where's your car parked?" she asked.

I had to think for a moment. "Uhhh… it's close to the Kincora. I think." I really didn't remember which street I'd parked my truck on.

We were heading somewhere but it wasn't anywhere near the Kincora. She parked in front of an old brick apartment building, shut off her car, grabbed my hand and said, "Why don't you just stay with me tonight and you can go home tomorrow?"

My heart started racing, I looked at her big, dark, enticing eyes and I was literally trembling. *She's so beautiful.* I collected my thoughts. "I really can't. I need to go home. I'm so sorry, but I… I can't do this. I'm married and I have three girls."

I got out of the car fast and began to walk away. She opened her door and shouted, "Hey! It's okay, I understand, no worries. I'll take you to your car."

I felt like a total idiot. I *was* a total idiot. I was so embarrassed, all I could say back was, "My truck is just a block away."

She shouted back, "Okay. It was nice meeting you. Be careful going home!"

I kept walking. I had no idea where I was going but I had to get away from a lethal scenario. I started to go in the direction I thought was west. I knew I was somewhere east of the Kincora. I walked for about ten minutes. It was dark and cold and I only had a thin fleece jacket on. I was shaking and I was drunk. *This is like being lost in the mountains, only I'm in Seattle on Capitol Hill. I was a mountaineer that had been corrupted.* I felt something in my jacket pocket. *My cell phone!* I pulled it out to see if there were any messages. Three… all from Debbie. *She'll probably never talk to me again.* I threw my phone back in my pocket. "What the hell just happened?" I said out loud. All I was going to do was have a beer with Ron.

I finally found Pine Street and walked past the college. I looked up the next street to the south, and there it was, all alone in the dark, my blue 1990 Ford Ranger. I was so happy to see it. I got in, fumbled with my keys, and started it. Right after I got on the freeway, while singing "In the End" by Linkin Park, my phone rang. I pulled it out, hoping it wasn't Debbie. It was a number I didn't recognize. I answered it. "Hi, Tim." It was Naomi. "I was worried about you. Are you okay?"

I was so happy to hear her voice again. "Yes, I'm good. How did you get my number?"

"Oh… I have my ways."

Then I said something that must've sounded really stupid to her. "You are the awesomist girl in the world… and, whatever happens, we will be in heaven together!"

"What?!"

I was so out of it. She asked me what I was doing next week and if Ron and I wanted to get together again. I said yes without even thinking. We said goodbye about three times. I finally made it home.

When I got in, everyone was asleep. I crept into the bedroom and slowly slid into bed next to Debbie. I was stinking of cigarettes and beer. She didn't move so I thought, *Yes! I'm home… unscathed.*

She wasn't asleep. "You do remember you were going hiking with Jeff and Amanda today?" Debbie said unhappily. "Where in the hell have you been until five o'clock?"

I didn't say anything. My mind was racing. *Holy shit!* I had forgotten that I'd made plans to go rock climbing with Jeff and Amanda. There was no way I could go now. I was still drunk. I thought about all that had happened.

It was early afternoon when I woke up with a splitting headache. I walked out to the kitchen and there was a note on the table. "Sorry Dad, we went without you. Love, Amanda." I had no idea where Debbie was. I went downstairs and checked the garage. Her car was gone. *Probably grocery shopping.* I really didn't care because… I was in love. Or maybe extremely infatuated. I was obsessed with Naomi, I was in love with Jo, I was in love with Ron. I was in love with all the people I had met. I sat down and wrote a song called "Fun."

Chapter 25

Uncle Roger's Cabin

"There's a light in the depths of your darkness
There's a calm at the eye of every storm.
There's a light in the depths of your darkness.

Let it shine"

— Dan Fogelberg

THE FOLLOWING FRIDAY AND SATURDAY nights were a repeat of that magical night. Ron and I would meet up for a beer at the Kincora, then go hang out at the Cha Cha. It got to be a routine. Sometimes we would hang out with Naomi, but it was never as over the top as the night of her party. I would usually get home around one or two. Debbie really didn't care, or at least didn't show that she did. She just seemed miserable.

Christmas came and went. The kids were happy. A couple days later, Debbie was busy putting things away. The phone rang. It was Ron. "Hey Timmy, want to go with me to hang out with my uncle Roger?"

"When?"

"Tomorrow. We can spend the night."

I wasn't too sure. "Just a second, I'm going to run it by Debbie." I covered the receiver with my hand and looked at Debbie. She was in the dining room, boxing things up. "Ron asked me if I want to go with him to meet his uncle and spend the night."

She forced a smile. "I don't care, do what you want to do."

I had no idea where I was going, what I was doing, or what I was getting myself into. You never knew what might happen while hanging out with Ron... I packed up a few things and left my house Friday morning and arrived at Ron's around 10:45. We stopped for lunch in Tacoma at some horrible diner, then grabbed some supplies: two cases of Black Label beer, cigarettes, cigars, and Hostess cupcakes. *What the hell were we thinking?* He told me his uncle lived in pretty primitive conditions. Well, we could survive on what we had just bought. Right?

It took some time to get there, and when we crossed the bridge onto Harstine Island it was dismal: rain, fog, and really dark. It had been a while since Ron had been there, so we drove slow for a mile or so looking for the place. We came to a sign that read "No Jehovah Witnesses!!" "This is it!" Ron said loudly.

I turned my truck into the lane. We went a few yards and there was another sign that read, "Enter only if you want to be shot!"

"What did that say?" I asked in a loud voice as I slammed on the brakes. We stopped and I looked at Ron. All you could hear was Pink Floyd's "Wish you Were Here" playing. Then I asked, "Did you tell your uncle that we were coming?"

It was dark but I could see the perplexed expression on Ron's face. He said, "No, he doesn't have a phone."

"Really? Is he going to shoot us?"

"Well, if I get out right when we get there and let him know it's me, we should be okay."

I was not feeling good about this. I continued on down the road, slowly. We came to a small clearing with three broken-down cars sitting on the side of the road. There it was, uncle Rogers cabin. It was a little cabin with a flicker of light coming through the windows. Notified by a big barking dog, a guy in a flannel shirt came running out on the front porch and pointed his rifle at us yelling obscenities.

I stopped the truck and Ron jumped out yelling, "Roger! It's me! Ron!"

Roger looked hard at Ron over the barrel of his Winchester with his finger on the trigger for about five seconds, then he slowly lowered the rifle a bit, peered through the dark, and said, "Ron?"

Ron had his arms up in the air like he was surrendering. "Yes! It's me!"

Roger lifted up the gun and pointed it at me and said, "Who's that?"

"It's my friend, Tim."

Roger looked at me long and hard squinting down the barrel and then said, "Why is his hair white?" "It's bleached!" Ron yelled back. Roger set the gun down next to the front door and said, "Come on in."

I grabbed my stuff and Ron said, "Better leave it until I ask him if it's okay if we stay."

"Any more surprises?"

"We just got here, just wait." The barking dog came up and sniffed my leg. I went to pat him on the head and he growled at me, so I just said, "Good dog." It looked like he had been mauled by a bear.

"Hey, Roger, I'm Tim," I said as I extended my hand. He shook it but all the time he was staring at my hair.

"Why is your hair that color?" he asked.

"I bleached it," I said.

"Why?"

I didn't have an answer. I just asked him, "What's wrong with your dog?"

"Oh, he got mauled by a bear."

Roger had an innocence about him. He was about six feet tall, very slim, with long dark hair and a full beard. He looked to be in his early sixties. He'd built his cabin from the trees on his property, left to him by his mother after she died. There was a peacefulness about him that made me feel like his home was my home. He was a recluse and an artist.

The cabin was about seven hundred square feet. Oil lamps were his only source of light and the wood stove was his only source of heat. There were three chairs arranged in front of the wood stove in a way that you could sit, stoke the stove, keep warm, drink beer, and smoke cigarettes. The cabin had no running water, no electricity, no cable… it was primitive as can be.

Ron and Roger were happy to see each other. They got caught up on things while I opened a beer and sat in front of the wood stove, trying to get warm. It was just above freezing outside and not much warmer inside. There was hole in the window right next to the bed, sucking the heat out. "How did that hole get in the window?" I asked.

Roger looked at me and then turned to Ron and said in a quiet voice, not knowing that I could hear him, "Why is your friend's hair that color? It's scary."

Ron laughed. I pulled out a cigar and lit it. Roger wanted to show us around, so we walked outside. He told us what he had done with the place. There was a bathtub out next to the front door sitting on four cement blocks. Under it was a fire pit. That was how Roger took a bath. There was a giant mountain of empty beer cans piled up next to an outbuilding that had a kid's bike hanging up on it. We asked him about that. He had been in a car accident a few years back and was taken to the hospital. When he woke up and realized where he was, he got nervous that they might put him in jail. So he got up and climbed out the window. It was late at night, and as he ran through the back yard of someone's house, he saw a small girl's Stingray bicycle. He grabbed it and rode it back to his cabin thirty miles away, at night, in a hospital gown.

His stories were amazing. He'd built a boat in his bedroom because he wanted to experience being on Puget Sound and sailing away. He ended up finishing this beautiful sailboat, but there was no way of getting it out of the house. So he took out the wall of his bedroom and slid it out onto the lawn. He borrowed a friend's trailer and pulled it down to the boat launch, launched it, and took off toward Canada. He didn't even know how to sail or swim. In the middle of the night, an orca whale tipped it over and it capsized. He clung to it, freezing, until a fisherman finally heard his calls for help and rescued him in the early morning hours.

Ron and I listened intently even though Ron had heard most of the stories before. The three of us sat down next to the wood stove and drank beers and listened to more of his stories. Roger would throw another log on the fire, then start rolling up a cigarette. Ron asked him about his daughter. Roger's voice changed a bit when he told us he hadn't seen her in twenty years. She was married and had children but he had never seen his grandkids. Unbeknownst to Roger, Ron frequently talked to his cousin and knew she really didn't approve of Roger's lifestyle. Ron and Ron's mother were the only family members that really cared for him.

He had many friends, though, and a few were coming to see him that night. The first to show up was his friend Foot. He was a big guy, with a full beard and long black hair, old worn-out jeans, flannel shirt, jean jacket with the sleeves cut off, black boots, and a blue and white bandana. He looked at me when he was introduced, shook my hand really hard, and said loudly in a deep, gravelly voice, "What the hell's up with the hair? Did you see a ghost? Har, har… What'cha got there? A cigar? Let me try that thing."

He grabbed it out of my hand and stuck it in his mouth before I could say a word. He swirled it around in his lips, licked it, got it all wet and slobbery. Then took a big long drag off of it. He blew out a huge cloud of smoke and said, "Hell, this ain't no cigar! You wanna try a good cigar?"

I just stood there with no expression. He looked at Ron. "No, no thanks," Ron mumbled and backed away.

Foot pulled an old, black, wet cigar stub out of his sweaty pocket and stuck it in my mouth. I could feel the germs crawling off it and onto my lips. I was trying to be cool; he was just being a nice guy, offering me his prize cigar. It was the most disgusting thing I have ever put in my mouth. He lit a match, held it up to the cigar and expected me to puff on it. I started puffing away, looking daggers at Ron.

"Is that not the best cigar you've ever smoked?" Foot asked.

Ron looked at me and started laughing. "Is it good, Timmy?" *You ass! You know I don't even smoke cigars. How in the hell would I know a good cigar from a bad one?* "Yep, that's a mighty good cigar," I said as I gulped, trying not to vomit.

"Are you hungry, Rog?" Ron asked Roger while he rolled a cigarette.

"I guess." Then he began to tell us how the hole got in the window.

"Yeah, I remember when that happened!" Foot yelled out.

Roger continued, "I was sitting on the bed and my friend was oiling up his .45 pistol. It was really oily and it slipped out of his hands. He grabbed it, and when he did, he pulled the trigger. The gun went off, the bullet went right over my head and out the window."

"Yeah!" Foot yelled out again. "It missed your uncle's head by a couple inches!"

Ron just said, "Damn, Roger, that was close."

I stared at the hole. *A bullet made that hole? Dear Lord, I hope no one brings any guns to this party.*

A few more of his friends showed up. It was quite the party. Roger's birthday was New Year's Day, so we were going to celebrate. It was around nine when Ron and I set out to get some pizzas for everyone. We jumped into my truck, I put in my Crystal Method *Vegas* CD, turned it up to maximum volume as we drove out of the primitive roads at excessive speeds. My truck caught air at one point and we slammed into a giant pothole. Water engulfed the whole front and I couldn't see anything for a couple of seconds. The music was blasting and Ron and I were laughing hysterically. *Was I losing my mind? Yes, I think so.* We found the pizzeria and ordered three large ones. I looked at my phone while we were waiting. I had three messages. Two were from Cyndi, thanking me for a Christmas gift, then asking me if I wanted to get together for a drink. One was from Sheila. She wanted to get together soon and play music.

We got the pizzas, and I drove back with a bit more control. There were more people in the cabin when we got there. I could sense that Roger was uncomfortable with the crowd. We ate and drank shitty beer and had a great time. After a while, people started to file outside to say goodbye. Roger asked if we were going to stay the night.

"Sure, we can stay here tonight," Ron said, as if we hadn't previously planned on staying. "We can just camp out on the floor."

Roger was okay with that. Then he looked at my hair again. "I still don't know why your hair is that color," he said as he began rolling another cigarette. I looked down at the floor. There was a fine smear of dirt on it. Roger got up to go get more wood and I asked Ron, "I don't know if I want to sleep on that floor… do you?"

"Well, I think there's a couch up in the attic," he answered back.

"Have you ever been up there?"

"Well… I once poked my head up there and looked around. But Roger didn't want me up there."

Roger walked back in with more wood and started stoking up the fire.

"Hey Roger?" Ron asked. "Is there still a couch up in the attic?"

Roger looked up at the attic door. "Yeah, but I don't want you going up there."

"Aw, come on Roger, it would be better than sleeping on the floor." Ron, pushing the envelope, made a move to get a chair.

Roger blurted out, "I… I don't know, Ron. It's dangerous up there. There's rats!"

Ron and I were on a mission, we were going up, and rats were not going to stop us. Ron slid the chair over, climbed up on it and pushed the attic door aside. We were overtaken with a rotten musty smell that reminded me of my grandmother's house. It smelled like old paper and garbage. He reached up with a flashlight and looked around. "There's the couch!" he yelled out. He began to climb up. "Wow! It's cold up here!"

"I think you should come down now, Ron." Roger sounded like he was getting annoyed.

"Come on up, Timmy," Ron said as he shined the flashlight in my face.

I pulled myself up and we both looked around with our flashlights. There was so much stuff everywhere: old pictures, books, collectables. The attic was a gold mine! Roger was still telling us to come down but we ignored him. We looked at the large comforter on the couch, covering up something that looked like a body. *Was this what Roger didn't want us to see? Is there a dead body up here that he was trying to hide?* We stood next to each other, flashlights fixed on the object. I looked at Ron, he looked at me. I could only see the faint outline of his face in the cold, dark, smelly confines of the attic.

"You guys shouldn't be up there! It's not healthy!" Roger pleaded.

Ron reached over, grabbed the end of the comforter and quickly pulled it off the couch. There it was, the mother lode, the holy grail, the dream of every teenage kid. Ron and I just stared in amazement, not saying a word, our mouths wide open, our eyes fixed on hundreds of vintage Playboy and Penthouse magazines dating back to the early seventies.

"OH. MY. GOD!" Was all we could say.

"I'm telling your mother!" Roger's threatening voice shouted out.

"I think she wouldn't care!" Ron shouted back. "And my dad would be with us on this one!"

Ron and I spent an hour or so going through all that we had missed for the last thirty years in the world of soft porn. Celebrities, famous models, Dallas Cowboy cheerleaders—you name it, they were all there. How wonderful to find such a treasure locked away in a dusty old cabin attic. Being artists, Ron and I could appreciate the art and beauty of it all. It was hard to turn the pages and see all the art and beauty with a flashlight, so we held them in our mouths, making unrecognizable sounds of excitement. Neither one of us could leave the freezing attic until we had looked at every one of them. We didn't want to miss anything.

Meanwhile, Roger had settled down to watch a movie on his battery-powered black and white TV. We climbed down to get more beer and warm up next to the fire. After deciding that the attic would not work for sleeping, the floor was our only choice. Ron rolled out his sleeping bag in front of the wood stove and climbed in. Roger asked me if I wanted to watch a movie. I really didn't want to sleep at all, so I said, "Sure."

We stayed up until four watching *The Jackal*. Roger kept turning up the volume. When there was an explosion, Ron would jump up out of a dead sleep, freaking out. Roger and I would laugh and then Roger would look at my hair again. He really didn't like it. Toward the end of the movie, Roger was nodding off, so I turned off the TV and sat by the fire.

I contemplated my life, staring into the fire. *What am I doing here?* I thought about all that had happened to me in the last six months. I missed Debbie, but I missed our time together before, when life was simple and the kids were young. I was getting pulled by something that I couldn't control or understand. The dreams about the monk, the dream about Garry, meeting Ron.

I dozed off, woke up around seven and went out to pee. It was cold and wet and dismal outside, but the clouds were clearing a bit and the morning sun was breathing light into a dark part of me. I wanted to go home. I went back in the cabin, stoked up the fire, and woke up Ron and then Roger. We decided to go out for breakfast. Foot showed up and went with us. Roger finally accepted my bleached hair, and I felt as though I had made a friend by the time we left.

I hugged Debbie when I got home… but there was nothing there. She just had that far-away look in her eyes. I was worried. I felt as though I needed to make a change to reconnect with her. I asked her if we could talk about things. She nodded.

We had a discussion a few days later but it turned into an argument. She was focused on her job, she wasn't listening to what I was trying to say. I was focused on climbing. I have never felt so distant from her. She finally asked me, "is this the last time you are going to climb Rainier"? I told her, "I don't know." She got quiet for a minute and then said, "Let me know when you do." Nothing more was said.

Chapter 26

Witchcraft

"Say, for the love of the goddess, to me again.
I'll say, the night is still young,
You say, right on, and then.
Take a moment to see yourself as I do, and you'll see
How I see the love in you.
And I know, love makes you happy, and I know love makes you smile.
And I know, love is now, and I know, now is eternal."

FOR THE MOST THINGS were going a little better between Debbie and I throughout January. Then, in early February, Sheila called and asked if we would be getting together soon to play some music. I invited her to come to our house with her flute and work on some songs together. Making music was a nice distraction. Sheila and I were becoming friends. A week later, we met at her small apartment. Cyndi, who played the drums, wanted to join us to make it a trio. Sheila got along with everyone. She was eloquent, she was garrulous, and she was a schmoozer. The more I hung out with her, the more I became taken with her. She loved to boast about her vegetarianism, paganism, and her ritualistic witchcraft. I thought it was cool.

Toward the end of the month, my friend and coworker Christy, invited me to her thirtieth birthday party. I wasn't going to go because Ron and I had planned to go to the climbing gym. We had just about climbed everything there and were talking about grabbing some beers afterward when a blonde woman who looked like Christy walked by. That reminded me. "The party! Hey Ron, do you want to go to a party?"

Ron looked at me cross-eyed as he packed up his climbing shoes. "Party? What party?" he asked.

"You know Christy from work? She's having her thirtieth birthday party tonight," I answered back excitedly.

"Are you talking about that cute blonde girl that works in customer support? I remember her. Where's the party and who's going to be there?" He was getting interested.

"It's at her house in Crown Hill. I have the invitation in my glovebox. What do you think? Free beer? Lots of women?" He was easy to convince.

We took two cars because he wanted to head home from there afterward. It was about nine forty-five when we arrived, so the party had been going on for some time. We walked up to the door just as a couple were leaving. They left the door open for us to just walk in. It was wall to wall people. There were stacks of beer, mixed drinks, people laughing, music, and then I caught Christy's eye. She started screaming at the top of her lungs.

"TIM! OH MY GOD! YOU'RE HERE!" I felt like a celebrity. I didn't think she liked me that much. She ran over to me and gave me a hug that about knocked the wind out of me.

"I think she likes you," Ron said in my ear.

I introduced Ron and then she started introducing us to everyone. Sheila was sitting at the bar along with her sidekick, Tara. Sheila signaled me to come over. She was drinking something blue out of a margarita glass. She smiled and said, "What's up?"

I smiled back. "Nada."

"Would you like to try my drink? I could have one made for you," she said, holding it up to me.

I took it from her hand delicately and took a small sip. It was sweet and syrupy. Not to my liking. "Ahh, that's okay, I'll just have a beer," I said as I handed it back. "You look great, by the way."

"Thank you."

She really did look amazing. Her light blonde hair was down and she was wearing makeup. It was the first time I really looked at her eyes. They were almost a jade color. She was wearing a long black coat and underneath, a hippie-type brown shirt with a flower print. She had on tight jeans and black boots. I was too fixated to care where Ron was at that point. "I really had no idea that you would be here or I'd have had you bring your flute," I said jokingly as I opened an Alaskan Amber.

"I did bring my flute!" she said excitedly. "It's in Christy's bedroom. And she has a guitar in there, too."

"Wow! That's awesome. Do you want to go play some music?"

We got up and went into Christy's bedroom. The music was loud even there, but we managed to play without being too distracted. It wasn't long before someone put the on the *Rocky Horror Picture Show* soundtrack and cranked it. People started shouting and cheering, so Sheila shut the door and locked it. "Sorry, but that music is a bit much when you're trying to concentrate."

I agreed. We worked on some arrangements that sounded really good, so I grabbed some paper and a pencil and began writing down chords and notes. As we were sitting next to each other, I dropped the pencil and we both reached down at the same time to grab it. Our hands touched. We looked at each other and started laughing nervously. I felt something deep for her in that moment. But I quickly changed the subject.

"What's going on out there?" I said in an exasperated tone.

"Who cares?" she said back. We played music for a bit longer.

Then I'd had enough of the competing noise. "Maybe we should join the party."

"Yeah, we probably should."

We got up, I opened the door and saw the impending debacle outside of the bedroom. Sheila's boyfriend, Dan, had been standing outside the bedroom door waiting for her to come out. He'd arrived late and someone told him his girl was in the bedroom with another guy. He thought the worst but was too nice to knock on the door. Meanwhile, Ron had been dancing with Tara to the Rocky Horror Picture soundtrack and they had stolen the show on the dance floor. They had everyone cheering them on and that was what the commotion was when Sheila and I had been playing music in Christy's room. Ron was totally shitfaced out on the deck smoking with his new buddies. He had his arm around Tara. We opened the patio doors and Sheila demanded, "What the hell is going on?"

"Nothing," Ron replied innocently.

"Aren't you married?" Sheila grilled Ron.

"Who are you?" Ron asked.

"Ahh… Ron, this is Sheila," I said, to break up the tension.

"Nothing is going on, I swear. We were just dancing together."

Everything was sorted out, Dan was put at ease, Sheila was civil to Ron, and we all hung out together like old friends, drinking beer, smoking cigarettes, and laughing out on the deck. The party wound down and everyone began leaving. Ron and I said our goodbyes, and as we walked to our cars, Ron grabbed my arm with this troubled look on his face. "Timmy, I did something really stupid."

"What, Ron?"

He looked like he was going to cry. "I kissed Tara. Oh my god! What was I thinking?" He was really upset.

"Don't worry, Ron. It's okay. It was just a harmless little kiss, right?" I tried to console him.

"It wasn't just a little kiss… I have to go home and face Joy, knowing that I kissed another woman. How am I going to do that? I can't see Tara ever again, okay?" He was really drunk, pleading with me to help him.

I began to feel bad. "I'm sorry Ron, this is all my fault. I never should have brought you here". He went on and on about how bad he felt. I said, "Look, Ron, you can do one of two things. You can tell Joy what happened and deal with that, or not tell her and believe it didn't happen. It's your choice. Personally, I would choose the latter of the two."

Joy was not someone who would be cool with you walking into the house and saying, "Hi honey, I'm home. Oh yeah, I kissed another woman. So how was your day?" Joy was a strong woman who you wouldn't want to get mad. And she was the extremely jealous type who would have probably hunted down Tara and shot her along with Ron. She never liked me or anyone who was friends with her husband. I never really could understand how the two of them worked together; they were complete opposites. I thought to myself, *I shouldn't have come here tonight. This was a mistake. Every time we get together, we sink further into badness.* When I got home, it was after one o'clock and Debbie was still up.

"So how was climbing?" she asked.

"It was good, I climbed a 5.11," I said excitedly to take the focus off the fact that the gym closed at ten. "We stopped for a beer on the way home."

She looked at me like she knew something was up. "Amanda said you guys were going to a party." I had forgotten that Amanda and Jeff were at the gym with us when we had decided to go to the party.

"Well, we changed our minds and decided to go get a few beers." The lying had just begun. I don't know why I couldn't tell her the truth, maybe because I felt guilty or because I just didn't want her to know. The lie just came out without even thinking. That was not me. The devil on my shoulder was taking control. It wouldn't be the last time.

That night, I had a weird dream that was the first of a series. Ron and I were climbing Rainier together. We had our foul weather gear on: climbing boots, crampons, ice axes, and we were roped together. We started out in the trees and we walked onto a golf course with people playing golf around us. We couldn't find the route so we went back into the trees and came upon a cabin. There were wands leading to the front door, so we followed them inside. The cabin was Roger's but he wasn't there. It was filled with all his stuff. There was another wand that led to the attic door. Ron climbed up and then belayed me up with a boot-axe belay. In the attic, there was a party going on with all these women in bikinis. On the rafters there was a sign like the one above Panorama Point that reads CAUTION - EXTREME CONDITIONS BEYOND THIS POINT - PROPER EQUIPMENT REQUIRED. Ron began chopping a hole in the roof with his ice axe. We climbed out onto the roof. There were more cabins close by and a deck with a hot tub. We climbed onto the deck and looked. There in the hot tub was Pat Sajak and Vanna White, both holding a glass of beer and a cigar. Pat raised his glass when he saw us, like he was toasting, and said, "Have a great climb, guys. Don't forget to spin the wheel."

We walked into the cabin, crampons and all, putting holes in the carpet. The rope kept getting stuck on things as we went up a spiral staircase that led to patio doors. We opened the doors and, there in front of us, was the Emmons/Winthrop Glacier leading up to the summit. The deck was too far away for us to climb down to it. The only way was to jump. Ron didn't say a word; he looked at me and jumped. I knew I had to jump because I was tied to him. I don't remember landing. It was like we flew down, landed on our feet and began climbing up. It wasn't very far and then we arrived at the summit. On the summit, there was a parking lot and hundreds of people sightseeing. There was a large visitor center and a McDonalds, and kids running around. Someone yelled in my ear really loud, "You're late!" Then I woke up sweating. *What the hell was that?*

I didn't hear from Ron for the next two weeks. I decided to just focus on my girls and riding my bike every day. Then, at the end of March, Christy asked if I wanted to meet up with her and some of our coworkers and her friends at an Irish pub called Murphy's.

I asked, "Who's going to be there?"

She named off a few people from work. I asked if Sheila and Tara were going to be there.

"No, I don't think so."

I told her I might come. I called Ron to see what he was up to. He said that he was going to play pool in Greenwood with his friend Lloyd. "Dude, you want to come? This place kicks ass. It's called the Crosswalk."

"Sure," I said.

Ron and I met at the Kincora at four o'clock and waited for Lloyd to get there. Finally at six, a really tall skinny guy showed up. It was Lloyd. We had a few beers then headed to Greenwood in Ron's BMW.

We had a great time at the Crosswalk playing pool, drinking beer, smoking cigarettes. "Hey! You guys want to go somewhere else and hang out?" I blurted.

"Where?" Ron asked.

"Murphy's." It was silent for a moment.

"Where's Murphy's?" Lloyd asked.

"It's not far from here, I think" I answered back. I had no idea where Murphy's was. Ron had no idea that Christy had invited me to go. He was adamant about not wanting to see Tara again. After getting lost and asking directions, we arrived at Murphy's around nine. We walked in and headed for the bar. Someone yelled my name and we turned to see Christy running up to me to give me a hug. "Come over to our table," she said.

We couldn't see the table at first, since the place was crowded and loud. We walked over with our beer and there they were, all of them. Ron made eye contact with Tara and went right over to her. It was like witchcraft and he was under a spell. Sheila had changed her hair to red. She was dazzling. She'd gone from looking Dutch to looking Irish. She smiled at me and said, "What's up?"

I sat down next to her and asked how she had been.

"Are we going to practice again?" she asked.

I told her I'd been really busy. Actually, I was trying to stay away from her. She was trouble. Or I was trouble. Maybe we were trouble together. I was jumping and not thinking or knowing or caring what I was jumping into. I just told myself, *everything will be fine, nothing could happen to change my life........Right?*

·   ·   ·

Garry, you told me not to jump, why didn't I listen to you? I didn't quite understand what you meant. Jump from where? From what? You were never specific. Now I know. That evening I jumped into darkness. That evening more than any other was the catalyst of the destruction of my marriage to Debbie. I looked at my hands and then looked all around Muir. I spoke out loud, "I had to learn this, didn't I, Garry? Everything that happened, happened, and there's nothing I can do." I closed my eyes and took a deep breath.

I thought about that fateful night.

.   .   .

It was loud at Murphy's. I drank a beer while listening to the chatter of seven women talk back and forth, not really listening to each other. Lloyd was at the end of the table just taking it all in. I finished my beer and went to the bar to order another one. Christy followed me. I walked to the fireplace to have a cigarette and Christy began to talk to me about something. I seem to remember her saying something about the teachings of Lao Tzu and Taoism. I had no idea what she was talking about. Then Sheila showed up. It was almost like she knew that I was clueless about what Christy was saying, so she politely interrupted and asked me if I had ever had my astrological chart done.

"No."

"Would you like me to do yours?"

"Sure."

"Well, I need your birth date and the hour you were born."

"I'm not telling you my birth date." No one in that group knew how old I was, not even Ron. They all thought I was in my mid-thirties. "I'll think about it and let you know." I knew Sheila was exactly fifteen years younger than me to the day, but she didn't. She just knew that we had the same birthday.

"Do you, Ron, and Lloyd want to get out of here and come over to hang out at my place for a while?" she asked. Ron and Lloyd were standing a few feet away, talking to Tara. I asked them if they wanted to go hang out at Sheila's place.

Tara's eyes lit up with excitement. "Sure," the guys replied.

The three of us drove to Sheila's place. We had to pee really bad so we stopped in the alley behind her large old brick building that was built in the twenties. We ran frantically over to the edge of the building, stood in a line, and peed, laughing like we hadn't a care in the world.

I rang her number at the guard gate and she let us in. As I walked down the old hall to Sheila's tiny apartment, the floor creaked under my feet. It smelled musty and I felt as though I was being pulled into a dark, unknown world. It was a direction that I knew was wrong but I thought, "Why not?"

There was an enormous amount of excitement when Sheila opened the door and let us in. Fleetwood Mac played on her stereo, "Don't Stop." She gave us the grand tour of her tiny studio even though I had already been there before. She had taken off the closet doors and crammed in her bed. There was a hodgepodge of hand-me-down furniture. The cigarette smoke was thick, and the windows that bordered the sidewalk on Fourth and Bell were open wide, with the sounds of cars and buses roaring in, drowning out the music.

Sheila's parents were hippies. She spent the first two years of her childhood on a commune somewhere in Virginia. She really embraced her hippie roots by dressing the part. She engaged in Wiccan rituals, and when her Siamese cat, Logan, would run out the door and down the hall she would say, "Oh, for the love of the goddess!" then chase after him. She intrigued me.

Tara had taken Ron to check out her apartment upstairs shortly after we arrived. When Sheila and I noticed they hadn't returned for a while, we took off upstairs to find them, leaving Lloyd alone listening to *The Lovin' Spoonful's Greatest Hits*.

When we got upstairs, we caught the two of them sitting together on her futon. "What's going on?" Sheila demanded. "Nothing," Ron pleaded. "We're just hanging out." Ron was showing signs of fear toward Sheila.

We all sat and talked for a while sipping on our beers. Tara spoke out about how she was sick of her apartment, "I look out my window to witness men standing out in the parking lot peeing." Ron laughed thinking about the three of us out there before we came in and said, "some of those men are my best friends." Then Sheila blurted out, "Hey, you guys should come to Tara's big thirtieth birthday party on Friday next week!" The more I watched her and studied her, the more I was becoming infatuated with her. There was this innocence, this little girl in her that was frightened and needed someone to love her. She was also fun and full of life, and I needed that in my life. I wanted to see her again so bad. As I looked at her, she looked at me out of the corner of her eye and smiled like she knew what I was thinking. I was under a spell and by the end of the night, I was completely taken with her. Ron and I made plans to come back the following Friday to Tara's party.

When we finally left, it was around one o'clock. I was on my way home when Sheila called to thank me for coming over and said she was looking forward to next week.

I said, "I was born September 5, 1955, at eight twenty in the morning. Now you know." It was silent for about five seconds while she calculated. I thought that maybe she wouldn't be too interested in me if she knew how old really I was.

Then she replied, "Right on!"

There is a delicate part of life that we are afraid to recognize because if we do, we ourselves become vulnerable. I don't know if I read that somewhere or made it up, but it describes Sheila. She was jaded and hardened by what happened to her growing up. It was difficult for her to understand, know, and truly love someone outside of her animals and her family. When she was two, her parents split up and she lived with her mom. She didn't get to visit with her dad very often because he spoiled her, according to her mom. Sheila would sit and gaze out the window of her mom's tiny apartment and dream about when her dad would come again. Sheila had to give up her surname, which was Moose, when her mother remarried. And then, in her early twenties, she lost her father to suicide. My heart ached for her. "I know that love is now, and that now is eternal," were the words I wrote to her.

Shortly after Tara's birthday party, Ron and I both knew we were in over our heads. He was having a full-on affair, and I was falling for a younger woman. So many signs told me that this was a bad choice. But did I listen? Infatuation is blinding. I was not the Tim Lewis who was a husband, father, a good son that my parents were proud of. I was jumping and not thinking. I was becoming someone else.

I told Debbie that I was in love with Sheila. The reaction was horrific. She knew something was wrong since I spent so much time away from home in the evenings, but my admission devastated her. She met with Sheila at the veterinary clinic where Sheila worked, to talk things out. Debbie asked Sheila to stay away from me and let me think things out for a while. Sheila agreed, but it didn't stop her from sending me emails every day with famous quotes that she hoped would help me get through the struggle. I was becoming more and more divided in my mind. *I love Debbie, I love my daughters, how is this going to affect them? I'm crazy about Sheila. What should I do?* I was torn inside out. I would get on my bike and just ride for twenty miles, or drive for hours.

It was four weeks before our planned climb up Rainier, and I desperately needed to get my mind straight. I thought it would be good for me to help my neighbors across the street move. It was therapeutic to load things in a large cargo truck; it took my mind off of Sheila. After we filled the truck, we went to their new house. I looked out the window of the truck while we were at a stoplight and noticed a cafe called "Sheila's Café. *Why is this happening to me?* As we drove farther, I glanced over to see a big sign that read, "Moose." *OMG! I am constantly being reminded of her. What am I going to do? I have to forget about her.*

After a while, we turned on a road I had never been on before. I asked, "What's the name of this road?"

My neighbor told me. I was stunned. The name of the road was Sheila's last name. Just then, my phone rang. It was Sheila. "What the hell is going on?" I said out loud.

"What?" asked my neighbor.

I replied, "Oh, nothing. Just a phone call from someone I wasn't expecting."

"Who?"

"I'm not sure if I really know," I replied.

I had to see Sheila again after that. There were too many things happening to me that I couldn't explain. Two weeks before the climb, Ron and I went to see Tara and Sheila. Sheila asked what we were doing that coming weekend, so I told her that Ron and I were going to Camp Muir to get ourselves acclimated for the climb. Sheila asked if she and Tara could tag along. I was hesitant at first, thinking it would conflict with our training. But then Ron and I talked about it and agreed to let them come with us. Not a good choice.

At four o'clock on Saturday morning, June 14, I picked up Sheila and Tara in my truck. I was surprised that they were ready to go when I got there. We met Ron at the park-and-ride just off the freeway near his house, and the three of us got into his BMW. I had packed everything the girls needed for the trip. We arrived at the Paradise parking lot around seven. It didn't take us long to get ready.

The girls hiked up with no complaining and we had no problems. I was surprised at how well they did. When we arrived at Muir, there were about two hundred people there. It was a beautiful day with no wind. It felt like summer. Ron and I had brought along a twelve-pack of Alaska Amber ale. "Three beers apiece," Ron yelled out when we got there.

There we were, the four of us basking in the sun, drinking beer, smoking cigarettes, having a party. I made a delicious vegetarian panini on my MSR stove. Ron and I were caught up in the magical moment, both of us in love, happy, having the time of our lives in one of our favorite places. We were in the now, and the now was amazing. I didn't want to go back. I didn't want to face Debbie. I knew what I was doing was wrong but I didn't care. I looked at Sheila, smiled, then kissed her. I felt a tingling inside like I had just broken something into a thousand little pieces. It was the Tim Lewis that was; he was no longer.

On the way home, Sheila and I sat in the back seat. She had gotten badly sunburnt from being in the sun for so long at high altitude. We stopped on the way and got dinner at a greasy spoon. Fortunately, they had an aloe vera plant that we sliced up and squeezed all over her face. When I dropped her off, I kissed her goodbye and she told me to come by before we left for Rainier. "I have something for you that I want you to take with you on your climb.

Chapter 27

The Tiger's Eye

"You can never conquer the mountain. You can only conquer yourself."
— Jim Whittaker

"Take care of each other. Share your energies with the group. No one must feel alone, cut off, for that is when you do not make it."
— Willi Unsoeld

"I believe that, with anything in life, if you have the patience, desire and passion, you can do whatever you set your mind to."
— Ed Viesturs

IN APRIL OF 2003 I'D GOTTEN A TATTOO on my right calf. It was a picture of my ice axe with some mountains behind it. I'd made a bet with Cyndi that, if I were to get the $100.00 prize for finding a mistake on a brochure before it got printed, I would get a tattoo. I found a mistake and got the money. "Remember what you said you would do, Timmy," she said when I got the cash. So I had to go through with it. It turned out better than I had imagined

•   •   •

269

With my leg stretched out behind me, I looked my tattoo. The ice axe handle wasn't as brilliant blue as when it was first inked on. "This is too painful for me to remember," I said out loud as I pulled my long underwear and pile pants down over my calf. I stood up. The wind was dying down and the sun felt warm for a minute. *I betrayed so many people, people I loved and people who loved me. How could I cause so much hurt?* I began to cry. The tears flowed hard and the pain in my heart was unbearable. Then I said out loud, "I will never love again."

I began to pull myself together as I took out an old crumpled paper towel from my pocket. I wiped my eyes and face. *I need to get out of here!* I then opened my pack and pulled out my old climbing logbook. I wanted to write down the events of this day and as I went through my climbing log I came upon the accounts of the last Rainier climb that I had written years earlier. The wind had stopped but I felt cold inside as I began to read......

Wednesday June 25th, 2003

Ron, Ron's friend Paul, Terry, Jeff, and I, were to meet at the Paradise parking lot. The weather couldn't have been better: sunny and warm, temperature in the high seventies.

We are going up our favorite—the Kautz Route. Terry, as usual, was getting ready with his funk music blasting. Jeff and I got out of his dad's Explorer and began to get our packs ready. It was about eight fifteen in the morning. We had all day to get up to our first base camp on the upper edge of Wilson Glacier at 8,600 feet. Then Paul and Ron showed up. It was all good, as Sheila would say.

As we headed up toward the Nisqually Glacier approach route, I reached into my pocket and grabbed the tiger's eye that Cyndi had given me for protection. I looked at its many different shades of gold and brown. It looked as though it was moving inside. I put it back in my pocket. Then I looked at the amber ring on my little finger. Sheila had given it to me the day before we left. It too had protection energy. The ring and the lock of hair she had given me made me feel as though her energy was with me.

I was in conflict, I still loved Debbie. She has been my wife for twenty-five years. We brought three beautiful girls into the world. She had been through so much with me. My family knew some of what was going on, but didn't understand why I was doing what I was doing. Sheila told me that if I were to leave Debbie, my girls would become stronger. Would they? Should I believe her? I was a mess inside. I knew what was right, but I didn't want to do what was right anymore. *My life is falling apart. How can I get through this mess?* I thought to myself. "I need to find a way to end this insanity." I said under my breath. *But how?*

Ron seemed fine with what he was experiencing with Tara. Or was he? Was he going to leave Joy? We had talked about it many times as we walked down the streets of Seattle. He told me, "I will be ostracized by my family if I leave Joy. I don't know what to do, Timmy! I am a principal of a company. All my clients like Joy. It could have an adverse effect on my career. I'm in love with Tara but I also love Joy."

We were both in the same boat and it was not good. I needed to make a decision. I just wish I knew. *What was that dream with the Buddhist monk about? Why do I keep having it over and over?* So many questions that consumed me.

I thought of Debbie and about what she might be going through. The lyrics of a song by Joseph Arthur came into my mind: "I picture you in the sun wondering what went wrong."

Then I thought of the song "By My Side" from *Godspell*. I had sung it at a wedding in the seventies so I knew it well when Sheila played it one night and began singing it to me. I began singing the harmony. "Where are you going? Where are you going? Will you take me with you? For my hand is cold and needs warmth. Where are you going?" *Where was I going?* I felt empty inside and sad, but I knew I had to maintain confidence for my climbing friends. I felt I was losing control.

We crossed Nisqually Glacier and unroped. Ron headed up the small narrow route that divides the two giant rock walls and heads up to Wilson Glacier. Terry was behind him and I was behind Terry. Ron was about halfway up when a giant, car-size slab of rock came tumbling out of nowhere.

It missed him by a few feet and headed straight for us. We ran to the right, and it kept going right on out onto the Nisqually. A bit of excitement always takes your mind off other things…

As the five of us walked out on Wilson Glacier, we found the drop-off tank that the park rangers had left for climbers to put their blue bags into. All climbers are required to poop into a small blue bag, then carry the bag with them until they find a drop-off tank. What do you do with this bag until you find a tank? Well, there are three logical things you can do: First, don't poop. Second, you can put the bag in your pack and let it get squished with all your stuff. Third, you can tie it on the outside of your pack. It looks very unattractive, swinging back and forth as you hike along, but it's far better than the second choice. I prefer the first choice.

Jeff set—or thought he set—his new GPS device that he had just purchased the day before. I don't think he really knew how to use it. It was about two o'clock when we reached the top of the Wilson and began to make camp. We arrived at a place we named "Camp Nixon" because it was next to a large rock formation that resembled Richard Nixon's head. We had plenty of time to rest and get ready for the trek up the Turtle in the morning. Paul was the last one to get up there, mainly because he was carrying about ninety pounds of luxuries. He brought a French press and a battery-powered coffee grinder. Ya gotta love him. It was good to have him and Terry there; they fed off each other's energy. It was hard to tell who was more excited.

After dinner, Ron asked me, "Hey, can I talk to you in private about the climb?"

"Sure." Jeff and Terry looked at us like there was a problem.

"We'll be right back," Ron said in his commanding voice.

We walked up to the large rock formations about a hundred feet away. He look at me like he wanted to say something but he couldn't. "What, Ron? Why the private talk?"

"What are you going to do when we get back?" he asked.

"About what?"

"What do you think?!" He sounded a bit agitated at my response. He pulled out a slightly squashed pack of Camel Lights and offered me one, then stuck one in his mouth. He lit mine first.

I looked at him long and hard. "What does your heart tell you, Ron?"

"It's telling me that I need to end this thing." He blew out a big puff of smoke. You get a bigger buzz at high altitudes. No wonder you always see cigarettes in the mouths of mountaineers in old photos. They knew what was going on.

I answered, "Ron, I'm going through hell right now. I am in so much turmoil internally that I can't think straight." I looked away and thought about my situation and the only words that came out were, "I just want to disappear."

"Disappear?"

"Yes. Disappear. Then I wouldn't have to worry about anything anymore. I wouldn't have to make a choice between Debbie and Sheila. It would be a win-win situation, Ron."

He looked at me angrily. "What the fuck! How can you say that, man? That's crazy shit, dude! You don't really want that, do you?" For the first time in our friendship he looked me straight in the eye, intently. "Do you?!"

"At this point, Ron, what difference would it make?"

We finished our cigarettes and walked back to our team of concerned climbers. "You guys were gone for quite a while. Everything okay?" Paul sounded a bit worried, like we knew something that he didn't. All three of them looked at us like they were worried.

"Don't worry, everything's great," I reassured them.

The sun was setting over the north side of the Olympic Mountains. It was amazing to watch. It was a few days after the summer solstice, so the day was long. It finally got dark around eleven and we all turned in. I lay on my back I thought about what I'd said to Ron. *Would I really just walk off on the glacier and disappear? Or I could just jump into a crevasse? If they found me they would think it was an accident. Yes, I think I could do this. I just have to slip away from them.* I couldn't sleep. I felt frustrated, angry and hurt. *No one understands me or what I'm going through. How could they? It's like I'm being manipulated by everyone in my life. My family, Debbie, Sheila.* I thought to myself, *Would I do this, I don't want to go back. I don't want to live anymore.* I crawled down deep into my sleeping bag and pulled out Sheila's lock of hair. I smelled it. She had put her fragrance on it: Amber. I finally fell asleep.

I dreamed I was in my house looking out the window and it was snowing hard. The house was dark and cold. I was alone and felt abandoned. The snow was coming down like crazy and the wind was blowing so hard that the house was creaking like it was going to fall down. I woke up to the wind blowing against the tent. *I have heard the wind howl so many times.* It was 4:05 a.m., probably starting to get light outside. I realized that I had lost Sheila's lock of hair. I panicked, frantically looking for it inside my sleeping bag. "You okay, Tim?" Jeff asked.

"Yeah, I'm… I'm okay."

It was down at my feet. I was relieved to find it.

The sun was shining on the east side of the mountain when I crawled out of the tent. The sound of Ron's MSR stove was not unlike the sound of a small jet airplane engine. "Tim! You need some hot water?" Ron shouted at me.

"Nah, I'm good." I replied.

Jeff was getting his stove set up and preparing his breakfast. He was quiet, not really engaging in any conversation, like something was bothering him. My breakfast consisted of two Clif bars and a cup of Paul's delicious coffee. Jokingly, I said, "All we need is some half-and-half."

"Oh, I have half-and-half right here in my pack," he replied.

"Holy shit, Paul! Is there anything you didn't bring?" I asked.

"I didn't have a pack big enough for a kitchen sink," he joked back.

We were ready to go around eight thirty. I was feeling anxious and unsettled. I just wanted to get up there and get this climb going. *Terry is always the last person to get ready.* I thought as I looked up to the mountain. The sun was gleaming off of the snow and rock. There was steam rising off the Kautz Ice Cliff. I looked over at the Führer Finger. *Ahhh, the infamous Führer Finger.* It's a large couloir between the Kautz and Nisqually Glaciers—one of the most direct routes up Rainier. Two brothers from Switzerland, Hans and Heinie Führer, climbed it in 1920. It was named after them for some unknown reason. Joseph Hazard led the climb, but I guess Hazard Finger doesn't sound as good as Führer Finger. I always thought that it was too reminiscent of Hitler. Not the best name.

"Tim! Are you coming?! What are you looking at?" Ron's shouting startled me. I acted like I knew what was going on. I followed close behind Ron in the last position. We didn't need to rope up because it was all snowfields up to Hazard.

We hadn't climbed more than twenty minutes when I passed Paul. "You should have left your French press, beans, grinder, and cream at Camp Nixon."

"Nevaaah!" He said as he stopped to take off his pack and get some water. He was already sweating profusely. I caught up to Ron and we began to talk about the climb. He quickly looked away and said, "Look, there's a group of climbers heading up."

There was a party of ten crossing the upper part of Wilson Glacier right below the Führer Finger. "Do ya think they're taking the Finger route?" I asked.

"No, I think they would have headed up sooner if they were doing the Finger. I think they're heading up to Hazard."

They were about two miles away from us. There are not many good camping areas up there, so I was concerned that we might have to stay on, or near, the Turtle.

"I'm going to try to catch up to the climbing party and get us a spot before they get there." I said to Ron.

"I don't know, Timmy. They're way up there. But if you could, that would be awesome."

That was all he needed to say. It was the ultimate challenge to pass them before they got to Hazard. I was on a mission. I caught up to Terry and Jeff in no time and told them what I was going to do.

"You're crazy!" Terry said excitedly.

"I'll go with you, Tim," Jeff said.

"Me too!" Terry added.

So the three of us took off. Whenever I get into a climbing rhythm, I can't stop. I was practically running up the Turtle and I wasn't even tired. After about thirty minutes, I stopped to see if Jeff and Terry were still behind me. They were about a quarter of a mile behind me, sitting down. I really don't know what was going on in my head but I couldn't stop. I just kept going up the Turtle. When I looked up, I could see that I'd gained on the climbers quite a bit; I could make out what they were wearing. My heart was racing. I didn't care if it exploded—I would just keep going. *I have nothing to go home to. If I go home I have to face the mess that I've gotten into.*

I couldn't stop thinking about Sheila and Debbie. I was climbing like I was possessed by some kind of demon that was pushing me from behind. The voice in my head kept saying, *You can't stop. Don't stop.* I didn't stop.

I heard voices ahead of me. I looked up, the climbers were sitting down in front of me taking a break. One of them shouted at me, "What's your hurry?" I thought I recognized him from pictures I had seen in the paper and climbing magazines. I wasn't one hundred percent sure, but it looked like Ed Viesturs. A climbing legend

"What's up?" I asked in a rather winded voice.

"We're up here training new guides," he said. "Are you climbing the Kautz Route solo?"

"No, my party is…" I turned around only to see my party about a mile behind me. "…right behind me." *What the fuck?! How did I get so far ahead of them? This is weird.*

"We're setting up fixed ropes on the Kautz Glacier today." Ed said. "You should be good to go tomorrow morning."

"Thanks!" I started heading up, then I stopped when I finally thought of something smarter to say. "Are you guys summiting tomorrow?"

"Nah, we're just doing some training," he answered back.

I smiled and nodded, then began to head up.

The last time I was at Camp Hazard had been with Rob seven years before. I walked around looking for the two best spots together for our tents. After I found the perfect spot, I took my pack off and sat under a large rock outcropping that would protect us from the wind. I pulled out my water bottle and guzzled down the last bit of it. I turned and looked up at the Kautz Ice Cliff. I could hear the little bits of water trickling down from the melting ice. *I'm not going up there again, the last time was a disaster. I'll send Terry and Jeff up there to get water.* I went around the rocks to see if I could get a better vantage point from which to see my comrades. I climbed up the back side and was able to see down the Turtle. There they were… way the hell down there. I knew I was going to be alone awhile. I felt fantastic: strong and alert. I pulled off the rope and threw it off to the side by the rocks and stuck my ice axe in next to it. There was a cool breeze taking the top off the heat of the summer sun. I waited and waited.

Finally, after about twenty-five minutes, Jeff and Terry showed up. "How long have you been here?" Jeff asked me as he sat on a rock by my pack, red-faced and exhausted.

"Oh, I just got here before you did."

He didn't say anything. He was either not feeling well or knew something was up with me. We began setting up the tent. Over the years, climbers had carved out small areas with rocks piled up around in large circles. The rocks help block the wind. There was snow everywhere and up above us loomed the giant Kautz Ice Cliff.

We were putting the finishing touches to the tent when Ron arrived. It took another thirty minutes for the pack mule Paul to show up. After a short rest, Ron began setting up the "North Face Hotel," as we nicknamed his tent. When he was sliding in his last tent pole, it slipped out of his hand and began heading toward the Turtle. "Oh shit!" he yelled.

I instinctively began running after it. It was picking up speed, so I dove for it and was able to grab it before it went off to Longmire. Before I began to climb back up, I noticed that there were clouds moving in. *That's just great.* "It looks like low pressure moving in, Ron," I said as I handed him the tent pole.

He seemed displeased, then said in his loud deep voice, "We'll see how it goes." Ron was out of it, like he really didn't care.

I felt like things were not meshing right. Terry was the only one of us who was happy, positive, and excited. We had to summit, get down, and get home tomorrow and the weather was not looking good. It was changing rapidly, as it does so often up there. The good thing was, the wind wasn't blowing. I still did not want to go home. I crawled into the tent to try to calm down and see if I could catch up on some much-needed sleep. The altitude was getting to Jeff. He crawled in too and said, "I'm not feeling that good."

"Did you take some aspirin?" I asked.

"Yeah, but it's not working. I'm going to lie down for a while." He started going through his pack looking for something and I could hear the other guys talking over in the other tent. I reached into my pocket to make sure Sheila's hair was there. I felt the rock that Cyndi had given me. I pulled out the tiger's eye and looked at it. It looked different. It was moving inside like it was fluid. I thought at first that I was hallucinating.

"Jeff, look at this rock. What do you see?"

He took it from me and looked at it. Then he dropped it. "What the hell is this thing?" he asked in a scared voice.

"It's a tiger's eye. It's a rock that Cyndi gave me. It's for protection."

"What's inside of it? It's moving!"

"I don't know… I really don't." I grabbed it and took it over to the guys to show them. They were amazed by what they saw. To this day I have no idea why it was doing what it was. I have talked to experts and they have no answers. Some kind of a weird phenomenon. Maybe the altitude. Maybe some energy that is only produced by the mountain.

We ate dinner and began to get ready for the climb. The clouds had moved up to about a thousand feet below us. It looked foreboding. They were churning and I was questioning whether we were going to attempt the summit in a few hours. Ron asked me if I wanted to go check out the route with him. Terry wanted to go, but Ron pulled out the same "I need to talk to Tim alone" card.

We went up to the ramp where the route starts up the upper Kautz Glacier. Ron pulled out his squashed pack of cigarettes and handed me one. I lit mine, then his. He looked at me and asked, "What do you think, Timmy?"

"I don't know, Ron."

"You're not going to try to walk off on us, are you?" he said, sounding worried.

"I don't know what I'm going to do, Ron. All I know is that I don't want to go back. I can't live this double life anymore. I can't hurt Debbie and the girls, but I feel like I'm going to hurt Sheila really badly and I really care about her. I'm at a crossroads and I'm going crazy. Why did I let myself get into this situation, Ron?" I took a big hit off the cigarette and blew out the smoke. It gave me a huge rush.

He looked at me sympathetically. "I'm sorry, Timmy. I feel like it's partly my fault. I should have never gotten involved with Tara. I'm ending this thing when we get back. We need to just get away from those girls. They are messing with our minds. Don't end your life, Tim. I need you man."

I knew he meant it. We had been through so much in such a short time. I looked down at the swirling clouds and then I looked up at the ominous mountain above us. Then, something just happened to me. The strength that is always there, but often obscured by my own self-pity, engulfed my spirit and I remembered who I was. *I am a climber!* I looked at my friend. "We have a mountain to climb, Ron. We have people relying on us to get them up there and down safely. Let's do this. Okay?"

He gave me a half-smile and nodded. I could see the same unparalleled confidence and strength of spirit in Ron. "Let's do this, Timmy!"

We headed back down and got ready for the climb. Set up the ropes, got all our protection pieces together, and, amidst all our inner turmoil, became climb leaders again. It was difficult to go to sleep with the sun shining bright, the wind gusting against the tent, and the sound of every movement of the person next to you. I tried meditation. It helped, and I finally fell asleep.

I dreamed about the monk again, only this time it was different. When I walked up the stairs in the monastery, he wasn't standing where he usually stood with his back to me. I turned around and saw someone outside. I walked back down the stairs and there he was in the bright sun, raking the gravel slowly. He looked up at me and said something in another language but I somehow understood. He held up three fingers and said, "Three gifts." Then someone pushed me in the back and I woke up. "Tim. Sorry, but you were really snoring," Jeff said. He rolled over and grunted grumpily.

It was 10:20 p.m. and still a little light outside. I went out for a pee. The golden glow of the sunset was faintly lighting up the tips of the clouds below.

I knew we were safe and ready to climb this mountain. I fell back asleep for about an hour, then it was time to get ready and go.

We all worked together like a machine. After getting our climbing gear on and ropes tied to each other, we headed out just after midnight. It was a quick thirty minutes to the ramp that leads up the upper Kautz Glacier. Ron started out first, then Paul after him. It was slow going. The glacier snow was frozen solid and it was very steep. The fixed rope was there, as promised the day before. Ron and I felt that it would be best for Jeff and I to be on the rope together and for me to be on the end to make sure we had everyone between us. I was cold from waiting so long. It was almost vertical going up and I was more or less toe pointing with my crampons, ice climbing for the first three hundred yards.

Around two in the morning we began heading up the steep Kautz Glacier. We were about thirty minutes away from where the Kautz and Nisqually Glaciers meet. We encountered a rather large crevasse and had to set in anchors and belay each of us to get around it. I belayed Ron, then he belayed us one by one. We didn't get far before we came upon another one and repeated the process. The sun was beginning to light up the sky around four o'clock and the view was incredible. A sea of clouds spread out infinitely in every direction. There was a soft, cold breeze blowing. I was sweating hard, so every time we stopped I would start getting cold.

When you are on the end of the rope, you have to stop many times and wait. Your mind wanders. I thought about Sheila and Debbie. I thought about when each of my daughters was born. Shortly after Melissa was born, I joined the Mountaineers—I was so young, only twenty-five.

"Tim! The rope is getting slack! Keep it tight!" Jeff yelled at me.

I remembered the times when I would lead a climb and a team member roped to me—usually Steve—would be right on my tail. It would piss me off and I would yell at him to keep the rope tight. "If I were to fall into a crevasse, I'd fall to the bottom before you could stop me!" I would say to him. If only we had been roped up on Glacier Peak, he wouldn't have broken his leg. Jeff was right to say something, I had been daydreaming and not paying attention.

I looked up and saw that Ron's rope team had stopped at a large outcropping of rocks. We had reached the area where the Nisqually and Kautz Glaciers meet. Terry was cold and shivering so we decided to eat, get some water, and try to warm up. We took off our packs, which was not a good idea. *I've stopped here before. It's 13,000 feet and we only have 1,411 feet to go.*

It was getting lighter. Jeff and Terry were both feeling cold and sick and wanted to rest a while. So I pulled out my sleeping bag, unzipped it, and they both got under it. I drank some water and looked over at Ron. My headlamp lit up his face. He had a pained look about him like he was annoyed. Especially when Paul said, "I'm cold too, can I get under there?"

Jeff just grunted out a "Yes."

We weren't talking much. I think we were in survival mode.

"What do you want to do, Ron?" I asked.

"Ahh…" he looked at the three under the sleeping bag. "Let's warm up here for a while and then take off in twenty minutes."

The temperature was hovering around freezing and I was getting cold waiting for them, so I started cramming myself under the sleeping bag too.

"What the hell! What are you doing, Tim?" Ron sounded pissed.

"Hey, we have twenty minutes, I'm getting warm," I shot back.

"Is there room for me too?" Ron whined.

"If you can fit," Paul replied.

So there we were, all five of us crammed together under my unzipped REI sleeping bag. Shoving against each other, one or another complaining that he was hanging out of the sleeping bag, crampons and ropes, practically lying on top of each other. It worked; we were getting warmer. Then something clicked in my mind, I started to think about the climb. I yelled out, "We've got to get going! What are we doing?"

"Timmy's right. Come on, let's go!" Ron commanded.

We got our shit together and headed up the Nisqually. We began going left toward Point Success, then we switched back right. It was slow going but we were getting up there. Jeff had to stop about every ten minutes because he was suffering from altitude sickness. He threw up at one point. I had to keep yelling at Ron to hold up because of Jeff's condition. "Jeff, are you going to make it up there?" I asked.

He looked irritated and replied, "Yes! I'm fine!" So I left him alone.

The sun was hitting the top of the mountain when we switched back to the left for the last time and headed up the last five hundred feet to the crater rim. There is an unexplainable feeling that you get when the sun hits you at that height. Warmth and security, confidence, and a feeling of excitement that is overwhelming. You know down deep in your soul that you are embarking on an amazing experience that will always be life changing.

About fifteen or twenty feet below the crater rim, Ron waited for us all to reach him so that we could all walk up together at the same time. It was glorious! Of all the times I have summited, this one was the most memorable. We walked across the top of the crater rim to Columbia Crest. I stood up there, took a deep breath, and let it out in a big roar. "Yeahhhhhh!" I yelled as loud as I could.

Ron yelled back. I walked over and gave him a big hug. We both got so emotional we couldn't talk. Then we all got together for a group photo.

At that very moment of my life, I wanted time to stop, and it did. I've always believed that when you are above thirteen thousand feet you are closer to heaven. Something spiritual possesses you and fills your soul. *This is why I am a mountain climber! There is nowhere on earth that you can achieve this euphoria, except on the summit of a mountain.*

As I walked down to the summit register, I noticed that the steam vents were spewing out hot steam. I went over to them and let the warm steam blow into my face. It felt so good. There was no wind and it had warmed up to a balmy thirty-five degrees. We spent quite a while up there, the longest time I have ever stayed on the summit. I found a steam cave and went down inside. It was dark and felt like a walk-in freezer. Then, I remembered that I had promised Cyndi I would bring her back a rock from the summit. I could have grabbed any rock from up there, but I had to find one from the very top—the highest point I could find. There was one sitting on the snow on the summit about the size of a softball. I grabbed it and put it in my pack. Then I decided to check my phone and see if I had reception. I did! First I called Debbie. It rang and rang and then went to our voice recorder. It made me mad. First of all, because I knew she was there. Secondly, because I knew she was sleeping and was too tired to get up and answer the call from her husband who was on the summit of Rainier. "Debbie! Pick up! I know you can hear me!" I yelled into the phone after hearing my outgoing message on the recorder. Nothing. So I hung up and tried again. Amanda was at Jeff's parents' house and Michaela was probably sleeping, too. I thought someone would answer the second time. Nope. So I called Sheila. She picked up on the first ring. She was so happy to hear that I was okay and couldn't wait to see me again.

"Just make it back safe!" she said before I hung up.

I let Ron use the phone to call Joy, then Jeff called his house and talked to his mom, dad, and Amanda. Paul called his wife, and we were done. I was still really upset that Debbie didn't answer. Jeff reminded us that he had to be at work the next day and that we needed to start down. So we began the trek down to our base camp.

It was smooth going until we came to the Kautz Ice Cliff. "I don't remember it being this steep when we came up here," Jeff said as he started backing down the steep wall.

"I don't either," I said back.

We reached the ice cliff around twelve thirty. It took another hour for all of us to safely get back down the fixed ropes and makeshift belays. At one point, I was in a position that if Jeff had slipped and fallen, he would have taken me with him. So I threw in an extra anchor. I had a loose snow fluke that I kept throwing in and clipping into. When Jeff belayed me down, if I had fallen, I would have taken him with me. It was not the safest decent, but we made it. I was exhausted when we finally made it to base camp. It was probably the most dangerous part of the climb at that point because if Jeff or I had fallen, there would have been no way the others could have done a team-arrest. It was too steep. We should have had anchors in and been tied off the whole way down.

We began to tear down and get out quickly. The clouds were moving up below us and I could tell the weather was deteriorating. It wasn't long before we were out of the warm sun and into a full-on blizzard. The wind was gusting and snow blowing in our faces so that we could barely see ten feet in front of us. We stayed close together so that we wouldn't get lost. I had my map, compass and altimeter handy so that we could find where we were. About every fifteen minutes, Ron and I stopped to check the instruments again. We tried using Jeff's new GPS device, but between the cloud cover and the low batteries, we couldn't find a satellite. It was not a good scenario. It was a whiteout and it was getting worse. I was feeling panicky, I felt desperate like had to do something. I couldn't go back now. My mind was racing with fear and I was shaking inside.

Ron and Jeff were desperately trying to get a satellite fix, so we stopped and hunkered down in an area where the rocks were shielding us from the wind. "Stay here, guys!" Ron yelled out as Jeff set a point on the GPS so they could find their way back to us. They hiked off and were gone.

This was it! This is my chance to disappear!

Ron on Jeff were out of sight when I yelled to Terry, "Terry! I saw a wand back there about a hundred yards, I'm going to see if there's another one. I'll be right back, okay?"

"I don't think you should be leaving, Tim!" he shouted back.

"Don't worry!" I didn't care, I knew he wouldn't do anything anyway.

I got up and started back toward Wilson Glacier. I could hear him yelling, "Tim! Wait! Don't go!"

It wasn't long before all I could hear was the gusting wind and the snow pelting my hat and parka. It was burning the exposed area around my face, but I didn't care. I was on a mission. I knew that this was it: the one chance I had to fulfill my desire to get out of the mess I was in, to make things right. *Debbie will be fine. I assured myself. Once they find me dead in a crevasse or somewhere up here, she'll get a huge amount of money. The girls can go to college and Debbie can pay for their weddings. This is my contribution: my life.* I was so sad.

I began to weep as I walked down to where I thought the Wilson and Nisqually Glaciers met. I knew there were multiple crevasses there. I stopped. I turned around one last time. The wind and snow had covered my tracks and there was no turning back. "I'm on my own," I said out loud. I took a deep breath, closed my eyes for a moment, and exhaled to clear my mind. The wind almost blew me over as I began plunge-stepping down. I knew I was heading toward Nisqually Glacier, and within five minutes I came upon a large crevasse. I approached it cautiously and side-stepped along the edge. The adrenaline was flowing and I was beginning to wonder if I was making the right choice. There was no going back; I could never find my party at this point. I quit thinking about the consequences and listened to the voice in my head saying *You have to do this, it's the only way.* I stood at the edge and looked down. It was not a giant crevasse, but it was big enough to go down and not hit anything for ten feet or so. It was so black that I couldn't see the bottom. The wind was howling and the snow was hitting my face hard. I closed my eyes and thought about the time Alan and I jumped into the Foss River. It was so cold and I knew it was not going to feel good when we went in. You just have to tell yourself to let go and jump. I opened my eyes and looked down in the crevasse. *Okay, this is it, just do it.*

As I started to go, the strangest thing happened. No one, to this day, believes me when I tell this story. I looked down at my red gaiters and pushed my ice axe into the snow. I crouched down to jump and a cat meowed right behind me. Yes, a cat. I was not hallucinating. It sounded like it was lost and it needed help. I turned around, expecting to see a cat. I heard it again about ten feet away. I got up and walked to where I thought I'd heard it calling from. I looked up and the clouds cleared for a few seconds. Just long enough to see Shark Fin Rock. I knew where I was. Then, the cat meowed again, only this time the sound echoed off the rocks like it was right next to them. I walked up farther. I really don't know why I was trying to find this cat. Something inside of me told me to go find it. It sounded sad and scared; it needed help. I heard it again to my left, a few feet away. I ran over. It was hard to run with a large pack in a blizzard and deep snow. I was determined to find it. I had to prove that it existed and that I was not imagining it. It meowed loud and long, and it echoed again right ahead of me. As I tried to focus through the blinding snow, I saw something that looked like rocks. I listened for the cat—just the sound of the wind and the snow. I started toward the rocks to sit down… As I got closer, I realized they weren't rocks. It was my climbing party.

Terry saw me first. "Tim!"

Then the rest of them came running over to me. "What the fuck were you thinking?" Ron yelled at me. "We've been looking for you! Why the hell did you leave? Where were you?"

They all had grabbed ahold of my coat like I was going to run off again. "Look, guys, we need to rethink this. I found a flat area up above us that I think we should go to and wait this storm out. Get in our tents and call Jeff's dad and tell him we might not get back until tomorrow. By the way, did any of you hear something that sounded like a cat?"

They just looked at me like I had really lost it, but Ron agreed it was a good idea to regroup and get warm, so we went back up to the area I had seen. We set up our tents and crawled in out of the storm. My phone battery was almost dead when Jeff called his dad. He told us he would call the Ranger Station and let them know that we were safe and that we'd be down Saturday. He called back and told us we were doing the right thing and that the weather report was for better weather in the morning. So we spent one more night up there.

The snow stopped that night around ten o'clock, and by morning it was just overcast. We were at around seventy-five hundred feet on the edge of Wilson Glacier. We packed up and began heading down, but still could not find the route to the Nisqually. Then we heard people coming down the glacier. It was Ed and his group of trainees. He told us to follow him, that the route was down farther. "We'll find it," he said in a confident voice. When we arrived at the parking lot, the clouds were above us and a misty rain that soaks you was coming down. There was a bone-chilling cold wind as I walked slowly with my ice axe in hand toward the cars.

It was a bittersweet feeling when I took off my pack and threw it into the back of Jeff's Explorer. Part of me was disappointed that my plan was foiled by something that I wasn't really sure existed, but then part of me was happy to be alive. I didn't want to talk about what happened to anyone, but they were being overly nice to me, like I had an illness or had returned from the dead. Paul kept asking me, "Are you okay?"

"I'm fine!

When we went into the lodge to get a beer, I could hear Ron talking to Paul and Terry quietly, "I think we should just leave him alone and let him figure things out."

I walked over to the giant fireplace in the lodge and put my hands on the large screen to warm my hands. There was a huge fire burning and I stared into the flames and let my mind go blank. I felt someone standing next to me. I didn't look at first, because I was annoyed that someone was crowding my space. Then he pushed himself against my right arm with his shoulder. I looked. There he was, the Buddhist monk who had visited me so many times in my dreams. He was dressed in red, his head shaved, and he had a big smile. I didn't know what to say. He didn't say anything. He nodded at me and then turned around and walked away slowly. *Did that really just happen? Am I dreaming?* I wanted to ask him a question, so I went after him but he was gone. Then I remembered the last dream. *Three things… what are the three gifts?*

I walked over to the guys and asked them if they had seen the monk.

"No, we didn't see a monk." The three of them looked at me like I was really crazy.

"He was right there by the fireplace! You didn't see him? He was wearing a red robe. How could you miss him?"

"Are you okay, Tim?" Ron asked.

I didn't say anything. I knew what I had seen was real, that there was a Buddhist monk and he had stood right next to me. I knew I had been saved from making the huge mistake of taking my own life by something that was paranormal. I know that there was something up on Wilson Glacier that sounded like a cat and led me back to my climbing party in whiteout conditions. There are things that happen on Mount Rainier that are unexplainable. Many climbers can back that up. We live in a physical world, and since we can't see the spiritual world, we tend not to believe in it. It is there undeniably, just like the air we breathe. We can't see it or feel it, but it exists.

I never dreamed about the monastery or the monk again after that. He had moved out of my dream, into my reality, and then left me to figure out what the three things were.

Chapter 28

Finding Myself Alone on a Mountain, Then Finding Myself

"I've been waiting patiently hoping for the sun to rise and waken,
The night can seem so long sometimes but soon the pain will all but be forgotten,
And when the sun finally comes you will find,
that we'll leave all the darkness behind,
And begin again, Let's begin again".

THE FOLLOWING MONTH, Ron broke it off with Tara and began to be a better husband and father. I was lost when I came back. I continued seeing Sheila even though everyone kept telling me it was wrong. I didn't listen. I just stared into the eyes of the sow… and didn't listen to what anyone was saying.

In July of 2003, I moved in with Dave. I thought that if I got away from Debbie, It might help us sort things out and possibly discover what our issues were, but seeing Sheila almost every day was keeping me from focusing on what was really important. I hadn't just left Debbie, I had left my daughters, my family, and the old Tim Lewis. I was confused. Debbie and I went to counseling together, but it was too little too late.

Two years later, we were divorced. I was living with Sheila and with the custody arrangement, I was too embarrassed to have Michaela come every other weekend and stay with us because of the lifestyle Sheila and I had adopted: drinking beer and smoking cigarettes. I was not happy, but continued this lifestyle because I was so depressed.

I married Sheila in 2007, thinking it would be good to show my commitment to her for my daughters to see. I realized later that marriage was not something that she'd really wanted and I think she reluctantly did it for me. It was one of the worst decisions I've ever made. Before our first anniversary, she told me that she felt that she had made a mistake and that she still had feelings for an old boyfriend in Santa Fe. It was not her fault, it was the two of us together. We hadn't thought it through. Sheila never knew that I was always feeling guilty for leaving Debbie and Michaela, and deep inside I felt that Sheila longed to be with her lost love. It was doomed. Most of time as we were drinking beer and smoking cigarettes together, I was angry at myself for getting into this mess. I was unhappy with the situation. I was resentful and wanting to be home in my nice house with the mancave and my family. I couldn't tell Sheila and I knew I couldn't go back to Debbie at this point because I felt she would never forgive me. I was a mess inside. I would get mad at Sheila and say things that I would later regret. I was desperate to find myself.

I thought if I climbed Rainier again, it would help me find my roots again. So in June of 2008, Ron and I made an attempt. On our way up the Muir Snowfield, a bad storm blew in. We had to get out of it fast. That night as we lay there in our shelter from the storm, I heard someone out in the distance yelling for help. I wasn't sure if it was the wind howling or if it was actually someone so I listened closely. I heard, "Help me! Please, someone help me!" off in the distance.

Ron flew up out of his sleeping bag and yelled, "There's someone out there!"

I calmly said, "I don't know, Ron?"

We listened again and heard nothing. It would have been impossible to find anyone in the storm; we both knew it. I lay there thinking and listening to the snow and the wind hit the tent, and Ron snoring. I felt inside like I was that voice out there calling for help. I have not attempted to summit Rainier since.

• • •

I closed my eyes tight and opened them. I thought to myself, *I should not have been in a relationship with Sheila because I could never get over the hurt I had caused to all the people I loved the most. Jumping into a crevasse was not the answer, but leaving Debbie wasn't either. I should have tried to fix what was broken instead of throwing it away. Where is the man that I was? I know where he is, he's inside of me!* I knew what I had to do, that I had to fight to put the pieces of my life back together. *And now I am here at Camp Muir looking for—*

"Are you okay?" I was startled at first. I turned around to see an older gentleman standing about thirty feet away. "You look lost," he said. I couldn't quite see him because the sun was shining in my eyes. "You were staring off in the distance like you were contemplating the secrets of the universe."

I laughed. "Where did—?"

Before I could finish the question he interrupted me. "I was up on the Ingraham and I just got here."

"Wow!" I said. I was so happy to see someone.

He smiled. "Great weather, right?"

We talked a bit then he stopped the conversation and said, "You look familiar. Do I know you?"

"I don't think so…"

He took off his pack and began pulling out a few things. I didn't want to stare at what was inside his pack so I studied his features and thought he looked familiar too. I stood up and walked a bit closer. "I'm heading down," I said in almost a questioning tone. "I've been up here for a couple of hours. I've never been up here alone. It's kind of weird, there are always more people up here."

He turned, looking me right in the eyes and smiled. "I thought the same thing when I got here." He had a small canvas bag of something in his hand, and offered me it to me. "Would you like some dried cranberries?"

Oh, my God! It's him! It was the guy that Ron and I had helped down from Disappointment Cleaver in 2002. *Could it really be him?* I asked, "Were you up here like ten, eleven years ago? There was an accident?"

He look at me and said, "It's your hat, I recognize your hat. You're that guy who helped me and my.. friends down from up above Disappointment Cleaver. That was quite the day, wasn't it?" he said, smiling.

"Yes it was. A day I'll never forget," I replied. "Where did you go after we unroped when we got to Muir"? He didn't say anything at first then said, "Your name is Tim, right"?

"Yes, you have a good memory." I said back.

He held out his hand and we shook hands as he told me how he and his friends were so grateful that Ron and I had brought them down safely. He had a firm handshake and I felt warm inside after I let go of his hand. What are the chances that I would run into him? What are the chances of anything that happens…

We are all spiritual beings having a human experience. I believe that mountain climbing brings us close to a spiritual realm. Our spirit is felt by others when we put ourselves in a place like Mount Rainier.

I had many questions for him but felt more compelled to tell him about what happened to me the following year, about the cat and the Buddhist monk in my dream, then he stopped me and said, "I know what he was trying to say to you, Timothy. We, as humans, must completely understand the true purpose of our existence to find fulfillment, happiness, and enlightenment. That is why you are here today. We can start to understand this purpose by knowing the three gifts within us that bring the light needed to find our true purpose." He smiled and continued. "The three gifts are in the three jewels of the Buddha, the Dharma, and the Sangha. What that means is how you find your true Buddha Nature. That is what the monk was telling you in your dream.". He looked at me intently and said, "You need to go find your true Buddha Nature.

"The cat was in you, Timothy". You knew that you didn't really want to take your own life.

"We are given life and the power to be truly happy. No one person can bring you happiness. You must first find the three jewels and make them your foundation. Your universe, and all that is within you, is yours. It is all you have, it is all-encompassing, it expands out into infinity, and only in this moment that is remembered for a lifetime. Remember this, if you feel trapped in a room and the door will not open, try opening it the other way."

As I heard the words come out of his mouth I realized that he was not just an ordinary person and that he was with me here for a reason. My eyes welled up as I smiled at him. "Thank you," I said, "Will I ever see you again?"

"Oh, I'm sure you will," he said.

I said good bye to the mysterious man, and turned to walk away. Then I heard him yell, "Hey, Timothy!"

I stopped and turned around.

"Thank you again for saving my life!"

I smiled and yelled back, "Any time!" I thought for a minute and looked back at him and said, "Thank you for saving mine!" I waved and walked off.

As I descended the Muir Snowfield, I thought, *who was he? Was he real? I never even got his name. How did he get there? I don't know.* I smiled and thought, *maybe his leader left him there.* I was smiling as I met a multitude of people heading up. *How strange that the mountain gave me this time alone. She chooses who she takes and who she gives back.* I felt so good inside. It was hard to find my truck in the full parking lot, but there it was, waiting for me like an old friend.

I sat in my truck looking at all the different vehicles still wondering, *Why did I come up here today? Oh... I remember why*! I had told myself many times that I would sell my soul to go back to 2003 and do it all over again, to be transported back in time to that moment of being lost in the snowstorm at the edge of the crevasse knowing what I know now. Could that even happen?

Maybe, I encountered some kind of a paranormal experience out on Wilson Glacier nine years earlier. I know I wasn't hallucinating—or was I? I may never know what it meant or why it happened. Some people have told me the cat was my spiritual guide helping me out of danger, that it wasn't my time to go and that I had to be saved. Some have told me that I am a cat and I have used all my nine lives. I just know that now is the time for me to let go of regret and start forgiving everyone, starting with myself. Love is unconditional and I learned that you can't go back and change the past. The only thing that really exists is the now and you have to make the best of every moment.

I inhaled deeply through my nose and out of my mouth in a big sigh. I thought about the dream in which Garry came to me. Then suddenly I had an epiphany. I said out loud, "He wasn't talking about one jump, he was talking about every jump!" "Think about what you are doing before you jump," he'd said. We are always making jumps in life, just like we are climbing mountains and we have all pet the sow. He hadn't been giving me a warning, he'd been giving me advice.

"I have everything to live for!" I said it loud, feeling such appreciation for my surroundings. It was so beautiful. I felt better about where I was going and who I was. "It's time for me to begin again." I turned on my iPod and Ulrich Schnauss's "Goodbye" came on.

Just as I drove out of the parking lot I thought about what had happened today. *Was it a dream?*

I stopped along the side of the road. I looked up at the mountain. There she stood in all her majestic glory, brilliant white against the sapphire sky. I thought about all the climbs I had made on those slopes, the pain, the glory, the fear, and the knowledge she had given me, and knew that the next time would be different. I would be different. I looked up to the summit and promised myself, "This is the end of my old story and the beginning of my new life."

THE END

AFTER WORDS

I REMEMBER ONCE WHILE FLY-FISHING on the Yakima River years ago, as I threw my line and pulled it back, I watched two leaves fall out of a birch tree and land on the river. It was a deep pool, so they moved slowly at first but then began to pick up speed. They were connected, floating down the river together side by side. They passed me and then they split apart and went two different directions where the river bifurcated. I began thinking about Alan and all the people I have known in my life, people who were so close to me. We created such memories together back in the seventies, eighties, nineties and 2000s. I thought about my brother John; I rarely see him now. I thought about Garry, no longer with us. Then I began to think about all the people I'd taken climbing and will probably never see again. I could see how relationships are similar to those two leaves.

We are side by side with someone we care about and we think it will always be that way. Then the unexpected happens, and we are pulled apart. Then gone in separate directions.

Looking back over the last thirty-five years, I can honestly say that I was never a world-class climber nor a famous climber. I am just a typical, everyday guy who rides his bike to work. Yes, I climbed many mountains and took many risks. I took people to the summit, and knew so many amazing friends. They could be any Alan, Ron, Steve, or Dave that you might meet. They were all my cherished friends who I loved. They went to the summit with me. I climbed for many reasons, but mostly because I loved to do it. Will I climb again? Yes. Will I die up there? I don't know, maybe... I can't think of a better way to die than while doing what you love.

But, I know now that I can't change the past or control the future, I can only be a part of the now with you. I will always be up and down about my choices in life. *Is my cup half empty or half full?* I have been an optimist most of my life, and I know that good things will happen if you have faith. I am a mountaineer and, in my heart, I will always be a mountaineer—not unlike an explorer, a soldier, or a Knight of Templar. My ice axe is like my sword and I can survive with what I carry on my back. I am confident when my ice axe is in my hand. That is why I had it tattooed on my right calf—as a reminder of who and what I am. I am always on Mount Rainier in my heart, and my spirit resides there. I know what it is like up there all the time. The mountain is alive and it waits. It waits for you and me.

People often ask me about my experiences. They enjoy my stories, but the question that is so often asked is why I climb mountains. I believe I have answered that. I wrote this book mainly to record the experiences of my life and hopefully to give an understanding of what climbing is all about for many of us unknown adventurists who live in the Pacific Northwest. I could be any one of the thousands of climbers who have lived and died, who have experienced similar experiences and never shared them with the world. For as long as there are mountains, there will be someone to challenge them, to climb, stand on the summit and say, "I did it! I climbed this mountain!" For all eternity, I will never forget the moments that are frozen in time forever in my heart and soul. For they are in the mountainside of my life. They have been cut into my foundation, and they are my Frozen Footsteps.

Made in the USA
Middletown, DE
01 May 2019